Fate of the Wild

Fate of the Wild

The Endangered Species Act

and the Future of Biodiversity

Bonnie B. Burgess

The University of Georgia Press   *Athens and London*

Published by the University of Georgia Press
Athens, Georgia 30602
© 2001 by Bonnie B. Burgess
All rights reserved
Set in 10.2 on 13.5 Electra
Printed and bound by Maple-Vail
The paper in this book meets the guidelines for
permanence and durability of the Committee on
Production Guidelines for Book Longevity of the
Council on Library Resources.

Printed in the United States of America

05 04 03 02 01 C 5 4 3 2 1

Library of Congress Cataloging-in-Publication Data
Burgess, Bonnie B., 1946–
Fate of the wild : the endangered species act
and the future of biodiversity / Bonnie B. Burgess.
p. cm.
Includes bibliographical references (p.) and index.
ISBN 0-8203-2296-2 (alk. paper)
1. Endangered species—Government policy—United States.
2. Biological diversity conservation—Government policy—
United States. 3. United States. Endangered Species Act of
1973—History. I. Title.

QH76 .B87 2001
333.95'22'0973—dc21   00-053657

British Library Cataloging-in-Publication Data available

This book is dedicated to God my mentor,

and to Jane, Marge, and Bob

my friends and supporters.

Contents

Acknowledgments

B Y THE TIME I started pursuing my interest in wilderness and wildlife in the early 1990s, I understood that the diversity of the world is part of the wonder of God. So this book was a collaborative process between God and me. She guided my investigation and inspired my fingers on the keyboard and would not let me give up when I received rejection notices from publishers.

I am grateful for the encouragement and support of the personal friends I call my East Coast family. Bob Rolls has been there for me from the beginning of this process. Everyone should be blessed with such a friend. Through him, I met Tom Blake and Joseph Konrad, and the four of us became family. After the book was written, two special women entered my life and also became family—Jane Gruenebaum and Marge DuMond. They, too, are priceless friends and supports.

Two people were early inspirations and role models for me. The first was Dr. Charles J. (Charlie) Stine, a dentist whose avocation led him to teach Ecology and Wetlands Conservation at the School of Continuing Education Studies (CES) at Johns Hopkins University, where I was studying before I began my master's degree in environmental science. He inspired me to dig deeper and deeper into environmental science and policy, and his field trips awakened my love for mucking around in wetlands and for all things natural.

Paul Torrence, an activist with the Maryland Sierra Club, directed me down the activist path and mentored me in protecting endangered species. He also introduced me to his favorite cause, preserving the Alaska National Wildlife Refuge. Another of my CES instructors was John P. Wolflin, supervisor of the U.S. Fish and Wildlife Service Chesapeake Bay Field Office. He advised me when I began this book and thought I was just writing a school paper, and he helped me gain interviews with such key resources as Jaime Rappaport-Clark, director of the Fish and Wildlife Service. Mr. Wolflin's encouragement was brief but invaluable.

Larry Silverman, an environmental attorney and adjunct professor at the School of Arts and Sciences at Johns Hopkins, mentored my interest in environmental law and policy—a more realistic path for me than scientific study. He, too, advised me on my master's thesis. I am grateful for his help along the way. Other Hopkins professors who supported and inspired me include Dr. Bjorn Gunnarsson, Dr. Tom Lovejoy of the Smithsonian Institution and World Bank, and Dr. Katelin Szlavecz.

I am grateful to Barbara Ras, executive editor at the University of Georgia Press, for believing in this book and seeing it to publication; and to Kathy Caveney, my first editor, who cleaned it up nicely; and to Sally Antrobus, who helped me express many points more clearly.

Finally, I wish to acknowledge the League of Women Voters. This organization helped support me while I was reeducating myself for my true vocation and allowed me to take the time off I needed to complete the first draft of this book.

A number of my references are transitory in nature in that they are fact sheets, letters, alerts, and memos put out by congressional offices or nongoverment organizations at the time of the writing. I suspect it will be hard or impossible to find these sources in a library or even at the organizations. I have kept copies of all these materials, should any scholar need access to them.

Abbreviations

AAAS	American Association for the Advancement of Science
ACE	U.S. Army Corps of Engineers
APA	Administrative Procedure Act
BCCP	Balcones Canyonlands Conservation Plan
BLM	Bureau of Land Management
BRD	Biological Resources Division
CBD	Convention on Biological Diversity
CEI	Competitive Enterprise Institute
CEQ	Council on Environmental Quality
CESD	Center for Excellence for Sustainable Development
CI	Conservation International
CITES	Convention on International Trade in Endangered Species of Wild Flora and Fauna
DOW	Defenders of Wildlife
DPR	Defenders of Property Rights
E&E Daily	Environment and Energy Publishing daily e-mail service
E&E Weekly	Environment and Energy Publishing weekly e-mail service
ECO	Environmental Conservation Organization
EDF	Environmental Defense Fund (now Environmental Defense)
EIS	Environmental Impact Statement
ENHA	Endangered Natural Heritage Act
EPA	Environmental Protection Agency
ESC	Endangered Species Coalition
FACA	Federal Advisory Committee Act
FHA	Federal Housing Authority
FWS	U.S. Fish and Wildlife Service
GBA	*Global Biodiversity Assessment*
GIS	geographic information system(s)

GSP	gross state product
HCP	Habitat Conservation Plan
ISC	Interagency Scientific Committee
IUCN	International Union for Conservation of Nature and Natural Resources, World Conservation Organization
MOU	memorandum of understanding
MVP	Minimum Viable Population
NBS	National Biological Survey
NCCP	Natural Communities Conservation Plan
NEPA	National Environmental Policy Act
NESARC	National Endangered Species Act Reform Coalition
NRC	National Research Council
NRCS	Natural Resources Conservation Service
NRDC	Natural Resources Defense Council
NWF	National Wildlife Federation
NWI	National Wilderness Institute
OCS	Outer Continental Shelf
PAHs	polycyclic aromatic hydrocarbons
PCBs	polychlorinated biphenyls
PCFFA	Pacific Coast Federation of Fishermen's Associations
ppm	parts per million
PVA	Population Viability Analysis
REA	Rural Electrification Administration
TEDs	turtle exclusion devices
TNC	The Nature Conservancy
TVA	Tennessee Valley Authority
USPIRG	United States Public Interest Research Group
UNEP	United Nations Environment Programme
USFS	U.S. Forest Service
VA	Veterans Administration
WOE	*Daily War on the Environment*
WWF	World Wildlife Fund

Introduction

P EOPLE ARE DAMAGING the earth that sustains us and millions of
other species at a greater rate than nature can replenish it. Visible
evidence abounds; but some of the most alarming indicators are invisible to the average person: these are in the ocean, in the soil, in drinking
water, in the cells of fish, birds, and higher animals, and in the new weather
patterns that sweep the earth.

Destruction is visible in clear-cut forests in the Pacific Northwest, in oil slicks
floating on oceans and rivers, in thousands of fish floating belly-up in the
Chesapeake and the Albemarle-Pamlico estuaries due to the Pfiesteria out-
break in 1997, and in smog clouds covering Los Angeles, Phoenix, and many
industrial cities. Piles of strip-mine tailings and rows of rusted barrels oozing
toxic waste are considered merely an eyesore. Concrete surfaces cover more
and more fields, forests, and floodplains as cities and suburbs expand. Huge
expanses of wildlands are sliced up by superhighways and access roads built
to haul away the natural resources. Many plants and animals succumb to introduced toxins and radically altered habitats; many human beings struggle
with the health effects of pollution but choose not to connect the cause and
effect.

Few consider the invisible damage. But it is there. It is there in the collapse
of natural fisheries. It is there in croplands so depleted by the chemicals used
to enhance crop growth and destroy pests that it now costs huge sums to produce the food supply that once grew with only human sweat. It is there in the
continued incidence of human cancers and the onslaught of new diseases such
as the AIDS and Ebola viruses. It is there in the rising human infertility rate.
Some pollutants, like the pesticide DDT, are passed up the food chain.
Through a natural process called bioaccumulation, they grow in strength as
they move up the chain. Located at the top of the food chain, human beings
all too often do not even discover there is a threat until damage has been done.

Many other indicators attest to the damage. The diversity of life has diminished in the streams, rivers, bays, and oceans that are poisoned by pollutants. Weather patterns have changed because of massive amounts of carbon dioxide and other greenhouse gases produced by human technology and consumption; moreover, the accumulation of greenhouse gases is exacerbated by continued logging of the trees that consume carbon dioxide and produce life-giving oxygen. Major flooding has increased because of the reduction in natural flood-control areas known as wetlands. The cost of the damage to life and property has escalated because people persist in developing and settling in floodplains. Incidence of skin disorders is on the rise because the reduced ozone in the upper atmosphere permits more ultraviolet light to penetrate. Most people have heard about at least some of these pieces of evidence but shrug their shoulders and assume that nothing can be done about it.

There must be hundreds of examples, around the globe, of places rendered uninhabitable or near uninhabitable. The Anacostia watershed in Washington, D.C., and adjacent Maryland counties is an example of severe environmental destruction. Fortunately, it is also an example of how collaborative community action can turn a problem around. The Anacostia is a tributary of the Potomac River, which in turn is tributary to the Chesapeake Bay. The river watershed once supported a dense hardwood forest, abundant wildlife, and streams filled with fish. In 1993–1995, the American Rivers organization named the Anacostia one of the two "Most Endangered" urban U.S. rivers. It was also one of the most ignored rivers in spite of its location in the federal government's backyard and its contribution to the highly popular and protected Chesapeake Bay watershed.

The deterioration of this river began in the nineteenth century with development of the national capital city and intensified land clearing for agricultural development. This led to increasing sedimentation due to erosion of the land adjacent to the river. By 1850, sedimentation was so significant that the port of Bladensburg closed. By the end of the century, extensive mudflats had formed along the banks of the tidal portion of the river. With expanding population during the twentieth century came many land use changes. A large percentage of the forests disappeared from the watershed and the loss of wetlands is estimated at 90 percent. Less than 15 percent of the remaining forest tracts are large enough to support the natural biodiversity (Anacostia 1997).

The river flow has changed and runoff pollution has increased. So have direct discharges of industrial waste. Such discharges should have ceased with the implementation of the Clean Water Act in the 1970s. However, a recent

Greenpeace study of government documents indicated that a U.S. Navy facility in southeast Washington, D.C., continued to discharge polychlorinated biphenyls (PCBs) in spite of the 1976 ban on this chemical. "Samples from the Anacostia [also] contain levels of heavy metals, such as mercury, lead and cadmium, and polycyclic aromatic hydrocarbons (PAHs) which are high above the national average" (Greenpeace 1997). Environmental Protection Agency (EPA) tests conducted in May 1995 reveal PCB levels in one sewer outfall at 227 parts per million (ppm). A discharge above 0.3 ppm is a violation of the Clean Water Act.

PCBs are carcinogens linked to breast, skin, and liver cancers in humans. Recent studies have shown that PCBs are also a human hormone disrupter. PCBs are linked to abnormalities in reproductive organs and can cause birth defects if consumed during pregnancy. The chemical can leach through the soil into groundwater or can be carried off the land by rain and snow into surface waters. PCBs are slow to degrade and therefore pose a threat for many years.

Most of the visible environmental damage is ugly and depressing, but people consider it unavoidable. Some label it progress. Others say it can't be helped or ask in defeat what one person can do. Can these destroyed areas return to healthy natural systems? Left alone, perhaps they can; but how can they do so if human demands remain as voracious as at present? Ultimately, every environmental problem can be traced to the growth of human demand, which is increasing exponentially with the growth of human population. Our increasing demand for fossil fuel energy is the reason that oil, coal, and natural gas deposits worldwide are close to depletion. The demand relates directly to the number of people on the earth. There are huge annual losses of rain forest to create livelihoods for growing populations, particularly in tropical, equatorial countries. (Ironically, tropical soils tend to be poor in nutrients and do not support cultivation for long.) Air pollution is largely a function of increased automobile traffic, increased industry, and increased energy production to meet the demands of more people demanding more goods and more convenient access to the goods. All of these problems are the result of overpopulation of the species *Homo sapiens*, but controlling human population growth is taboo in almost every culture in the world. In the United States, where population growth is caused more by immigration than birth rate, there is disproportionate demand for natural resources relative to other countries because our current standard of living promotes the use of more and new technology and the continued acquisition of goods. While we continually hear from the fossil fuel energy industry or its political supporters that new sources of fossil fuel are located all the time, we must question whether their desire for this to be true is driving these claims.

One of the most threatening environmental changes is the loss of the variety of life. This loss of biodiversity is a function of the demand for more land to support humans as well as of the pollution. Some species die in the destruction process; those capable of migrating move on to more habitable areas; some simply stop reproducing when the habitat can no longer support a population. People console themselves with the knowledge that a lost species still thrives in another place. Perhaps it does; but it no longer contributes to the quality of life in the place where it has been extirpated, and the number of areas remaining where it can thrive continues to diminish. It is hard to take comfort in knowing that the only surviving members of a species are in zoos or exist in potential form as frozen sperm or eggs in a gene bank.

Many argue that change is the way of the natural world. This is true. However, when the change is destructive, it requires the geological time scale, measured in millions of years, or at least the evolutionary time scale, measured in generations, to solve the problem. But the human time scale is measured in decades. Destruction of the earth is proceeding at a pace that far outstrips the planet's ability to recuperate in the human time scale.

Being a nature lover—and I confess, the kind who often prefers animals to people—I could not understand why one of the strongest environmental laws, the Endangered Species Act (ESA), was languishing without reauthorization and often with too little funding. Looking into this, I uncovered a drama unfolding around the nation over reauthorization of the act.

This book is about the social and political issues hobbling the ESA. It explains the science that supports the need to conserve biodiversity—the science behind the endangered species policy—and addresses some of the scientific conflicts. Although I touch on economic issues because they are key to some of the strong emotions swirling around the law, I leave in-depth coverage of this topic to economists.

There is no single policy on biodiversity in the United States. Instead, there are fragments of policy scattered through the statutes that have created and sustained many federal agencies. The Endangered Species Act is often considered U.S. biodiversity policy. However, it covers only a tiny facet of biodiversity—species on the brink of extinction.

Conservation biologists concur that the earth is experiencing the sixth great extinction event in its history. Five others are described in chapter 3. All previous events resulted in the loss of a large number of species. One can only speculate on the reasons for those prehistoric extinctions, but the cause of the sixth event is known—the activities of humankind. The American public, individually and through our elected representatives, must realize that the problem can no longer be deferred for more immediate economic issues. Time and again, the environment loses to the perceived need for jobs and growth. However, human health is dependent on a healthy environment. The real issue is not jobs versus the environment but rather jobs versus human health and survival. Although *Homo sapiens*, or an evolutionary form of *Homo sapiens*, probably will survive beyond the extinction of most other species, such a world is not pleasant to imagine. Ultimately, however, humans will not be able to replace all the natural life support services lost, and we too must go extinct.

It is probably too late to repair within the human time scale all the damage to the biosphere that we have wrought. It would take tens of millions of years, for example, to replenish the fossil fuels we have extracted. Furthermore, the toxic chemicals already introduced into the environment will remain long after they cease being used. Each species that has been lost formerly filled an ecological niche, so each loss creates a functional gap in the web of life. The "average" life span of a species, or of the human species, is not known, but recorded history spans only ten thousand years and fossil evidence of humanoids goes back only about two million years. If people start now to protect the biosphere, there is a reasonable chance that it can be saved for future generations. Life is resilient, but it needs natural resources in a natural state to rebound. In economic terms, the remaining natural capital must be allowed to regenerate itself to support human life.

The Problem

The ESA is in trouble. It needs to be strengthened in order to protect endangered species better; it needs to be improved to assure consistent application of policy on public and private lands in the United States; and it needs to be expanded to foster private protection of a vital national resource. Above all, it needs guaranteed annual funding that is not subject to the vagaries of politics. Yet even these changes would only protect endangered species. Species cannot be protected from becoming endangered unless they are managed in the context of their ecosystems, and this requires implementing an additional discipline: ecosystem management. Some have suggested that the United States should dispense with the ESA altogether and create an EEA—endangered ecosystem act—but I believe that approach only continues the fragmentation of biodiversity policy. Rather, what is needed is a comprehensive biodiversity policy that pulls all the fragments together under one conservation policy umbrella.

Before the future of biodiversity can be improved, however, prevailing social and economic mores must change. As Stan Shetler so aptly puts it, "The biodiversity crisis is not so much a crisis of species as a crisis of lifestyles" (1991:38). Along with the change in belief systems must come new practices that consider and protect the earth and all its inhabitants. While there is a general consensus that it is undesirable to lose species, there is also a strong fear of the changes that may be necessary to stop the losses.

The 104th and 105th congresses (1995–98) fought regulatory interference by natural resources laws with "business as usual." Yet the laws had been enacted because business and industry were destroying natural systems. These congresses were led by strong conservative personalities who believed jobs and economic growth were the key to continued prosperity. The reaction of such leaders to diminishing supplies of oil, coal, timber, and some key minerals is to explore, mine, and log more land, regardless of the losses. This approach addresses today's problems at tomorrow's expense.

Biodepletion is global problem, but my focus is on the United States. It is indicative of the ESA struggle that the United States is the only major power that has not ratified the international Convention on Biological Diversity (CBD). In the domain of biodiversity awareness, the United States is the lagging world power. Why?

Human abuse of the earth is the core of the trouble, and it is compounded by human ignorance and resistance to the facts. But there are promising signs: scientists and environmentalists are being joined by a growing number of members of national, state, and local governments in recognizing the problems. The problem-solving process has started. While much of this book addresses the problems, my underlying purpose is to suggest possibilities for solutions. There are options. Strides have been made to stop biodepletion. My goal is not, however, to provide the answer. There is no single answer to the huge array of problems contributing to the biodepletion crisis. Furthermore, there is no best answer. There is an overwhelming lack of biological information available. Nevertheless, solutions must be devised and implemented. It will take continued collaboration, coordination, communication, and cooperation to resolve the problems. Multiple stakeholders representing state, local, and federal public land managers, private landowners, and public interest groups must work together using an adaptive management strategy to begin the change.

The human species has awesome creative power: we can develop a modified, earth-friendly lifestyle—and we must—or we will pass to future generations an unhealthy, dirty world, devoid of diversity. Evolution is the engine of life; its imperative is survival. The first step is the realization that if other life forms are destroyed now, the future earth will not support human life.

The story of the Endangered Species Act is a real-life drama with fascinating characters, breathtaking action, and heartbreaking inaction. Part 1 describes the history and the science behind the law. In part 2 the opposing players are introduced, and the main action is in part 3—the recent reauthorization attempts, the lack of progress toward more comprehensive biodiversity policy, and the continuing vortex of indecision. Unlike in a well-conceived drama, the denouement keeps dragging on.

The story of the ESA stalemate is tragic in that our system has proven unable to address a crucial national and global problem. In many ways it is the story of overall U.S. environmental policy; there are many parallels between the conflicts over the ESA and those over the Clean Air Act and Clean Water Act. Part 4 proposes a national biodiversity policy that would protect all life systems while also improving the ESA's ability to protect troubled species, acknowledging the rights of private property owners, and encouraging sound public and private land stewardship. I aim to offer ideas for obliterating indecision and resolving the stalemate.

Part One

Setting the Stage

Chapter One

History of the Endangered Species Act

Nothing is more priceless and more worthy of preservation than the
rich array of animal life with which our country has been blessed.
It is a many-faceted treasure, of value to scholars, scientists, and
nature lovers alike and it forms a vital part of the heritage we all
share as Americans. —Richard M. Nixon, as he signed the law, 1973

THE ENDANGERED SPECIES ACT of 1973 (ESA) makes a strong, un-
equivocal statement of national policy on species protection
[§1531(b)]: "to provide a means whereby the ecosystems upon which
endangered species and threatened species depend may be conserved, to provide a program for the conservation of such endangered species and threatened species and to take steps . . . to achieve the purposes of the treaties and
conventions set forth."

In writing the ESA, the authors planned to "make a bold collective statement of moral and legal conviction regarding endangered species" (Kohm
1991:15). The House worked on fourteen different versions; the Senate worked
on three. Congress clearly wanted a strong act to prevent species extinction.
The bill passed both houses of Congress (by a vote of 99 to 1 in the Senate)
and was signed into law by President Richard M. Nixon in December 1973.
"[It] has been regarded as one of this country's most important and powerful
environmental laws and an international model" (Corn 1995, summary).

The story of the ESA is dramatic, eventful, and frustrating. Since passage
of the act, private developers and federal planners have had to review their
plans and activities carefully and make changes to protect listed species. The
law's power to slow and even stop development has made it unpopular with
landowners and land use businesses. Some people feel it threatens jobs; others feel it reduces profits because it requires expenses to protect one species
in order to harvest another.

On the other hand, environmentalists contend that the ESA is only a self-perpetuating emergency response. Some say that it is limited because it does not stop species endangerment; they believe it would be better to change customs and activities in order to avoid or prevent species endangerment in the first place.

The ESA has been challenged by both sides many times in federal courts but has been upheld by the judicial system. The 1990s, especially, were a decade of reaction to the law and its prohibitions. Anti-ESA groups have come head to head with pro-environment forces. The statute is in trouble and species continue to disappear. The conflict, however, makes sense only in the context of the statute's actual provisions and its early history. A summary of the statute by section here clarifies the issues and sets the stage for the discussion in this book (for the full text of the current law, see the URL http://endangered.fws.gov/ESA.html).

Summary of the Endangered Species Act of 1973

Although some sections of the original bill were deleted, the current law retains the original section numbering, thereby producing gaps in sequential numbering. Thus, sections 13, 14, and 16, which appear to be missing from the summaries below, simply do not exist. Of the fifteen sections that remain, four serve as the major "workhorses" of the ESA and play the largest role in conflicts over the law. Section 4 is the listing process and requires the development of a plan to recover the species. Section 7 is the consultation process used on public lands and for federal activities. Section 9 defines taking of a species and is applied to activities on private lands. Section 10 describes the mechanism provided for incidental takings permits on private property—the Habitat Conservation Plan. (Unless otherwise noted, reference throughout the statute to "the Secretary" means the secretary of the Department of the Interior.)

Section 1 (§1530) states the name of the act, and Section 2 (§1531) declares its purpose, as given at the beginning of this chapter. The text states that some species of fish, wildlife, and plants have become extinct as a result of economic growth and development, while populations of other species are in danger of becoming extinct. It asserts that "these species of fish, wildlife and plants are of esthetic, ecological, educational, historical, recreational, and scientific value to the Nation and its people." This section further declares the policy of Congress to be that "all Federal departments and agencies shall seek to conserve endangered species and threatened species and shall utilize their authorities in furtherance of the purpose of this chapter."

Section 3 (§1532) defines the terms used throughout the law. According to Congress, *conserve* and its derivations mean "to use and the use of all methods and procedures which are necessary to bring any endangered species or threatened species to the point at which the measures provided pursuant to this chapter are no longer necessary." Among many other terms defined, the following are especially important to today's issues:

Critical habitat refers to the "specific areas within the geographical area occupied by the species, at the time it is listed . . . on which are found those physical or biological features (I) essential to the conservation of the species and (II) which may require special management considerations or protection." The statute states that the designated critical habitat cannot include a species' entire range.

An *endangered species* is "any species which is in danger of extinction throughout all or a significant portion of its range other than a species of the Class Insecta determined by the Secretary to constitute a pest whose protection under the provisions of this chapter would present an overwhelming and overriding risk to man." A *threatened species* is any species "likely to become endangered within the foreseeable future." *Take* means to "harass, harm, pursue, hunt, shoot, wound, kill, trap, capture, or collect, or to attempt to engage in any such conduct."

Section 4 (§1533) specifies the listing and recovery plan processes. A twelve-month period after receipt of petition is provided for the investigation and listing of a petitioned species. The public notification process requires public listing of the species and their critical habitats as well as public notification of removals of species from the list. Species can be listed as endangered or threatened. The causes of endangerment are defined as modification or reduction of habitat, overutilization, disease or predation, and inadequate regulations. The listing determination must be based "solely" on "the best scientific and commercial data available." Critical habitat is to be determined and listed at the same time a species is listed unless the critical habitat is "not then determinable." In the latter case, the Secretary has another year to declare critical habitat. Unlike the listing determination, critical habitat must be designated "on the basis of the best scientific data available and *after taking into consideration economic impact and any other relevant impact*" (emphasis added). In addition, listed species are required to have a recovery plan. This plan must include a description of necessary site-specific management actions, objective and measurable criteria for determining when the species has recovered sufficiently to be removed from the list, and an estimate of the time and cost involved to carry out the plan.

Section 5 (§1534) authorizes the acquisition of land, water, or interests that will further the conservation of a species.

Section 6 (§1535) directs federal cooperation and consultation with states on land or water purchases. The Secretary can enter into management or cooperative agreements with states that further the goal of conserving endangered or threatened species when the state's program meets federal goals for conserving the species. The effect of such cooperative agreements is to give the state responsibility for the species' program management, research, and monitoring. Federal funding is provided for up to 75 percent of the state's program costs if one state is involved and up to 90 percent of costs if two or more states work together. Congress allocates funds for the Cooperative Endangered Species Fund, where state cooperative agreement monies are reserved.

Section 7 (§1536) directs that all federal agencies assure that no action "authorized, funded, or carried out" by them will jeopardize a listed species, this to be determined in consultation with the U.S. Fish and Wildlife Service or National Marine Fisheries Service. No action may "result in the destruction or adverse modification of habitat of such species." This section requires a written statement of findings to be provided by the Department of the Interior and, if jeopardy is found, written suggestions for alternative courses of action to avoid jeopardy. The agency requesting the consultation must conduct a biological assessment of its project if the Secretary indicates that an endangered or threatened species may be present in the area. Consultations result in one of the following decisions: (1) The planned action will not jeopardize a listed species and may proceed; (2) the planned action may proceed with specified modifications that will avoid species jeopardy; or (3) the planned action may not take place.

Also in this section is a process for obtaining an exemption for federal activities from ESA regulations through the Endangered Species Committee. This committee is defined in the statute and is composed of the secretaries of the Interior, Agriculture, and the Army; the chairman of the Council of Economic Advisors; and the administrators of the Environmental Protection

Agency and the National Oceanic and Atmospheric Administration. The president appoints one representative from each affected state. The section also defines the rules for the meetings and decisions of this committee.

Any of the following may apply to the Secretary for an exemption in writing: the federal agency, the governor of the state in which the agency action is to occur, or the permit or license applicant. The application must set out the reasons an exemption is warranted and must be submitted within ninety days after the final action from a consultation. The applicant must make "a reasonable and responsible effort to develop and fairly consider modifications or reasonable and prudent alternatives to the proposed agency action." The applicant also must have conducted a biological assessment and must not have committed any "irreversible or irretrievable resources to the project." The Endangered Species Committee may not exempt a project from the law permanently if the project will result in the extinction of a species; nor may the committee exempt a project that is in violation of an international obligation. However, projects determined to be necessary for national security may in fact be permanently exempted from the ESA regulations.

In Section 8 (§1537) the law designates the Secretary of the Interior as the management and scientific authority of the Convention on International Trade in Endangered Species of Wild Flora and Fauna (CITES) and the U.S. Fish and Wildlife Service (FWS) as the implementation authority.

Section 9 (§1538) defines prohibited acts in relation to endangered and threatened species. These include importing or exporting any listed species into or out of the United States; taking any species within the territorial (land or sea) United States or on the high seas; possessing, selling, or transporting any species taken in violation of the ESA; engaging in international trade in such species; or removing any such species from federal jurisdiction. Individuals of listed species that were held in captivity or within a controlled environment as of the date of the act were exempted. This is the section applied to private property activities. Until 1982, there was no provision for any exceptions to be made to the full implementation of the ESA on private property.

Section 10 (§1539) specifies exceptions that may be made to the law and under what conditions. For example, the Secretary may permit actions that are for scientific purposes or that "enhance the propagation or survival of the affected species" or any taking that is incidental to an act that is otherwise lawful. The Habitat Conservation Plan (HCP) provision was added to the statute in 1982 to enable the Secretary to grant a permit for incidental takings on private property. An acceptable HCP must include (1) the impact of a taking, (2) what steps will be taken to minimize and fund the mitigation of the impact, (3) what alternatives were considered, and (4) any other measures required to conserve the species involved. An incidental take permit is granted on private property if the Secretary finds that the plan submitted is scientifically sound, well funded, and certified not to result in reduction of the likelihood of the species' survival and recovery in the wild.

Section 11 (§1540) defines the civil and criminal penalties for violations of the act. The civil penalty for knowingly taking an endangered or threatened species is $25,000 per violation. The criminal penalty is $50,000 or imprisonment for up to a year or both. For knowingly violating any other section of the law, the civil penalty is $12,000 and the criminal penalty is $25,000 or six months in prison or both. If one can prove that the taking was done to protect oneself, a member of one's family, or another individual, an exception will be made.

Federal agencies are authorized to carry out their own enforcement of the law. Property may be inspected and, if an endangered species is found, the person holding it may be arrested. The illegal articles and any equipment used in taking the animals may be confiscated.

This section also permits anyone to file a civil suit on his or her own behalf to enjoin another (including the United States) from an action that may harm an endangered or threatened species.

Section 12 (§1541) directed the secretary of the Smithsonian to review the plant kingdom within a year after the passage of the act and to determine which plants should be listed and the methods to be used to conserve them. (Sections 13, 14, and 16 do not exist.)

Section 15 (§1542) authorizes appropriations to fund this law and sets appropriation ceilings for 1988–92 for the Departments of the Interior, Commerce, and Agriculture. It separately authorizes a ceiling on funds for CITES implementation. In practice, Interior funds tend to be broken out for the following activities: prelisting, listing, consultation, permits, recovery, and the Cooperative Endangered Species Fund. Commerce funds tend to be lumped with appropriations for the Marine Mammal Protection Act.

Sections 17 (§1547) and 18 (§1548) set the relationship between the Endangered Species Act and the Marine Mammal Protection Act and require an annual accounting of expenditures by the Fish and Wildlife Service for listing and conserving endangered and threatened species, respectively.

Since the ESA's passage, nearly every state has enacted its own endangered species law and established its own program that parallels and/or supplements the federal program. Conservation of endangered species has been integrated into most federal programs. The law has also stimulated major conservation initiatives by private organizations. Over time, however, the ESA has challenged American traditions and practices, most notably the pursuit of unlimited economic expansion and the perceived right of private property owners to use their land in a manner the owners deem beneficial to themselves.

The act was amended six times—in 1976, 1977, 1978, 1979, 1982, and 1988. The 1976, 1977, and 1979 amendments were primarily concerned with procedures on how to consider and post information, adding to scientific data the use of catch records (commercial records) as a resource for determining endangered status. The substantive changes occurred with the three reauthorizations in 1978, 1982, and 1988.

The 1978 Reauthorization

The first major amendments required the listing of critical habitat for a species concurrent with its listing as endangered. Although the listing of a species may not take economic impact into account, the Secretary must take economic impact into consideration in determining the critical habitat, with the result that the species' entire range may not be designated as critical. Critical habitat designation is one of the more controversial and unpopular elements of the statute. It is intended only to limit any land uses that would endanger the targeted species, but critics of the ESA contend that critical habitat designation stops almost all land use.

The 1978 amendments also prohibited the "irreversible or irretrievable" commitment of agency resources to a project before the ESA consultation was complete. In addition, a written biological opinion was required as the result of formal consultations. The most notable change, however, in these amendments was the creation of an exemption outlet, the Endangered Species Committee. The exemption process in the original act involved a review board; the process was amended with the Endangered Species Committee structure and responsibility (Corn and Baldwin 1990).

The events leading to the 1978 reauthorization and to the creation of the Endangered Species Committee (quickly dubbed the "God Squad") are indicative of the conflicts the ESA has stirred up during its lifetime. Two dam projects opened the political floodgates on the ESA, exposing the law's full power for the first time and surprising many in Washington, D.C.

The first was the Tellico Dam project of the Tennessee Valley Authority (TVA). TVA had built sixty dams, reservoirs, and flood-control projects in four states. Tellico was its sixty-first. It was a $110 million project on the Little Tennessee River. Local and national opposition to the dam had been intense throughout the planning and development cycle.

Congress authorized Tellico Dam in 1966. The project was halted for twenty months in the early 1970s due to a lawsuit charging that its Environmental Impact Statement (EIS) was inadequate and violated the 1969 National Environmental Policy Act (NEPA). It resumed in 1973. That same year, David Etnier of the University of Tennessee discovered a small fish called the snail darter in the portion of the Little Tennessee that would be impounded by the dam. In January 1975 a University of Tennessee student, Hiram G. Hill, and his professor, attorney Zygmunt J. B. Plater, requested an emergency listing for the snail darter.

According to Lynn A. Greenwalt, then head of the Fish and Wildlife Service, Plater saw the snail darter as a way to apply leverage to stop the dam. The FWS advised TVA to stop development, but the latter maintained that the act did not apply to them and continued work on the dam. Greenwalt urged TVA to look in nearby creeks for other populations of the fish, but they did not take his advice on that either (Greenwalt 1995).

The FWS listed the fish on an emergency basis in October 1975 and ruled that TVA could not finish the dam. TVA continued construction and committed another $78 million. Plater filed a lawsuit arguing that Tellico violated the ESA. In April 1976 the district court dismissed the case on its merits, and an appeal was filed. While waiting for the appeal, the circuit court issued an injunction against closing the floodgates of the dam but allowed construction to continue. The appellate court held that the ESA did apply to Tellico and granted an injunction to stop the remaining 10 percent of construction. TVA appealed to the Supreme Court in January 1977.

Greenwalt (1995) recalled this case as the first time two agencies of the federal government faced one another before the Supreme Court. The FWS continued to work with TVA to find a way to allow both the dam and the fish to survive. The battle became a David versus Goliath drama. Attorney General Griffin Bell, in an unusual action for his office, chose to argue the case for TVA himself. Plater represented Hill. Furthering the David and

Goliath image, Bell showed the court the three-inch fish in a test tube and compared it to the hundreds of millions of dollars that had been spent on the Tellico Dam.

The law held. In June 1978, the Supreme Court affirmed the appellate court's ruling for the snail darter. "The plain intent [of the ESA] is to halt and reverse the trend toward species extinction, whatever the cost" (*TVA v. Hill*, 436 U.S. 187 [1978]).

Simultaneously, a less sensational but equally intense battle was occurring over the Grayrocks Dam and Reservoir in Wyoming. The Fish and Wildlife Service determined that the construction of Grayrocks would jeopardize the downstream Platte River habitat of the whooping crane. In 1976 two suits were filed in Nebraska alleging that the Rural Electrification Administration (REA) and the U.S. Army Corps of Engineers (ACE) had failed to consult the FWS under Section 7 of the ESA and might have violated NEPA as well.

On the eve of House passage of the 1978 ESA reauthorization, the federal district court found the ACE and REA in violation of the law. Then the Eighth Circuit Court stayed the lower court injunction against the dam. In December of that year the parties reached a settlement that placed constraints on the operation of the Grayrocks Reservoir and, at the recommendation of the National Wildlife Federation (NWF), established a permanent trust fund of $7.5 million for maintaining the crane's critical habitat. The trust was to be permanently funded by the power companies involved at Grayrocks.

Meanwhile, the members of Congress from Tennessee were in an uproar over the Tellico Dam stoppage. At first they tried to do away with Section 7 of the ESA. Failing that, in 1978 Senators Howard Baker (R-Tenn.) and John Culver (D-Iowa) introduced a bill in the Senate to amend the ESA so as to create a method of exemption or an escape hatch—namely, the Endangered Species Committee, which would be empowered to exempt federal projects from ESA regulations. The plan was to provide a mechanism for dispute resolution outside the court system. The Senate passed the reauthorization bill in July that included the Endangered Species Committee but without a specific exemption for Tellico or Grayrocks.

In the House, Representative John Duncan (R-Tenn.) proposed an amendment to the House reauthorization bill to exempt Tellico. That bill also contained an exemption process and a specific exemption for Grayrocks. It passed in October. The bill reported out of the conference committee excluded the specific exemptions but required the Endangered Species Committee to meet and decide on the two dam projects within thirty days of enactment or the two projects would be exempted automatically. President Jimmy Carter signed the bill in November 1978.

The Endangered Species Committee was empowered to exempt a federal project from the ESA if they judged the economic and social benefits of the project to outweigh the biological consequences. In cases where they declared an exemption, they were required to establish mitigation procedures to offset the resulting jeopardy. The applicant was responsible for funding the mitigation.

The Endangered Species Committee first met in December 1978. In January it rejected the exemption for Tellico but granted the exemption for Grayrocks because of the negotiated mitigation measures, which included the trust fund settlement. Cecil Andrus, chair of the Endangered Species Committee and secretary of the interior at the time, stated in reference to the Tellico decision: "Frankly, I hate to see the snail darter get the credit for stopping a project that was ill-conceived and uneconomical in the first place" (Corn and Baldwin 1990:25).

Later in 1979, when the House considered the Energy and Water Development Appropriations Act, Representative Duncan slipped in an amendment to authorize TVA to finish the dam regardless of the ESA or any other law. This amendment was accepted without recorded vote. The Senate, however, threw the amendment out. The bill was sent back from conference committee, repassed by the House, and after heated debate finally passed the Senate with the amendment to authorize Tellico's completion. The Tellico floodgate was closed on 29 November 1979, allowing the reservoir to fill. Ironically, shortly after the Supreme Court decision was handed down, populations of snail darters were found in other creeks in the Tellico area.

The first two serious challenges to the Endangered Species Act were over. Fortunately, other snail darter populations were found in nearby streams. Otherwise, the Tellico decision would have meant the extinction of the fish. As it was, the crisis raised public awareness of the power of the law and damaged its image because the research had been insufficient. The mitigation plans for Grayrocks were sufficient to protect the whooping crane by providing alternative habitats, thus making the Endangered Species Committee exemption moot. The power of the Section 7 consultation process was demonstrated in the negotiated mitigation plan, which preserved both the species and the dam.

The 1982 Reauthorization

The 1982 amendments relaxed some listing requirements and required the Secretary to issue a preliminary finding on listing within ninety days. The critical habitat listing, which in practice often lagged behind, was formally allowed to follow species listing. Political pressure on federal agencies often intervened to delay critical habitat designation.

Experimental populations—"any population (including any offspring arising solely therefrom) authorized by the Secretary for release . . . when . . . the population is wholly separate geographically from nonexperimental populations of the same species" (*TVA v. Hill*, 436 U.S. 187 [1978])—were also authorized, and Section 9 takings restrictions were relaxed for such populations. The most significant change in 1982 was the permission of incidental takings on private property using a permit application if a mitigation-conservation plan was submitted and accepted.

A key criticism of the ESA was that it did not treat the federal and private sectors equally. Section 7 worked well for government agencies and federal projects on public lands. The consultation process encouraged the discussion of alternatives and cooperative development of mitigation steps to avoid species jeopardy; consequently, the vast majority of the consultations resulted in project authorization and protected the species concerned. Permits for incidental takings (members of the species killed inadvertently as a result of the development process) were routinely granted with these authorizations. Moreover, the bulk of the consultations occurred informally, often by telephone, between agencies on federal projects.

By contrast, Section 9 was applied in the private sector; it had no consultation process and, initially, no mechanism for incidental takes. In fact, it prohibited any taking of species. In addition, in the late 1970s the legal council for the Fish and Wildlife Service said no federal action could be taken to protect a listed species on private property unless there was a taking—a dead body—or unless Section 7 could be invoked by establishing a federal nexus, or a connection to an existing federal project or procedure. Prior to the 1982 amendments, therefore, when endangered species were found on private property, the FWS was forced to be creative. Joe Dowhan, then a biologist with FWS assigned to the California-Nevada region, shared two illustrative stories.

In the first, the taking prohibition was enforced. A small company in the Antioch Dunes of the San Joaquin Valley owned land at the confluence of the American and Sacramento rivers just above San Francisco Bay. The company was mining the sand from the area. Because the dunes were home to the Langes metalmark butterfly, the FWS tried to acquire the land as a wildlife refuge, but the owners showed no interest in selling. Although it was difficult for the FWS to prove that the butterflies were being chased away, biologists knew that once a year the butterflies deposited their eggs on a species of wild buckwheat, a plant on which the hatched larvae would feed. Therefore the destruction of these plants with the larvae could be considered a taking. Dowhan and a law enforcement officer he described as a "ten-foot, three-inch giant" went to the dunes; the officer stood in front of a bulldozer and halted it. Dowhan advised the company that the larvae were in front of the bulldozer and any further action would be an "intent to take with a $20,000 fine for each violation." That stopped further excavation. When negotiations with the landowners were reopened, the owners were willing to sell the property. The FWS used the statute's Section 5 authorization to purchase lands for conservation and paid the landowner for his property. The area is now a national wildlife refuge (Dowhan 1995).

In the second case, that of the San Diego mesa mint, Dowhan sought a federal nexus to save an endangered plant because plants are not protected under the ESA from taking on non-federal lands by private actions. The vernal pools on the mesas around San Diego hosted the mint plant during the rainy season, but the pools dried up after the rain. These pools also contained fairy shrimp and a variety of invertebrates. Developers would have to destroy the pools in order to build. The federal nexus Dowhan found was with the Federal Housing Authority (FHA). The FWS maintained that home mortgage loan approvals were, in this case, a federal action that was contributing to the jeopardy of an endangered species and therefore in violation of the ESA. It was a long battle between developer and federal agency and between the agencies, but eventually the VA and FHA denied home loans. This forced the developer to prepare a conservation plan (Dowhan 1995).

In 1982, Congress created Section 10a of the ESA, which permitted incidental takings on private land with the submission and acceptance of a conservation plan. This later became known as a Habitat Conservation Plan or HCP. HCPs were created to help private landowners with the process of accommodating endangered species on their land. This amendment created a means of identifying alternatives to permit conservation of species and desired owner land use. It was intended to create equity in the treatment of private property owners. Owners could specify in the HCP the actions they would take to offset any negative effects on endangered species. When the plan was judged financially and biologically sound by the Fish and Wildlife Service, the FWS issued an incidental take permit for the project. As with Section 7, however, a project could not imperil a species as a whole.

The idea for habitat conservation plans came from Lindell Marsh, a California lawyer who "had long worked at the confluence of private property and endangered species" (Mann and Plummer 1995a:45). In the early days of the ESA, Marsh brokered a deal on San Bruno Mountain near San Francisco in which the developer created a plan to protect three species of butterflies. He believed in the approach and recommended it to Southern California developers to consider given the potential listing of the coastal California gnatcatcher. The first formal HCP was submitted in 1986 for the Coachella Valley in Riverside County, California, the home of the fringe-toed lizard.

This approach seemed like a good answer to the problem of dealing with endangered species on private lands. In practice, however, the system is riddled with difficulties and inequities. For example, the expense of developing an HCP makes such a plan almost impossible for small landholders. The time-consuming nature of the plan adds frustration, cost, and sometimes significant delay for private owners. This has become a key source of controversy today.

The 1988 Reauthorization

The next triennial reauthorization (1985) did not happen. Congress held it up largely because of concern in the western states over management of two major predator species: gray wolves and grizzly bears. Senator Alan Simpson (R-Wyo.) helped block reauthorization in 1985. In 1987 Representative Ron Marlene (R-Mont.) tried and failed to block the listing of the gray wolf. Wyoming put pressure on the Reagan Administration to postpone the Environmental Impact Statement for the reintroduction of wolves into Yellowstone. Another proposal put forth by Senator James D. McClure (R-Idaho) would list the wolf within the recovery area only and delist it outside that area. This was defeated because it would return control to states in the delisting area (Ernst 1991).

Wyoming was concerned over "nuisance" grizzly bears, and the reintroduction of wolves was perceived to be a major threat to livestock operators in other states as well. Wyoming and Montana excluded themselves from the recovery plans for the wolf, and Idaho would not permit use of state funds for wolf recovery. The story of one Montana rancher illustrates the issue. He leased public land on Chief Mountain east of Glacier National Park and grazed eight hundred sheep on it. Five grizzlies occupied the area and attacked his sheep; he found eighty-four dead. Although he could not legally shoot the bears because they were listed as federally threatened, there were other options for discouraging the bears from attacking his flock, such as fencing; but he did not use them. He shot one bear as it approached his flock. After this incident, the rancher sold off the rest of his sheep for, in his reckoning, a $10,000 loss. He was fined $2,500 for shooting the bear and spent $60,000 in legal fees to appeal his case (Chadwick 1995). The rancher believed he had a right to protect his personal property from predation, but the ESA provides no such permission. Predator control and reintroductions in the West continue to be major points of controversy.

Another issue in the 1980s was the inconsistent funding for cooperative agreements with the states. Although the act calls for federal funding of state cooperative agreements, the appropriations for Section 6 were frequently reduced by Congress, leaving insufficient funds for this program. The 1988 ESA amendments provided funding for state cooperative agreement programs equal to 5 percent of the combined amounts in the Federal Aid to Wildlife Restoration Fund and the Sport Fishing Restoration Account. Congressional allocations were to be held in the Cooperative Endangered Species Fund. Federal Aid to Wildlife Restoration and Sport Fishing Restoration funds come from sales taxes on hunting and fishing equipment, respectively. Nevertheless, funding remains an issue today because the Cooperative Endangered Species Fund is still subject to annual appropriations (Ernst 1991).

The 1988 amendments also recognized the backlog of candidates waiting to be listed and required the Secretary to monitor the status of candidate species and, if necessary, to make use of emergency powers to list them. Amendments strengthened the protection of plants by prohibiting the private collecting of endangered plants on federal lands and the harming of endangered plants on private land.

Endangered Species Case Law

Judicial decisions have generally supported the ESA and further shaped endangered species law. Case law affirms the statutory intent to balance species existence with economic development. In fact, "the courts have invariably upheld land management agency actions intended to protect listed species even though the effect on human economic and recreational interests was substantial" (Coggins 1991:66). U.S. Circuit and Supreme Court cases fall into three broad categories: those challenging conservation of habitat as a mechanism for conserving species or challenging the taking of habitat as a form of species taking; those demanding that an executive agency enforce the law; and those challenging the intent of the law.

Statutory intent challenges began in 1978 with *TVA v. Hill* (436 U.S. 187) in regard to the Tellico Dam project, when the Supreme Court ruled that the ESA intended to stop species extinction whatever the cost. In *Carson-Truckee Water Conservancy District v. Clark* (741 F. 2d 257 [9th Cir. 1984]), the circuit court of appeals rejected the argument that the ESA required the Secretary to avoid "only those actions that jeopardized the bare survival of the species." In *Sierra Club v. Clark* (755 F. 2d 608 [8th Cir. 1985]), the court outlawed a sport hunting season on gray wolves in Minnesota, thus affirming that the ESA prohibits public taking of listed species (except in "extraordinary circumstances where it is the only way to relieve population pressures").

Several times over the history of the ESA, environmental organizations have provided legal support to local groups to force either the Forest Service or the Fish and Wildlife Service to enforce the law. In *Cabinet Mountains Wilderness v. Peterson* (685 F. 2d 678 [D.C. Cir. 1982]), the court allowed a prospective mining operation to proceed in a grizzly bear habitat only when the FWS and the Forest Service imposed mitigating steps on the prospector to protect the animal. In another case, *Foundation for North American Wild Sheep v. U.S.* (681 F. 2d 1172 [9th Cir. 1982]), the court enjoined the construction of a new road because the mitigation procedures were not found to be sufficient. Enforcement of the law with ongoing project operation as opposed to new development was addressed in *Carson-Truckee Water Conservancy District v. Watt* (549 F. Supp. 704 [D. Nev. 1982]). The court held that the secretary of the interior had a duty to operate a California reservoir located in Pyramid Lake Indian Reservation to protect endangered and threatened species. The issue addressed the degree to which fish requirements should be preferred over human needs, and the court held that all other uses had to be deferred until the fish were safe. Finally, in *Northern Spotted Owl v. Hodel* (755 F. 2d 608 [8th Cir. 1985]), the court ruled that based on the available scientific evidence, the FWS acted arbitrarily by refusing to list the owl.

Four cases addressing the importance of habitat to species protection stand out. In *Palila v. Hawaii Department of Land and Natural Resources* (471 F. Supp. 985 [D. Hawaii 1979], aff'd, 639 F. 2nd 495 [9th Cir. 1981]), the Sierra Club brought suit on behalf of the Hawaiian finch known as the palila. The court found that the state's game management practice of allowing feral sheep and goats to graze in protected palila habitat resulted in the destruction of the nesting areas of the palila. The case tested the question of whether habitat modification could constitute a species taking and found that it could. Later the FWS promulgated their clarification of the word "harm" in the ESA takings definition, formalizing the court's decision into regulation.

In *Nebraska v. REA* (12 ERC 1156 [D. Neb. 1978]) and in *Riverside Irrigation District v. Andrews* (758 F. 2d. 508 [10th Cir. 1985]), the courts held that the ESA protected the temporary habitat of migrating birds even in areas downstream from the project at issue. The former case was part of the Grayrocks Reservoir and Dam controversy, ultimately settled out of court, and the Riverside case concerned the Wildcat Dam and Reservoir in Colorado: both dams affected the Platte River stopover habitat of the whooping crane.

In *Friends of Endangered Species v. Jantzen* (760 F. 2d 976 [9th Cir. 1985]), the court interpreted Section 10(a) to mean that a valid conservation plan can reduce the extent of a species' existing habitat while improving the remaining habitat and creating a trust fund for maintaining that portion in the future, as long as the plan and project do not appreciably reduce the total population of the species.

In 1995, in *Babbitt v. Sweet Home Chapter of Communities for a Great Oregon* (63 U.S.L.W. 3500 [1995]), the Supreme Court handed down a 6–3 decision, ruling that "the Fish and Wildlife Service had not exceeded the intent of the Endangered Species Act by prohibiting the modification or destruction of wildlife habitat on private land in order to protect threatened and endangered species from 'harm.'" The suit involved timber industry interests in the Northwest and Southeast claiming that the FWS interpretation of "harm" to a species was too broad when it imposed logging restrictions on private land. The two species involved were the northern spotted owl and the red-cockaded woodpecker. Industry had won this case in the D.C. Circuit Court of Appeals. The Supreme Court overturned the decision. The case focused on the interpretation of the word *harm* as used in Section 3 of the ESA and as clarified in FWS regulations to mean "significant habitat modification or degradation [that] actually kills or injures wildlife by significantly impairing essential behavioral patterns including breeding, feeding, or sheltering." This case was not a direct private property rights "takings" assault on the act, but it was brought by private property rights organizations.

More recently, the Supreme Court heard *Bennett et al. v. Spear et al.* The case was argued on November 13, 1996, and decided on March 19, 1997 (case no. 95-813). In this case, the petitioners were irrigation districts and private ranchers whose water allocations were being curtailed to protect two endangered species of fish. They claimed that the jeopardy determination, and the subsequent imposition of minimum water levels determined to be a "reasonable and prudent" alternative permitting continued access to the water without jeopardizing the fish, constituted an "implicit critical habitat determination" without a consideration of the economic impact. The district court dismissed the complaint on the grounds that the petitioners lacked standing to sue. The court of appeals upheld this conclusion. The Supreme Court, maintaining that the petitioners did have standing under the ESA and under the Administrative Procedure Act (APA) and did have sufficient grounds for suit, reversed the district court decision and sent the case back to be heard. The environmental community has portrayed this decision as a loss for endangered species because it opens the door for judicial review of more ESA-related cases. However, inasmuch as the ESA already offers citizens fairly liberal standing, it is difficult to see how this will impact FWS decision making significantly.

There have clearly been conflicts over the Endangered Species Act throughout its history, many of which have been resolved in the courts. It is an intrusive law, and it can interfere with plans of private developers, with access to water, and with economic expansion. More often than not, it has delayed plans rather than stopping them. These historical conflicts, however, are the base from which today's dilemma grew.

Chapter Two

The Endangered Species Act Today

As the world's most potent single piece of environmental legislation,
the Endangered Species Act is reshaping the way our society lives
upon the land, and it is fueling bitter debate over economic balance,
property rights and the limits to growth.—Douglas Chadwick, 1995

A
FTER TWO DECADES of change through congressional amendments
and judicial decisions, the Endangered Species Act of 1973 has remained unauthorized since October 1992. This is the longest it has
languished since its enactment. The 104th Congress (1994–96) attempted to
reduce the muscle of the law dramatically and to make it friendlier to private
property owners, even though there was no evident mandate from the voters
in 1994 to do so. That Congress failed to pass such legislation, and it took the
105th Congress (1997–98) the entire first session to introduce two reauthorizing bills, one in each house. The House bill was the better legislation because it addressed the needs of most endangered species and began to equal-
ize the differences between public and private land policy. The Senate bill
was a bipartisan compromise between environmentalists and private property
rights proponents—a large step toward ending the polarization—with an excellent public education component. Neither bill survived. The House bill
from the 105th was reintroduced in the 106th Congress, but no action was
taken to address it. Before his death in late 1999, endangered species supporter
Senator John Chafee (R-R.I.) ushered two ESA amendment bills through the
Senate Environment and Public Works Committee. Neither was a reauthorization bill. Late in the first session, Rep. Don Young (D-Alaska) introduced
another ESA reauthorization bill. Hearings were held on it in the House in
the first quarter of 2000. Just before the end of the Congress, Sen. Frank
Lautenberg (D-N.J.) introduced a Senate companion bill to Miller's House

bill from the first session, a positive ending note for this Congress. Still, there was no resolution.

Although the ESA is a model law in its regulation of harmful activities on public lands, it is also an intrusive law that interferes with human endeavors. Chapter 1 shows how conflicts over the law were greatly magnified when endangered species were discovered on private property in the 1980s. Emotions ran high when owners were required to modify or stop their development plans. By 1990, parties in the conflicts had coalesced into two main camps: those propounding the citizen's right to manage private property without federal interference, represented by the private property rights movement, and those expressing the human desire to protect other species from extinction, represented by the environmental movement.

Environmentalists had begun to coalesce into a cohesive movement in the 1960s. Within this movement are a number of organizations that have not wavered in their support of a strong ESA. The private property rights movement took root in the early 1990s after a decade of strain between private property owners and the ESA. These two movements are discussed in depth in later chapters.

The courts have upheld the law through many challenges. Developers now accept that they may have to alter their plans or mitigate for the consequences if an endangered or threatened species occurs on the land in question. From a legal viewpoint, however, the ESA is a limited remedy focusing on a single species and only when the entire population of that species is in jeopardy (Coggins 1991). Therefore, under political pressure, it is easy for federal agencies to water down legal requirements.

Endangered Species Update

Although the law helps stave off species extinction when implemented promptly, its implementation has been subject to political whims throughout its twenty-seven-year history. As a result, its effectiveness has been sporadic and incomplete. On the whole, the ESA has protected species identified as threatened or endangered on public lands but has been less effective for species on private lands. Though no law can prevent all species extinction, the scientists who conducted the National Research Council's 1995 study on the scientific validity of the ESA concluded that "fewer species have become extinct than would have without the ESA" (NRC 1995:11). The U.S. Fish and Wildlife

Service (FWS 1997b) noted that of all species listed between 1968 and 1993, less than 1 percent—only seven species—had become extinct. Moreover, only 35 percent of the listed species were still in decline, and 64 percent were still "critical" but their status was improving. The NRC report named some of the species for which status had improved: Utah prairie dog, piping plover, Oregon silver-spot butterfly, Aleutian Canada goose, Gila trout, greenback cutthroat trout, least Bell's vireo, California least tern, Virginia big-eared bat, and red wolf.

Scientists disagree on how many species are going extinct and how fast. However, there is unanimous agreement that the current extinction rate (percentage of species dying off per year) exceeds that in any past episode and that the cause this time is assuredly humans. Opinions on the crisis vary across a wide spectrum. At one extreme is the economic growth–private property view. Journalists Charles Mann and Mark Plummer contend that "saving all species everywhere would cook our society to death" (1995b:113), meaning destroy our society as we know it today. At the other extreme is the moral perspective: Paul and Anne Ehrlich of Stanford University maintain that "it is an offense against nature to eliminate a race of living beings from the Earth" (Mann and Plummer 1995b:25). In between are more moderate perspectives. The editor of the *Journal of Conservation Biology*, David Ehrenfeld, argues that species should be cherished "because they exist and have existed for a long time" (in Mann and Plummer 1995b:25). Senator John Dingell (1991:26) says: "Living wild species are like a library of books still unread. Our heedless destruction of them is akin to burning that library without ever having read its books."

In the early 1970s, overhunting, collecting, and pollutants were the recognized sources of species endangerment. Scientists had already discovered that the use of the pesticide DDT was decimating populations of bald eagles, peregrine falcons, ospreys, and other predatory birds. DDT weakened their eggshells so that the eggs broke under the weight of the incubating adult; in time, the lowered birth rates caused populations to crash. Overhunting had taken its toll on wolves, grizzly bears, American alligators, and whales. Tigers, elephants, rhinos, and spotted cats were being killed simply for their hides, tusks, or horns. Even butterfly species were disappearing because they were so popular among collectors.

These problems were addressed in the takings restrictions of the ESA, and a few species—like the eagle, the American alligator, and some whales—have recovered well, apparently because the major source of the problem was curtailed. The recovery of the bald eagle is cited as an example of how the law has succeeded *and* how it has failed. The U.S. national symbol has recently been downlisted from endangered to threatened and will soon be delisted altogether. ESA opponents contend that the law had nothing to do with the eagles' recovery; instead the banning of DDT saved them. ESA supporters agree that removal of the direct cause of destruction saved the birds from extinction but assert that provisions of the ESA enabled eagles to find nesting sites, protected the birds from hunters, and safeguarded their habitats from other anthropogenic interference.

Limitations of the ESA

The effectiveness of the ESA is limited not only by failure to implement its provisions but also by the lack of appropriate provisions to implement. Section 2 (§1531) of the Endangered Species Act (1973) clearly states that it is national policy to conserve endangered and threatened species *and* the ecosystems on which they depend. The balance of the statute, however, deals only with species and species habitat. The ESA does not protect the ecosystems that support multiple habitats and species.

Even in its consideration of single species, the law is imperfect in setting unequal levels of treatment and protection for different biological groups. Vertebrate animals receive the most protection; plants and invertebrate animals receive considerably less. Among invertebrates, insects that are considered pests are excluded from protection. According to the National Research Council (NRC 1995), there is no scientific basis for this treatment distinction. Discrimination between plants and animals and between vertebrates and invertebrates ignores the scientific importance of the trophic levels in the food chain as well as the value of ecosystem services, such as the role of plants in climate and pollution control and the role of insects in recycling waste material.

Similarly, the law is imperfect in its treatment of habitat, possibly because the problem of habitat fragmentation and degradation was not well understood in the early 1970s. Today, scientists concur that habitat fragmentation by deforestation, agriculture, road building, and urban development is the primary cause of species endangerment. The ESA does not adequately address habitat disturbance or fragmentation.

The ESA was written to address emergency situations. Hence, it takes effect only when a species is already in serious trouble. Speaking metaphorically, one could say that it takes effect when the species is so sick that it needs emergency hospital care, an analogy Mollie Beattie used as director of the Fish and Wildlife Service (1993–96). As in any emergency room, some patients get help in time to be saved, and some do not. Taking the analogy a step further, a biodiversity policy would function like preventive care: it would minimize endangerment by protecting the natural system that shelters multiple species, including species on the endangered list and also human beings.

Chapter 3 addresses the scientific aspects of biological diversity, or biodiversity. For now the term can be defined as the variety of life on earth. Biodiversity and its importance to humankind were not well understood until almost a decade after the ESA was enacted, although the concepts of ecosystem, ecology, and the interaction of life forms began to enter the national consciousness in the late 1960s. The science of conservation biology has also evolved since 1973. Knowledge of the scope of biological diversity and its role in human well-being is growing. Unfortunately, today's bureaucrats, politicians, and even environmentalists tend to think of the ESA as a national biodiversity policy, but it is not. Endangered species are an important element of biodiversity—but only one element. In reauthorizing the law, therefore, it would be appropriate to expand it into a biodiversity policy or to pass a separate statute as an umbrella policy on biodiversity. Logically, most of our land use laws would fall under this biodiversity policy. The difficulty with subsuming these laws under a single umbrella policy is that much of our economy relies on land use such as forestry, fisheries, agriculture, and the extraction of fossil fuels and minerals.

Western society, especially in the United States, stresses economic growth and development and assigns all things monetary value. Often, when the monetary value is not readily evident, the item in question is not deemed valuable. It is difficult to place a cash value on biodiversity, although many are trying. Environmental economists, scientists, and government agencies responsible for the ESA have struggled to assign values to species and natural services and to make them fit the mold of today's economic models.

But there is more to this. Although biodiversity is necessary to the ultimate survival of the human race, the time it will take on our present trajectory for life to become impossible for humans is unknown. The political and economic issues can hence all be reduced to one basic dilemma: should decisions be made for humanity's needs today or for the needs of future generations? I suggest that this conflict cannot be resolved until society recognizes that biodiversity is the basis for all survival and thus transcends all other economic and political measures.

International Perspectives

Biodiversity is truly a global issue, as are most environmental problems. At the National Academy of Sciences Conference on Nature and Human Society in October 1997, Undersecretary of State Tim Wirth noted that globalization is occurring at an increasingly rapid pace. Fostered by crises such as biodepletion, stock market crashes, and the economic and ecological effects of El Niño, relationships between countries are rapidly becoming as important as the individual identities of those countries (Wirth 1997).

The United Nations has focused on endangered species and biodiversity issues for several decades. The principle that nations must not harm the international environment was first defined in 1941 by the International Court of Justice and was codified in 1972 in the Stockholm Declaration on the Human Environment. In 1982 the UN adopted the World Charter of Nature, which stated that natural resources must be used "in a manner which ensures the preservation of the species and ecosystems for the benefit of present and future generations" (Norse 1993:208).

The best known of many UN sponsored organizations focusing on endangered species and biodiversity issues is the International Union for Conservation of Nature and Natural Resources (IUCN), also known as the World Conservation Organization. It consists of more than six hundred government research institutions and private conservation groups. In the 1960s, IUCN began defining the status of plants and animals and created three categories of species: endangered, threatened, and vulnerable. It also began publication of the Red Data Books (or Red Lists) giving listings of the species in each category. These books continue to be updated and used today. The IUCN goal for the preservation of natural ecosystems is to preserve a cross section of all major ecosystems around the world. That should include at least 13 million square kilometers, or 8–10 percent of the world's land surface. About 4.25 million square kilometers, or 2.8 percent of the earth's surface, is protected today (Meffe and Carroll 1997).

Two important international conventions specifically address biodiversity and species conservation. The Convention on International Trade in Endangered Species of Wild Fauna and Flora, commonly known as CITES, came first. CITES (pronounced "sy-tees") became effective in 1973—the same year as the ESA—with 56 signatory nations, including the United States, and 139 parties. This convention regulates international trade to prevent extinction of endangered species. At the same time it recognizes that individual nations are in the best position to protect their own wildlife. CITES includes three species lists:

> Appendix I contains species threatened with extinction that are or may be affected by trade. This list is analogous to the ESA's "endangered" designation.
>
> Appendix II includes species that *may become* extinct and species similar in appearance to an endangered species, needing to be regulated in order to protect the endangered species. This list is analogous to the ESA's "threatened" designation.
>
> Appendix III includes species that any party nation identifies as being subject to regulation to prevent exploitation.

Regulating international trade of endangered species involves a system of permits: specimens of species listed in Appendixes I and II must have both export and import permits. For Appendix I species, these permits signify that the specimen was not taken illegally, that its export does not jeopardize the species' survival, and that the primary use of the specimen will be for noncommercial purposes. For Appendix II species, the permit signifies that the specimen does not reduce the species' population to the level at which it would become eligible for Appendix I protection.

The second international convention—written almost twenty years after the first—is the Convention on Biological Diversity (CBD), developed under the aegis of the United Nations Environment Programme (UNEP). The eighty nations that negotiated the convention recognized that the distribution of biological resources crosses state boundaries and that preserving biodiversity therefore requires the cooperation of all nations. Signed at the Earth Summit in Rio de Janeiro in June 1992, the CBD went into force in 1993 with 184 signatory nations and 169 parties.

These did not and still do not include the United States. Though President Clinton signed it, Congress has not ratified it. The outlook for the United States signing this convention is bleak for the near future: Senator Jesse Helms (R-N.C.), chair of the Senate Foreign Relations Committee, the congressional versity remain in limbo. Species, ecosystems, and genetic diversity continue in jeopardy. Regulatory implementation, when carried out, remains inequitable. The dilemma is exacerbated by strong emotions; parties have been polarized and are only beginning to cross the polar divide. The United States Congress is currently at a stalemate over environmental policy, with no resolution in sight, and the Clinton Administration moved on its own to make some policy headway to protect species.

committee charged with recommending ratification of international agreements, has clearly stated that he will not address the CBD.

The CBD is the first international protocol to address all aspects of biodiversity: genes, species, and ecosystems. It has three primary goals: (1) the conservation of biological diversity, (2) the sustainable use of biodiversity components, and (3) equitable sharing of the benefits of the use of genetic resources. To attain these goals, CBD articles call for national biological assessments; national biodiversity inventories and ongoing monitoring of biodiversity; research and training; impact assessment; and technical and scientific cooperation between nations. While it affirms "the sovereign right" of nations to use their own resources based on their own environmental policies, the convention calls on all nations to identify and monitor their biodiversity and to integrate consideration of the conservation and sustainable use of resources into national policy (World Bank 1997a).

Two years after the passage of the convention, UNEP produced the Global Biodiversity Assessment. This comprehensive document, which includes the contributions of fifteen hundred scientists worldwide, provides a baseline of current biodiversity knowledge, issues, and theories and underscores the urgent need for further research (World Bank 1997; see Watson and Heywood 1995).

When considering endangered species legislation in 1973, Congress envisioned addressing the problems of such "charismatic megafauna" as grizzly bears, whales, and bald eagles. A great deal more is now known about the extinction problem, and it is far more extensive and complex than was recognized in 1973. Species often need more space than people want to provide, especially when their habitats include private property. When economic plans are interrupted, delayed, or thwarted, it is hard to remember how important other plant and animal species are to human existence. Rain forest biologist and chief biodiversity advisor at the World Bank Thomas Lovejoy said: "Conservation is sometimes perceived as stopping everything cold, as holding whooping cranes in higher esteem than people. . . . the choice is not between wild places or people, it is between a rich or an impoverished existence for Man" (Lovejoy 1997).

For eight years, Congress has failed to act on endangered species and biodiversity issues at the national or international level. The Endangered Species Act and the question of ratifying the Convention on Biological Di-

Chapter Three

The Importance of Biodiversity

It is from the earth that we must find our sustenance; it is on the
earth that we must find solutions to the problems that promise to
destroy all life here. —Justice William O. Douglas

THE WORD *biodiversity*, the shortened form of biological diversity, was
introduced by Dr. Thomas Lovejoy at the first Forum on Biodiversity
in September 1986. Biodiversity is a descriptive word and one that is
relatively easy to learn: "Probably few words have entered the vocabulary of
science and attained widespread acceptance with such ease and speed"
(Shetler 1991:37). The challenge is to assure that it becomes a common household term, as well understood as, for example, *cost of living index*.

Put simply, biodiversity refers to the variety of life forms, the variety of ecological roles, and the diverse genetic composition of the life forms. Biodiversity
embraces all aspects of the natural world: genes, ecosystems and landscapes,
and species. Biodiversity encompasses not only all life forms but the interactions among these life forms. It includes large, familiar land and sea animals,
small songbirds and insects, and the flowering plants they pollinate. Just as
important to the functioning of the biosphere are the fungi that facilitate
the processing of nutrients; the algae, bacteria, and viruses; and the host of
unknown or unclassified microscopic organisms. Biodiversity applies to the
total variety of species in the whole universe as well as to the assortment of
weeds in one's own backyard.

Biodiversity is used most frequently to refer to species variety in an ecosystem. An ecosystem is a community of living organisms interacting with one
another and with the nonliving, physical environment. The physical environment includes the climate, landforms, atmospheric conditions, and nutrient
sources.

Biodiversity also refers to the variety of ecosystems in the world, from Arctic tundra to deciduous and evergreen forests, to desert scrublands, and to coastal beaches. Amazingly, even the desolate landscapes of the Sahara Desert and the Antarctic glaciers have thriving life forms. The art of nature lies in its diversity, the complexity of its diverse interconnections, and the transparent and seemingly effortless interactions among species and between species and the physical environment. The concept of biodiversity involves everything from minute genetic structures and processes through species, populations, ecosystems, and landscape processes.

Conservation of biodiversity may be the most difficult environmental problem the world faces today because the interactions between life forms and between living and nonliving elements are so complex and so little understood. Although scientists know that every species has a function within its ecosystem, we do not yet know what roles most species play or what the impact would be if a particular species became extinct. Not all species in an ecosystem are critically important to its functioning, but no one knows how much diversity can be lost before the ecosystem will collapse.

Conservation of biodiversity is also one of the harder concepts for people to grasp in its entirety. Water and air pollution can be seen and experienced, but biodepletion—the loss or reduction of biodiversity—is harder to detect. Extinction occurs in subtle increments and is usually not perceived until it is too late. For conservation measures to succeed, we need broad public awareness of what biodiversity is and what difference it makes to human life.

The basic value of biodiversity was identified by the National Research Council (1995:vi): "The earth's non-human biota are crucial to humans' long-term survival. We depend on the photosynthetic capability of green plants for the oxygen that we breathe and for virtually all of our food and energy requirements." This statement is so important that it bears restating for clarity: the long-term survival of humankind depends on plants, which are not only our primary food source but also the source of the oxygen in our atmosphere. There was no oxygen in the earth's atmosphere until the first green plants appeared and began the process of photosynthesis. The animals that provide carnivores and omnivores with their source of meat feed on plants—grasses, leaves, or microscopic marine vegetation.

Biodiversity provides people with other critical services, for free. These ecosystem services include natural medicines and the prototypes for synthetic pharmaceuticals, natural flood and pollution control, natural soil fertilization and pest control, climate control, the breakdown of waste material into elemental nutrients that are recycled for plant consumption, and the absorption of pollutants such as carbon dioxide. Moreover, prudent use and conservation of such natural resources as fossil fuels, fish, shellfish, trees, and marshes promote economic well-being with continued employment opportunities.

Unfortunately, there are obstacles to understanding the value of biodiversity. With technological intervention creating synthetic foods and medicines, with drinking water filtration systems making polluted water drinkable, and with electronic gadgets providing synthetic outdoor recreation, people are losing awareness of natural ecosystem services. Technological services work, however, only because they mimic the natural systems — at a price. Worse yet, economic systems undervalue or ignore depletion of natural resources and encourage their exploitation.

Still another obstacle is lack of proximity: if the problem is not in the immediate geographical neighborhood, it is hard to recognize the danger. For example, we who live in temperate climates find it difficult to understand how the loss of millions of acres of tropical rain forests will impact us. We urgently need public education to overcome all these obstacles in order for people truly to understand the necessity of biodiversity for the survival of the human race. Only then will the conservation of biodiversity become a priority.

To address the wide range of issues involved in biodiversity conservation, a new area of scientific study began in the 1970s and has evolved into the multifaceted discipline known as conservation biology. Shetler (1991:38) described the interdisciplinary nature of its subject: "Conservation is not simply an academic matter of comprehending and ranking the scientific worth of various parcels of nature, but also a matter of human motive and a function of how people behave. It ultimately depends, therefore, on social more than scientific factors." Conservation biology is an umbrella science that incorporates biological, physical, and social science disciplines.

Members of these various disciplines are working together to acquire missing knowledge and to develop methods for working with incomplete knowledge. As a group, conservation biologists endorse three guiding principles:

1. Biological conservation must be carried out within the framework of evolution.

2. Ecosystems are not in equilibrium and therefore must be managed to maintain their natural dynamics.

3. Human actions will always have an impact on the rest of nature and must be considered part of any management strategy

Unique to the science of conservation biology is a value statement—that all life is important and must be conserved. Some politicians view the science skeptically *because* it professes values and because it encompasses so many disciplines.

To conserve and sustainably utilize biodiversity, conservationists need answers to a number of questions: What species exist? How abundant is a particular species? Where is it found? What abiotic and biotic factors are necessary for it to survive? What contribution does the species make to its environment? If the species is endangered, why is this so and what can be done to recover it? Both taxonomic and ecological disciplines are required to answer these questions.

Species: Biological Building Blocks

The earth is dynamic and our current biological diversity is the result of its 4.6-billion-year history of change (NRC 1995). Species are the results of adaptations over time to physical and biological changes in the environment. The extinction of a species, therefore, is the "irreversible loss of a suite of unique genetic adaptations" (NRC 1995:vi) acquired over a long history. Species represent an evolutionary continuum.

A species—defined as a naturally occurring group of individuals, genetically related, capable of interbreeding, and sharing a common evolutionary history—is the basic biological building block of the taxonomic hierarchy. Taxonomy is the scientific classification of living organisms based on their natural relationships and ordered from the least inclusive category (species, and sometimes subspecies) to the most inclusive (kingdom). In between are the genus, family, order, class, and phlyum.

The total number of species on earth is estimated to be between 3 and 10 million, with the majority of species still undescribed. Although there is some scientific quibbling over the actual number of species that have been described and classified, the 1.4 to 1.8 million range is fairly narrow. More than two thirds of these are invertebrate animals, most notably mollusks and insects, and a quarter are plants, algae, and fungi. The charismatic vertebrate animals (fish, reptiles, birds, mammals) represent only about 3 percent of known species.

"Species are the unmistakable bricks of biodiversity and yet they have various perspectives that are not easily categorized" (Stork et al. in Watson and Heywood 1995:486). Sometimes it is difficult to distinguish between species and subspecies or between subspecies and populations because of the ongoing process of speciation. Speciation, the evolution of a new species, is ultimately a genetic divergence between populations or a genetic cohesion of once diverse populations. Because speciation occurs over evolutionary time, it is difficult to detect even with genetic analysis. Therefore, on occasion a subspecies is deemed a species or the reverse applies. Sometimes a single population is split by a geographical barrier as large as an ocean strait or as narrow as a forest road; if the separation is total and each group survives, the two new groups may evolve into subspecies.

Chance genetic changes, called mutations, are the raw material of evolution. Natural selection, the process by which the genes that promote survival through successful reproduction are passed to offspring, is the engine of evolution. Genetic drift, which is the chance loss of genes from one generation to another, also contributes to evolution.

Understanding the interrelationships among species and between species and the physical environment is part of the science called ecology. Within the ecological hierarchy, which moves from individual organisms up to the overarching biomes and the biosphere as a whole, species live in populations that are normally part of multispecies or biotic communities. Biotic communities interact inseparably with the nonliving, or abiotic, elements around them. This set of interactions is called an ecosystem.

Another set of species classifications has more practical use for species management. There is disagreement among scientists, however, as to which of the following classifications is most valuable for species conservation.

A *keystone species* is one that makes a contribution within its ecosystem that is disproportionately greater than its population size might indicate. Its loss usually results in a significant change to, or even the collapse of, the ecosystem. Three examples of keystone species are the starfish, a marine predator that limits the population of its prey; palm trees that produce fruit when other plants do not and thereby sustain the animal population through lean times in some tropical ecosystems; and nitrogen-fixing bacteria.

The case of the California sea otter provides a good example of the ecosystem consequences of loss of a keystone species. The otter is a predatory mammal that eats sea urchins. When the sea otter population declined, the kelp beds that had previously thrived in otter habitat almost disappeared, as did several other marine animal species. Scientists now know these other species were fed and housed by the kelp. Without the otters consuming and controlling the sea urchin population, sea urchins destroyed the kelp forests that housed the diverse biotic community. Many ecosystem consequences are in such a chain-reaction form.

Keystone species can create ecosystems as well as maintain them. Habitat modifiers like the beaver change stream riparian areas into pond habitats that favor very different types of plants and animals. The African elephant can turn forests into savannas, creating the grazing environment that supports herds of zebras, gazelles, and wildebeest. One approach to conservation is to identify any keystone species in an ecosystem and develop conservation management plans around that species. Conservation of the keystone species in turn protects all species living within the ecosystem.

A *flagship species* is one with which the public readily identifies. It is popular and charismatic and often serves as a national symbol to stimulate conservation awareness (e.g., the bald eagle in the United States, the golden lion tamarin in Brazil, and the giant panda in China). Flagship species are usually more important to public cooperation and public relations than as a contributor to an ecosystem. But the value of public cooperation is enormous in conservation.

An *indicator species* has a highly specific function or a narrow ecological tolerance. It is tied to its community or to a stage of succession. As such, any change in the abundance, distribution, or demographic characteristics of these species is an indication that there may be problems in the entire ecosystem. Amphibians, mollusks, fungi, corals, and some birds are often indicators of the health of an ecosystem. The idea here is exemplified by the canary in the coalmine: if a caged canary died, miners knew they must abandon the mineshaft because the oxygen level would soon be too low to support them. The 1970s die-off of oysters in the Chesapeake Bay was an indication of problems with the entire estuarine system; oysters are an indicator species for that ecosystem.

An *umbrella species* is one that often thrives only in a large area or home range, such as the grizzly bear and many large cats. Protecting these species and their full ranges would help other species within the range, but protecting such a vast range is impractical in our world.

Populations: Ecological System Units

To focus only on species is to neglect a critical biological unit: the population. A *population* is a group of individuals evolving independently of other groups because of limited gene flow. *Metapopulations*—populations that are geographically separated but dependent upon each other for survival—are included in this definition. They tend to be scattered in subpopulation units around a landscape and may seem geographically isolated, but in fact the dispersed units are nevertheless all part of the same gene flow. Metapopulations are linked by migration. The link can be critical to survival of the metapopulation because some subpopulations exist in sink habitats—areas that barely or insufficiently support them without immigration from source habitats, where there are abundant resources and where such populations tend to thrive. The population is the ecological system unit; ecosystem services are delivered by populations (Hughes et al. 1997).

Using Robert May's estimate that there are probably 7 million species worldwide, Hughes and her colleagues (1997) estimated that there are 1.5 billion populations, which are going extinct four times faster than species. Small populations are the ones that usually end up being classified as endangered or threatened; indeed, population status is one of the criteria used by the IUCN to determine their Red List categories (Watson and Heywood 1995). The definition of "small" varies by species, but as a rule of thumb, scientists consider one hundred or less breeding individuals to be a small population. Population measures include birth rate (natality), death rate (mortality), immigration and emigration, and numbers of organisms at different ages and sexes, a critical measure for reproduction. A population that consists only of nonreproducing adults or only of individuals of one gender is dead-ended.

Other factors that contribute to population size are density (the number of organisms per unit of space or volume) and the organisms' dependence on a specific density; the resources available; predation, parasitism, and disease; and the intensity of intraspecies social interactions. Resources are reduced when there is a large number of consumers. Moreover, the greater the density, the greater the mortality from disease or predation.

The behavioral patterns of one species can interfere with the success of another species with which it shares a habitat. For example, the house wren punctures the eggs of competing wren species, lowering the competitor's reproduction capacity. The genetic diversity of the population is also an important factor. The greater the diversity of the breeding individuals, the greater the overall fitness of future generations will be.

Small populations are affected by four random, or stochastic, types of occurrences. The first is demographic stochasticity, which includes changes in sex ratio. The second is environmental stochasticity, which includes climate changes, changes in food supply, and the presence of competitors and/or predators. The third is natural catastrophes, such as fires, floods, earthquakes, storms, or outbreaks of disease. And the fourth is genetic stochasticity, which includes genetic drift and inbreeding. All four effects tend to be detrimental to the survival of small populations (Meffe and Carroll 1997).

Understanding population patterns over space and time is as important as understanding population trends (Watson and Heywood 1995). Gathering trends requires only repeated counts that reflect population size; determining population patterns over space and time requires estimates of population size and demographic information from multiple sites at different times. Conservation biologists use two types of models to analyze populations—Minimum Viable Population (MVP) and Population Viability Analysis (PVA).

By looking at genetics, demographic dynamics, and environmental dynamics, MVP attempts to establish the minimum size at which any population can persist. PVA builds on this information to determine the probability of extinction within a specified time frame. There is still much information needed to make the PVA models more effective, but the base concept has been established as a useful one.

Extinction: Permanent Loss of Biodiversity

Some ESA skeptics do not believe that there is a serious extinction problem *because* extinction is a natural process. Scientific disagreement on the number of different species on earth fuels this skepticism, since these estimates feed the estimate of the number of species going extinct each year. However, as Tom Lovejoy (1997) pointed out at the National Academy of Sciences Conference on Nature and Human Society, there is "virtual unanimity among present scientists about the loss of biodiversity" today. The only disagreement involves the magnitude of the problem, not whether an extinction crisis exists.

Fossil records indicate that there have been living organisms on earth for the last 3.5 billion years. Five mass extinctions have been documented. Two types of extinction have emerged from the data: extinction without replacement, when a species reaches a dead end; and taxonomic extinction, or evolution, when a species changes through geological time to the extent that it is classified as a different species (NRC 1995). The five mass extinctions were dead-end events, and many scientists believe the current crisis is the beginning of the sixth dead-end event (Ehrlich and Ehrlich 1981, Myers 1990, Raven 1990, Soulé 1991, Western and Pearl 1989, and Wilson 1989, 1992, all cited in Meffe and Carroll 1995b:123).

In the first documented event 570 million years ago (mya) 50 percent of the existing species died off. In the following four mass extinctions—345 mya, 290 mya, 208 mya, and 65 mya—60 percent of species or more disappeared (geologic ages from Press and Siever 1993; percentages from Meffe and Carroll 1997).

The reasons for the first five extinction crises are unknown, but the current crisis is due to the explosion of the human population and its appropriation of excessive natural resources to support it. Specific causes of extinction include overhunting or overharvesting; introduction of nonnative species, including those that cause diseases; habitat degradation, fragmentation, or loss; and pollution. Habitat degradation means that the habitat supports less natural diversity than it once did. Problems such as air and water pollution and climate change affect the viability of natural habitats, but these phenomena often work so subtly that the consequences do not become evident until the damage is significant. After each of the five great extinction events shown in the geological record, biodiversity expanded. It took 1 to 8 million years to return to the species richness (the number of different species present) of the period prior to the extinction. By geological standards, this is rapid renewal. By human time standards, however, extinction is forever. Robert May (1997) estimates that species life spans range from 1 to 10 million years, with the average being 4 million. The human species has been around less than 2 million years.

During the past 2 million years, there have been a series of glacial-interglacial cycles. The cool intervals last 80,000–120,000 years and the warm interglacial intervals span 10,000–20,000 years. Species survived glaciations because of the ability to move gradually across habitats to more amenable climates and habitats. The migration response during the next glacial interval, however, may be insufficient to protect species because anthropogenic habitat fragmentation will impede them (NRC 1995).

More recently, another less sweeping extinction event occurred between 5 million and 100,000 years ago. It apparently affected mostly large mammals. North America lost glyptodonts, ground sloths, two bear species, saber-toothed cats, cheetahs, beavers, capybaras, mastodons, the mammoth, a horse, a tapir, peccaries, camels, some deer, a pronghorn, and other bovids (Martin, in Meffe and Carroll 1997). It is unknown whether these losses were due to human hunters or changing climates or both. Most assume this loss was anthropogenic since the extinctions were game species.

About 5,000 to 6,000 years ago, agriculture came to North America. It reduced plant species and modified landscapes, soils, and water supply through deforestation, erosion, channeling, flooding, draining, and siltation. From prehistoric times to the present, human activities have been the primary source of extinction. It is estimated that 484 animal and 654 plant species have disappeared since 1600, and tens of thousands more species are probably already on the irrevocable path to extinction because of the habitat loss or degradation that has already taken place (Watson and Heywood 1995).

Extinction Rates

The present extinction rate is believed to be 100,000 times higher than the background, or normal, extinction rate. In 1992, Wilson estimated that 20 percent of all species would be lost within thirty years (by 2022) and 50 percent would be lost thereafter. However, scientific understanding of the mechanisms that drive increases in extinction is incomplete.

Extinction rates are based on the estimated number of species and the rate of habitat loss. (Current estimates of species range from 3 to 10 million; Robert Mays's estimate of 7 million is used here. Annual habitat loss is estimated to be 0.5 to 2 percent, based on deforestation rates.) The proportion of species found in tropical rain forests is another variable. Scientists generally agree that rain forests house the greatest species richness, but estimates range from 25 to 75 percent of the total global species. The rate of tropical rain forest loss is also very high. Because these baselines differ enormously, the variation in estimated extinction rates is naturally large. Furthermore, because estimates are based on models developed for tropical and neotropical rain forests where the largest amount of biodiversity exists, the extinction rate in temperate-zone nations such as the United States is likely to be much lower because the amount of biodiversity is lower.

There is an empirical relationship between area and number of species that derives from R. H. MacArthur and E. O. Wilson's 1967 theory of island biogeography. Simply stated, the larger the area, the more species are likely to occupy it. Furthermore, "the number of species approximately doubles with every tenfold increase in area" (Wilson 1992:221). Conversely, a tenfold decrease in area halves the number of resident species. The mathematical formula expressing this relationship is $S = CA^z$, where S = the number of species, A = the area, and C and z are constants fitted to the data; the value of z depends on the type of organism (bird, reptile, insect) and the distance of the area from sources of new population.

Wilson ignores C for the calculation of the rate of species extinction. The z value, which ranges from 0.15 to 0.35, is important, and the higher it is, the greater the number of species that will be lost as the area is reduced. Using an annual reduction in rain forest area of 1.8 percent to calculate the extinction rate with the minimum and maximum z values yields rates of 0.27 percent to 0.63 percent a year. The actual number of species that the percentage represents depends on the number of species estimated to exist, their ranges, and proximity to replacement populations.

Using conservative parameters, Wilson (1992) estimates that we are losing about 27,000 species a year in neotropical rain forests. In describing the difficulty of estimating the rate of extinction, Wilson states unequivocally that no precise estimate can be made because the number of species is not known; diversity reduction depends on the size of the habitat fragment and the distance between fragments, both factors that vary enormously; and the geographical ranges of most species are unknown.

Ecosystems: Ecological Communities

Now the focus turns from species and populations to the ecological relationships of species: species interacting with species and species interacting with their nonliving, or physical, environment. As already noted, this interaction is called an ecosystem. The whole ecological hierarchy of different systems making up the biotic earth with its support systems is known as the biosphere; continents and oceans are biogeographical regions; and a cluster of ecosystem types along temperature and rainfall gradients is a biome. While preserving a representation of the variety of biomes is important to the conservation of biodiversity, the ecosystem is the primary ecological unit of conservation. Many species living and interacting together with the nonliving elements of the landscape form an ecosystem. A single species cannot function well, if it can function at all, outside its ecosystem; and an ecosystem cannot retain its character without its indigenous species.

The word *ecosystem* for a biotic community and its abiotic environment is attributed to Sir Arthur Tansley, an English botanist and a founder of the British Ecological Society (Odum 1993). An ecosystem is four-dimensional. It includes the surrounding atmosphere as well as time. The components of ecosystems include climate, specific landforms (e.g., wetlands, mountains, or rock formations), soil, water, and the biota (Lapin and Barnes 1995). An ecosystem has different forms or functions at different times in its life span. The temporal dimension can be as brief as a day (an ecosystem may include diurnal and nocturnal biota) or a year (seasonal life stages or life spans of biota) or it can be as long as evolutionary time.

Complete ecosystems—even those that have been anthropogenically altered—are self-contained life-support systems. Few ecosystems are pristine, or unaltered by humans. The human species is ubiquitous and its population has been booming for centuries. Therefore most ecosystems today are modified and fragmented. Natural ecosystems are patchy and form a landscape mosaic. NRC defines *patches* as discrete spatial units detectable on certain scales. They can result from changes in physical environment or biological composition. A pond is a patch; so is a tree island in the midst of a wetland or an agricultural field in the midst of a forest. Organisms in one type of patch might depend on organisms in another contrasting patch, such as pollinators of certain tropical vines. There are patches of productive habitat where organisms settle, reproduce, and die, separated by less productive areas across which organisms move. Within an ecosystem, there are both suitable and unsuitable patches for each species, and there is variation in the ecosystem services and activities within patches.

Plants are key to all ecosystems, even marine systems supported by microscopic plants known as plankton. *Succession*, the process of a community's development, is an important ecosystem characteristic and is centered on plants. On an abandoned farmer's field in the southeastern United States, for example, the first organisms to recolonize are weedy plants such as crabgrass and ragweed (Odum 1993:188). Within a few years perennial forbs and grasses appear, followed later by shrubs and pine seedlings. A pine forest develops within a hundred years. Gradually, hardwoods overtake the pine forest. During each stage of this succession a different group of animals is present. In other climates and latitudes the succession would be different, but the concept remains the same.

Nature remains in disequilibrium (Meffe and Carroll 1997). The "balance of nature" is, in fact, imbalance. Disturbance regimes, an important and natural part of the ecosystem, influence the probability of extinction and colonization—and therefore the overall biodiversity of the landscape. Disturbances range from a small soil disturbance caused by a fallen tree to larger disturbances such as landslides, fires, and floods. Fire frequency, especially, has a large impact on the biodiversity of an area.

Conservation Strategies

One of many conservation strategies, captive breeding may be the most familiar to the general public. Captive-bred animals that populate zoological parks have important educational and research value. Conserving animals under captive conditions produces volumes of data that are useful to understanding the needs of animals in the wild, and captive-bred animals can help buffer declining populations. However, because of the value of species to their natural ecosystems, retaining the only remaining members of a species population in a captive environment does not preserve ecosystem biodiversity.

There is a place for captive breeding when species are in dire circumstances, such as in the cases of the black-footed ferret or California condor. For the most part, however, species do not do well outside the ecosystems in which they belong. Furthermore, to be effective ultimately, captive breeding must be followed by the reintroduction of captive-bred animals into the wild. There is a great deal more to be learned about reintroducing species successfully.

According to Ben Beck (1998), director of biological programs at the National Zoological Park, of the 146 reintroductions of 126 different species from among more than 13 million captive-born creatures (mostly fish), only 16 have succeeded. Captive-bred animals have a difficult time adapting to life in the wild and often do not survive. Also, the natural habitats of these animals must be restored, or the threats to the species removed, before attempting reintroduction.

Another conservation strategy, single species management, has an important place in the preservation of natural diversity as a crisis discipline. This is the strategy underlying the Endangered Species Act, and the ways and means of this strategy are discussed in detail in chapters 1 and 2.

Ecosystem management, by contrast, is a conservation discipline. Organisms do not exist in isolation: "Biology without ecological context is dead" (Barnes 1993:17). Inasmuch as biodiversity is a product of patch dynamics, any conservation plan must maintain ecosystems in a changing state of succession to mimic nature (Meffe and Carroll 1997). The ecosystem management approach, discussed in depth in chapter 10, focuses on the entire landscape and its assemblage of resident species. Hence it is a conservation process that can prevent species from becoming threatened or endangered.

Since the ESA was passed in 1973, a phenomenal amount of scientific information on species survival has been accumulated. Even with all this knowledge, it is still impossible to assess the probability of survival (or extinction) of species populations with any degree of accuracy. Scientists have learned, however, what kind of information they need to make conservation decisions. More research, inventorying of species and ecosystems, and monitoring of managed areas is needed to shed light on what works and what does not.

The value of inventorying is recognized and codified internationally in the Global Biodiversity Assessment and the Convention on Biological Diversity (CBD), and organizations are developing plans to carry out the inventories globally and nationally. Although slower to recognize the value of inventorying biodiversity, the Congress of the United States created the National Biological Survey in 1993. Now called the Biological Resources Division (BRD) of the U.S. Geological Survey, this group is charged with mapping the land cover, or vegetation, of the United States. The BRD also maps distributions of vertebrates, documents species types in managed areas, and makes this information available to scientists, educators, natural resources managers, planners, and policy makers.

It is a monumental task to identify all species, and it probably will never be complete because so many species are poorly known and difficult to identify. Nevertheless, the information is critical, and the way to tackle the task is step by step. The only way to protect biodiversity is to forge ahead with conservation efforts in the face of inadequate information and constant uncertainty and thus begin the change process that will be necessary for society to protect the biosphere that sustains it. Gary Gray (1993:221) recommends some general strategies: "Conservation biologists can perform a vital role by focusing attention on biodiversity as a management goal, by providing necessary information to guide management, by teaching and training agency personnel, . . . and by making sure that conservation biology practices are implemented on the land."

The following specific recommendations for conservation efforts that can be implemented at the present time have been culled from various sources including Gray (1993), the National Research Council (1995), and Meffe and Carroll (1997)

Implement ecosystem-based conservation measures and focus on the management of landscape-scale ecosystems.

Avoid further fragmentation or isolation of natural areas.

Cluster and minimize development for human purposes, resource extraction activities, and other land uses so that large blocks of natural habitat remain intact.

Protect large areas and create connecting corridors between fragments when planning reserves.

Plan in collaboration with government agencies, private owners, and all effected stakeholders: biodiversity cuts across lands with a variety of ownership.

Investigate and select decision-making models that minimize error and consider all issues: endangered species and ecosystem decisions are inevitably based on limited information.

Modify federal agency and national political cultures to permit errors and learn from them.

Educate wildlife managers in the systematic, taxonomic, and evolutionary biology disciplines while assuring that they retain their knowledge of wildlife behavioral patterns.

Raise public awareness of the issues; assure public participation in land and species management and at planning meetings. Begin a broad educational program, primarily through electronic media, including the Internet

Nature will take care of itself if allowed to do so. It is time to accept that the human role is only a part of the procedure—at most we are stewards and not controllers of natural processes. The answers to the problems are all present in nature, to be discovered and used. This is the challenge and the opportunity. In the 1940s human beings uncovered the tremendous destructive power of nature with the splitting of the atom. Now it is time to uncover the tremendous constructive and regenerative power of nature—in biodiversity. It is up to us to recognize it, permit it to function, and help it wherever possible.

Part Two

Characters

Chapter Four

Protagonists and the
Environmental Argument

Endangered species listings and law suits are the primary tools
being used [by the environmental movement] along with an
enthusiastic campaign of intimidation, guerrilla tactics and
monkeywrenching.—Reed F. Noss, May 1995

NOW THAT THE STAGE is set, it is time to meet the characters of
the endangered species drama. The protagonists—the people
fighting for a strengthened ESA—are led by environmental and
conservation organizations that represent millions of individuals who want
species protected. The antagonists, discussed in the next chapter, do not want
to see species disappear, but they fight resolutely for the right of property
owners to do with their lands as they wish. For many years the sides have been
polarized; only recently have signs of a thaw in their relationships begun to
appear.

The strength of the environmental movement may well lie in its diversity.
Hundreds of local, state, and national organizations with differing strategies
make up the movement. Nationally, the movement can be divided into two
categories of organizations: the conservationists and the activists-advocates.
Conservation organizations, concerned with on-the-ground conservation and
based in scientific skills, work with the local inhabitants of a targeted conservation area to preserve the ecosystem and natural ecology. The major organizations in this category are the World Wildlife Fund (WWF) and the Nature
Conservancy (TNC). Both have strong international and domestic programs.
Two others, the Wildlife Conservation Society and Conservation International
(CI), focus almost exclusively on conservation work outside the United States.

Activist-advocate organizations, on the other hand, use their significant

47

national memberships to influence national environmental policy through lobbying and local activism. There are three echelons of organizations in this category. The first echelon consists of national bodies—the Sierra Club, Audubon Society, National Wildlife Federation (NWF), Wilderness Society, and Defenders of Wildlife (DOW). Some of these, like Audubon and Sierra Club, are active at the state and local levels as well. The primary focus of these organizations is on monitoring and influencing policy making on Capitol Hill, with the executive branch of government, and on maintaining and stimulating grassroots activity. The second echelon—consisting of the Natural Resources Defense Council (NRDC), Earthjustice Legal Defense Fund (formerly Sierra Club Legal Defense Fund), and Environmental Defense (formerly Environmental Defense Fund, EDF)—is just as active in influencing policy making as the first but is defined separately because of its legal orientation. All three organizations are staffed primarily by lawyers and use litigation to maintain the integrity of environmental laws and/or to assure that they are properly enforced. The third echelon contains dozens of smaller groups that move in and out of the national limelight. Very active are the door-to-door canvassing specialists like the Public Interest Research Group (PIRG), Clean Water Action, and Friends of the Earth. Two organizations still active today but receiving less publicity than they once did are Greenpeace and Earth First!

Noss's remark opening this chapter involves the tactics of the first two echelons of activists-advocates, often referred to on Capitol Hill and in the present work as the "Enviros." Leaders of these organizations do not spike trees or bind themselves to the hulls of ships to stop logging or whaling. They are mainstream, white-collar professionals who take a hard-line, often uncompromising approach to all environmental laws. These leaders are knowledgeable in the science and policy of ecology and ecosystems. The Enviro organizations evolved among committed naturalists and outdoor people, stubborn idealists unwilling to budge on their issues, and they had to fight for every inch of ground gained in order to protect the environment.

Rodger Schlickeisen, president of Defenders of Wildlife, sums up the position of environmentalists regarding biodiversity and endangered species:

Call it a land ethic, a conservation ethic, an ecological ethic: its central requirement is that humans accept an obligation to maintain the strength of functioning natural communities that sustain the distinct elements of biological diversity, and that we value these elements not solely for their contribution to human well-being but also for their benefits to the health of the natural system. . . . We must rethink our role in the global natural environment and our relations with the other species that are passengers on Spaceship Earth—or as some have said, Lifeboat Earth. A conservation ethic requires that we recognize that the welfare of each passenger, or species, depends on the welfare of all. (DOW 1993:i)

Outside the policy mainstream but still very effective are the conservation organizations. The World Wildlife Fund maintains a presence in the Enviro community by participating in multi-organization coalitions such as the Alaska Coalition, which focused on saving the Arctic National Wildlife Refuge. However, they minimize active legislative advocacy. The Nature Conservancy stays out of these coalitions and out of the advocacy arena completely, but it often makes advisory contributions. TNC also functions on many ecosystem management teams and has mediated the development of Habitat Conservation Plans. The conservation organizations focus on purchasing land in order to restore it to its full ecological value and on sending scientific teams out to the field, often overseas, to work with local communities to develop sustainable ecosystems and economies. They are dependent on donations by large funders, private and government. Some, like TNC and WWF, have broad public membership bases, whereas others restrict their membership more to those in the scientific professions.

Evolution of the Environmental Movement

Protecting the environment became a national compact between citizens and Congress in the 1970s and remained one until the 1994 election. The environmental movement developed to fight the appalling levels of air and water pollution that had accumulated by the late 1960s, to stop toxic waste dumps, and to save the whales, eagles, and grizzly bears. Diminishing numbers of charismatic animals, a burning river in Cleveland, and the Love Canal calamity—where toxic waste seepage into drinking water supplies caused serious illnesses among residents—all assured the sympathy and backing of the general public for the cause.

Early in his first term, President Nixon created the Citizens Advisory Committee on Environmental Policy. By August 1972, the committee had created the Task Force on Land Use and Urban Growth, which produced *The Use of Land: A Citizens' Policy Guide to Urban Growth*. The task force started to challenge the prevailing idea that economic growth and unregulated development meant prosperity. The Council on Environmental Quality (CEQ) published *The Taking Issue: An Analysis of the Constitutional Limits of Land Use Control* in 1973, focused on the Constitution's Fifth Amendment taking clause. Mann and Plummer (1995b) interpreted the theme of both reports to be that private property was an anachronism the nation could ill afford.

People believed that the number of species facing extinction was at crisis proportions. In 1979, Norman Myers published *Sinking Ark*, warning that continued logging of tropical rain forests would expunge species at a rapid rate. In 1980, the *Global 2000 Report to the President* was published. In it, Dr. Thomas E. Lovejoy concluded that between 15 and 20 percent of species would be lost by the year 2000. In 1981, Ann and Paul Erhlich published *Extinction*, indicating that the increase in world population and the resulting deforestation would extinguish many tropical species by 2025 (Mann and Plummer 1995b). Today, many believe that the estimates of species extinctions made in the 1970s and 1980s were scientific hyperbole. Environmentalists believe the answer to the extinction crisis lies in better land use policy and enforcement; this belief is diametrically opposed to that of the advocates of private property.

The environmental movement flourished during President Reagan's and President Bush's administrations. The movement lobbied for and helped to write the strong pro-environment laws enacted between 1969 and 1980. Again and again, activists prevailed against attempts to dilute the ESA. The attempts "resulted in procedural changes . . . and some provisions that allow greater flexibility in implementation, but never a substantial lessening of the nation's commitment to conserve its biological heritage" (DOW 1993:5).

Environmental legislators and lobbyists prevented Congress from eliminating Section 7 (federal consultation) in 1978 when the shock of Tellico hit. In 1982, environmental pressure enabled Congress to avoid weakening Section 9 (no takings) by creating HCPs as a means for private property owners to obtain incidental take permits. Environmentalists have influenced the delay of reauthorization several times when anti-ESA forces threatened to weaken the law. Throughout the Reagan years, it was a struggle to protect the ESA.

The Enviros lost some of their political control with the listing of the northern spotted owl in the Pacific Northwest. The resultant loss of jobs presented their opponents with an opportunity to emphasize the destructive capacity of the ESA. The listing of the owl occurred at a time of national recession with an associated increase in unemployment. The prevailing popular mood was one of fear for the economy and for individual economic welfare. Emotions ran high and the ESA became a convenient target. Newspaper headlines accused the ESA of cruel and inhumane treatment. Environmentalists fanned emotional flames by answering that with old growth trees gone, jobs would be lost anyway.

When Clinton took office, the Enviros relaxed their vigilance. With Vice President Al Gore on one side of the president and Secretary of the Interior Bruce Babbitt on the other, environmentalists expected great things from the administration. A Democratic president to complement the Democratic Congress was a real win after years of hard work to keep all environmental laws strong. However, Congress took a turn to the right about the time Clinton took office. Environmentalists did not adjust quickly to that fact (Wicker 1994).

Early in his administration, Clinton disappointed Enviros by backing down on environmental commitments. Then came the totally unanticipated election results of 1994—the Republicans won the majority of seats in both houses of Congress. Republicans took over key environmental committee chairs. The new chairmen had some old axes to grind with environmentalists, and long-time environmental lobbyists lost their supporters and much of their influence on the Hill.

Just as the private property movement used takings litigation to challenge the power of environmental laws, environmental organizations used litigation to preserve the integrity of those laws. Environmental groups sued the agencies that failed to implement the ESA with new endangered species listings or by developing and implementing recovery plans. When the U.S. Fish and Wildlife Service failed to implement the international components of the ESA, it faced a lawsuit. The Natural Resources Defense Council, Environmental Defense Fund, Earthjustice Legal Defense Fund, Defenders of Wildlife, and National Wildlife Federation often led these suits.

Continual litigation was and remains an expensive outgrowth of the political cycle. Presidents from Reagan onward imposed their political penchants on federal agencies with insufficient budgets to carry out the laws or by direct action (executive orders) or tacit mandates. Implementing agencies such as the FWS and the National Marine Fisheries Service (NMFS), responded with lackluster regulatory enforcement. The result was a judicial system clogged with cases. Some cases uncovered the truth about a situation using the Freedom of Information Act; some forced the agency to fulfill its statutory obligations. The 104th Congress tried to eliminate the right of citizens and citizen organizations to file suit against ESA violators in order to "relieve the judicial backlog" or to "avoid costly and unnecessary litigation." Litigation, however, is the natural outgrowth of the system.

Long before private property rights supporters formed grassroots organizations, Enviros had perfected the art of grassroots politicking. For close to twenty-five years the organizations of the environmental movement had built and nurtured their memberships and taught people how to make their opinions known effectively to their legislators.

After the 1994 election, some of the spirit seemed to go out of the national movement. During 1995 and 1996, little creativity emerged from the then two-hundred-member Endangered Species Coalition (ESC), the organization formed to protect the ESA. ESC Membership in 2000 exceeded 400 conservation, scientific, business and religious organizations. The political influence of the movement waned, and its strategy in Congress was vulnerable. Rather than try proactive tactics, the movement relied on its grassroots to stop any damaging legislation.

The Enviros had lost many congressional supporters in the 1994 elections, and the remaining seated Democrats were in disarray and ineffective. It took time to rebuild alliances in Congress after the Republican takeover, but by 1996, a strong moderate Republican block that was pro-environment had coalesced and was becoming a force. Enviros cultivated affiliations with these legislators.

The ESC did not attempt to get a species-friendly ESA reauthorization bill on the floor. The coalition's strategy was to fight the damaging bills as they were introduced. Representative George Miller (D-Calif.) stated that Enviros were "living off old capital" and were unable to mount sufficient political pressure on Congress. "The president will sign any bill environmentalists can get to his desk" (Wicker 1994:52). In spite of the temporary disorganization within the movement, the environmental platform relating to the Endangered Species Act and biodiversity remained robust.

The 104th Congress, on the other hand, responded to years of stifled Republican aspirations and started its crusade of deregulation with environmental laws. The *Contract with America*, published early in the first session, contained no specific plan to attack environmental regulations, but that is just what the Congress did.

Although Enviro tactics needed reinvigoration, the public remained solidly pro-species and pro-ESA. The principles on which environmentalists based their arguments fell into three categories: moral, scientific, and economic. Public support came from a variety of nonenvironmental organizations and included doctors, pharmacists, religious leaders, small businesses, the fishing and sport hunting–sport fishing industries, scientists, and educators.

The Moral Principles

The Endangered Species Coalition made a clear statement of the moral basis for their public stance: "We as Americans have a moral responsibility to safeguard our natural heritage and protect species from human-caused extinction. The Endangered Species Act ensures that each of us does our part to uphold this obligation" (ESC 1995:5).

Representatives of Christian, Jewish, and Buddhist religious groups have also declared in favor of preserving species and biodiversity. Persuasive testimony was delivered by Rabbi David Saperstein, director of the Religious Action Center of Reform Judaism, at the Endangered Species Task Force hearing: "Religion and science alike agree that there is a profound integrity to the natural order, a marvelous ecological complexity that even now, with all our growing ecological understanding, remains beyond our comprehension. The biological integrity of the world and its spiritual integrity are stunningly intertwined. . . . When we exterminate a species, through actions direct or indirect, we erase a part of the sacred, stating through our actions that we know the value of the world better than does its Creator" (Saperstein 1995:2).

In February 1995, Paul Gorman, executive director of the National Religious Partnership for the Environment, sent an editorial memorandum to the editorial boards of many newspapers expressing the joint concerns of this coalition of major faith groups. The partnership serves over 100 million Americans, including the U.S. Catholic Conference, the National Council of Churches of Christ, the Evangelical Environmental Network, and the Coalition on the Environment and Jewish Life. In the memorandum, Gorman stated that the group represents an "overwhelming consensus . . . that environmental protection is a fundamental religious duty and moral imperative transcending political partnership." He continued: "The broad consensus and range of activities among diverse mainstream faith groups . . . testifies to some-

thing far more fundamental than 'environmentalism' conventionally understood. . . . Environmental protection is too fundamental a part of who we are
and what we believe as Americans to be identified with 'environmentalists'
alone" (Gorman 1995).

No description of moral position would be complete without the perspective of Native Americans and other indigenous peoples worldwide. David
Suzuki and Peter Knudtson, in *Wisdom of the Elders* (1992:5), found "often
striking parallels between traditional Native ecological perspectives and Western scientific ones. . . . As biologists, one specializing in animal behavior and
the other in genetics, we have found ourselves increasingly intrigued . . . by
the shared truths, as well as the undeniable differences, in these two distinct
. . . ways of knowing about the natural world."

Native peoples tend to see the land and all its inhabitants as one whole.
Unlike those in Euro-American cultures, they do not separate spiritual and
secular or economic and ecological. Their economic base is their ecological
base. Their cultures are built around the animals and plants with which they
share space. Even though the words of Chief Seattle, as we know them, may
have been changed from the original speech of this Native American, they
still eloquently express the beliefs of most indigenous peoples: "The air is
precious to the red man. For all things share the same breath—the beast, the
trees, the man, they all share the same breath. . . . What is man without the
beasts? If all the beasts were gone, men would die from a great loneliness of
spirit. For whatever happens to the beasts, soon happens to man. All things
are connected. . . . Whatever befalls the earth befalls the sons of the earth"
(Suzuki and Knudtson 1992:xx).

Scientific Principles

E. O. Wilson (1992:15) defines biodiversity as "the key to the maintenance
of the world as we know it. Life in a local site struck down by a passing storm
springs back quickly: opportunistic species rush in to fill the spaces. They
entrain the succession that circles back to something resembling the original
state of the environment. . . . This is the assembly of life that took a billion
years to evolve. . . . It holds the world steady."

The Endangered Species Coalition maintained that "the loss of species
should trigger alarm bells in the minds of responsible citizens. The dramatic

dying off of animal and plant species is telling us something: ecological systems have been so contaminated, degraded or disrupted that they no longer support their native wildlife and may not long support us either" (ESC 1995:13).

The medical and agricultural fields have long benefited from discoveries of medicines and genetic material in both plants and animals. In a June 15, 1995, letter to Representative Jack Metcalf (R-Wash.), ten medical doctors spoke out in support of the ESA: "As medical professionals, we strongly believe the Endangered Species Act (ESA) protects not only endangered species but human health as well. Nearly one-quarter of prescriptions distributed annually in the U.S. are based on substances derived from plants and animals." According to some statistics, as many as 40 percent of prescription medicines today are derived from wild plants and animals. Similarly, an article in the *Networker/Interfaith Impact* explains how agriculture depends on wild species of plants for the development of new crops that thrive in poorer soils and for remedies for plant diseases: "Wild relatives of common crop species provide a genetic reservoir from which new pest and disease resistant strains are developed. For example, in the 1970's, genetic material from a wild corn species found in Mexico was used to stop a leaf fungus that had wiped out 5% of the U.S. corn crop" ("Preserving Environmental Justice" 1994:2).

The National Research Council's Committee on Scientific Issues in the Endangered Species Act concluded in 1995 that "the ESA is based on sound scientific principles." The scientific advances made since its passage "provide opportunities to improve the act's implementation." It affirmed that the definitions of "species" and "distinct population segments" are "soundly based on science" and "should be retained"(NRC 1995:3). The report recommended that the ESA expand its species definition to include taxonomic units below subspecies for invertebrates and plants. "Biological differences between animals and plants underlying their taxonomic separation offer no scientific reason for lesser protection of plants." It continued: "there is no scientific reason to have different standards for determination of 'jeopardy,' 'survival,' or 'recovery' on public and on private lands" (71).

The scientists who contributed to the NRC report verified that habitat, "the physical and biological setting in which organisms live[,] . . . is a basic requirement of all living organisms. . . . [The ESA] reflects the current scientific understanding of the crucial biological role that habitat plays for species. . . .

Habitat (in the broadest sense) thus plays a crucial role in protecting individual target species and ultimately, in reducing the need for listing additional species"(NRC 1995:5).

Economic Principles

Economic considerations are the real source of all ESA issues. "In a world increasingly dominated by the growth imperative of global economics, the infatuation with technology, and the ever expanding demands of an exploding human population, we cling to assumptions founded on the inadequate Cartesian and Newtonian world view" (Suzuki and Knudtson 1992:xxxi). Because modern civilization and Americans in particular place so much value on the growth imperative, any changes to practices that further this imperative are threatening. The ESA brought change to the practices; it has also brought economic value with it.

The story of shrimper Sinkey Boone of Darien, Georgia, as related in materials published by the Endangered Species Coalition, demonstrates that there is often economic value to be gained from the implementation of an endangered species protection mechanism. In Boone's case, the mechanism was the mandatory deployment of the highly contested turtle exclusion devices (TEDs). Before installing TEDs, Boone could drag his shrimp net for twenty to thirty minutes before he had to stop to remove fish and turtles caught in the net. The other animals smashing them in the net would ruin much of the shrimp catch. With TEDs, Boone could drag the nets for up to three hours and the quality and quantity of his catch improved. Boone was so pleased with his new productivity that he started his own company to manufacture and market TEDs.

The environmental perspective presented by the Endangered Species Coalition included economic considerations: "We need long term jobs that are part of sustainable economy, rather than jobs based on short-sighted destruction of our resources, a scenario that would eventually lead to economic collapse. Furthermore, we need to ensure that extractive industries work in a way that doesn't hurt the environment" (ESC 1995:17).

Several industries rely heavily on the implementation of the ESA, such as pharmaceuticals, fishing, and tourism. Some industries, however, experienced an economic pinch when endangered species protection was enforced, and it was easy for them to blame the ESA during the economic downturn in the early 1990s. One of the often difficult truths about the environment is that any change has ramifications elsewhere. If the practice of clear-cutting timber along major passageways to salmon spawning grounds had not been curtailed to protect the northern spotted owl, salmon would have been jeopardized as well as the owl. Salmon fishing provides tens of thousands of jobs and some $1 billion in personal income annually ("Preserving Environmental Justice" 1994).

The Defenders of Wildlife maintained that the country's "economic well-being depends on a healthy environment. The most important economic consideration we can make is the value of maintaining our nation's biological diversity to us and our descendants. This biological 'warehouse' includes our food supply, medicinal necessities and other treasures" (DOW 1993:11).

Zeke Grader, executive director of the Pacific Coast Federation of Fishermen's Associations, and Liz Hamilton, executive director of the Northwest Sportfishing Industry Association, identified an even more direct economic benefit: "The ESA is merely the messenger. The real problem is the destruction of the basic natural resources—like salmon—upon which ours and many other industries are ultimately based" (Grader and Hamilton 1995:3).

While economic considerations provoked the debate over the ESA, the private property rights advocates became the primary provocateurs. The environmental position on this issue is generally defensive, but the ESC (1995:21) also made the positive claim that the ESA "protects our private property from corporations that benefit financially from the destruction of our natural heritage."

A more common environmental position is the argument that private property rights groups are "trying to limit our ability to protect public health, the environment, and civil rights. The private property movement fails to address the question of how do private rights coexist with public rights? Does an individual's right to property outweigh a community's right to clean air or water?" ("Preserving Environmental Justice" 1994:3) However, the Enviro perspective fails to address the question of public versus private rights. In an excellent example of the extreme and inflammatory language found on both sides of the issue, the Endangered Species Coalition (1995:22) summarized the private property rights issue:

Clean air, clean water and the nation's wealth of species are our right as Americans. We should not be required to pay selfish individuals not to destroy them.

Proponents of "takings" legislation claim to represent the "little guy" and back up their claims with "horror stories" of regulatory abuses that are often exaggerated or just plain untrue. Those who stand to benefit most from this type of legislation are large landowners and wealthy corporations seeking regulatory relief and freedom from restrictions on their exploitation of our nation's natural resources.

Many people consider such statements rigid and sanctimonious.

Endangered Species: A Public Trust

One difficulty with the Enviro position on private property is that it avoids a central issue: are species a public trust, and if so, should their protection be at public expense? Richard Stapleton submitted: "We are running out of land, and public policy is shifting, . . . setting up the fight over property rights" (Stapleton 1993:26). In the West the issue is over public land; in the East it is over private land. Holmes Rolston (1991:51) also addressed the public trust argument: "If the public is gaining a good, government ought to compensate, but if government is protecting from harm, it can prohibit without compensation." In a case addressing denial of a permit to fill wetlands, the Supreme Court of Wisconsin found that destroying the natural habitat constitutes doing harm to the natural ecology and therefore to the public (*Just v. Marinette County*, 56 Wis. 2d 7, 201 N.W. 2d 761 [1972]). In Section 2 (§1531) of the Endangered Species Act of 1973, Congress effectively declared endangered species a public trust. Property rights advocates argue that if species are a public trust, the public should pay the cost to protect them.

The concepts of property are evolving and this evolution brings serious food for thought. On the one hand, Rolston (1991) maintains, there is a long legal tradition to support the position that property holders do *not* own vertebrate wildlife, even if it resides solely on their property, because wildlife is a common good. On the other hand, plants traditionally belong to the landowner. In a Michigan case, *Kerschensteiner v. Northern Michigan Land Co.*, standing timber was declared to be "part of the realty." Private property arguments would be even louder if plants were protected on private property because there would be so many more cases of perceived invasion rights (Rolston 1991).

Rolston called the struggle one of new values versus long-ensconced values. Environmental values, however, are often difficult to see, and environmental impacts are seldom immediately evident. "Property rights were instituted to protect individuals from harm; now we must institute a law to protect individuals from harming species and in so doing harming other persons" (Rolston 1991:53).

Disagreement within the Environmental Movement

Perhaps the most disturbing division in respect to the reauthorization of the Endangered Species Act is within the environmental community. Two camps have developed based on two different approaches to supporting the ESA. One camp could be called the pragmatists and the other the purists. Both groups want to strengthen the law; both agree that the bills introduced in the first session of the 104th Congress were insupportable. The split occurred over the strategy and components for an acceptable bill.

The purists include the Sierra Club, Earthjustice Legal Defense Fund, Defenders of Wildlife, Friends of the Earth, Humane Society of the United States, Fund for Animals, the Grassroots Environmental Effectiveness Network (the Defenders of Wildlife's subsidiary dedicated to ESA reauthorization), and USPIRG. They developed proposed legislation entitled the Endangered Natural Heritage Act (ENHA). The trial bill emphasized the prevention of species endangerment and required federal agencies to conserve declining species proactively. It emphasized *recovery* of listed species, whereas the existing law emphasized *survival*. The trial bill did not, however, include any recommendations to address the private property issue.

The pragmatists include Environmental Defense, Center for Marine Conservation, Nature Conservancy, World Wildlife Fund, the Western Urban Water Coalition, Plum Creek developers, and Georgia Pacific. Also affiliated with this camp were the Western Governors' Association, International Association of Fish and Wildlife Agencies, and from Capitol Hill, staff members from the offices of Representatives Jim Saxton (R-N.J.), Nathan Deal (R-Ga.), Jack Kingston (R-Ga.), and Wayne Gilchrest (R-Md.). The group agreed on a set of provisions for improving protection of endangered and threatened species while addressing the complaints of the regulated community about the disincentives to cooperating with the law. Among the provisions they proposed were simplification of the process for the Habitat Conservation Plan (HCP) and the creation of incentives for landowners who manage their land for species recovery, such as estate tax deferrals and tax credits for lands managed under conservation plans. This group also wanted to codify the Clinton Administration's "Safe Harbor" and "No Surprises" policies (see chapter 8) and allow the secretary of the interior to make prelisting agreements. The effort of this group was evident in the Endangered Species Recovery Act of 1997 (see chapter 6), introduced in the Senate during the first session of the 105th Congress.

Property rights advocates seldom deny the importance of saving biodiversity and species; it is the current regulatory methods that they dislike. According to the Defenders of Property Rights (DPR), "the Federal Government has been bankrupting private individuals by taking their property without compensation through wetland regulations, threatened and endangered species listings, and a host of other regulations. These regulations benefit the public, without regard to the costs they impose on individual landowners" (DPR 1995a). Property rights advocates say that the government should purchase any private property on which use is restricted. Environmentalists believe that property owners should welcome preserving their land, regardless of any economic hardship.

This kind of emotion demonstrates the reason for the polarization of the sides over the ESA. It is unrealistic and unreasonable to expect the U.S. government to purchase all private land inhabited by members of endangered species. It is equally unrealistic and unreasonable to expect private citizens to sacrifice their economic support in favor of a public goal. A middle ground is needed that enables the protection of species, financially acknowledges species as a national public trust and helps private owners bear any proven economic burden.

Chapter Five

Antagonists and the Private Property Rights Argument

Nature and wildlife are part of the American Dream. So is the right to own and make decisions about one's home and property. Protecting these two principles requires a delicate and perpetual balancing act that should be facilitated, not obstructed, by federal law. —*Seattle Times*, April 23, 1995

P RIVATE PROPERTY rights advocates lead the movement to stop ESA intrusion into the plans and decisions of private landowners. Societal reaction to the Endangered Species Act and other environmental protection statutes that demand behavioral changes ranges from indignant protest to outright disobedience of the law. The Endangered Species Act, however, does not treat private and public property equitably, so there is a basis for strong reaction. The takings compensation movement is one response by private property owners to ESA intrusion; another fear response occurs when an owner clears the land—quickly, before the law can be enforced—of any vegetation that might attract an endangered or threatened species.

Takings proponents and private property rights advocates seek to weaken the ESA's power over private property inhabited by an endangered or threatened species. The Enviros react strongly to the damage done by private owners. Both sides can justify their perspectives. Both consist of multiple component organizations with different strategies for success. Both sides present popular polls indicating that the nation is concerned with the environment, with endangered species, and with private property rights. Unfortunately, the average American does not fully understand the issues or the relationship between saving species and private property rights.

Strong emotion has fueled the conflict between the factions. It appears that it has been easier to stoke the emotional fires with hyperbolic claims than to sit down and discuss the issues rationally; certainly, it is easier to react to those claims than to work on their resolution.

Ike Sugg of the Washington, D.C., free-market think tank Competitive Enterprise Institute noted that only since 1992 has anyone perceived there to be two sides to the ESA. Before that, it was considered political suicide to touch an environmental law (Sugg 1995). The private property rights movement has gained strength as a major grassroots and political entity since 1991, but its inspiration dates to the early 1980s, when the list of endangered and threatened species began to interfere with activities on privately owned land. Before 1980, ESA implementation focused on public lands and federal projects. As more species were listed, those with small geographic territorial requirements were added, and many were on privately owned lands. Then the Endangered Species Act began to intrude on individuals. Some of the landholders affected were angered by what they perceived to be callous enforcement of a law that was insensitive to people.

There are many private property rights organizations, including Alliance for America, a loose coalition of property rights activists, and Defenders of Property Rights (DPR), which publishes the movement's critical propaganda and encourages activists to speak out and contact legislators. There is also the League of Private Property Voters (comparable to the environmental League of Conservation Voters),which tracks and publishes an annual Congressional voting record (Adler 1995).

In 1984, Fred L. Smith founded the Competitive Enterprise Institute (CEI). Smith had been a senior policy analyst at the Environmental Protection Agency and saw the growing environmental interest as a threat to individual liberties. He and his organization are committed to advancing the principles of free enterprise and limited government. Their contributors include the Coca-Cola Company, the E. L. Craig Foundation, Ford Motor Company Fund, Philip Morris companies, Pfizer, Texaco, and many anonymous donors. CEI devotes about half its time to environmental issues. Its position is that the Endangered Species Act is a failure because so few species have been taken off the endangered list (except because of data error or extinction) and also that the cost of implementing the law should not be borne by private landholders.

The property rights movement became a political force by 1994, growing from a dispersed collection of grassroots groups. The movement certainly had the attention of the 104th Congress. While its hold on the 105th Congress was weaker, it continued to remind Congress and the public about the citizen's constitutional right to private property and to fight to preserve that right. While bipartisan in nature, the movement has a philosophy close to that of the Republican Party.

The private property rights movement is not the same as the "Wise Use" movement. The issue of private property infringement is a convenient platform for the industry-backed Wise Use movement, but the two entities are distinct, although sharing similar goals and strategies. They are easily confused because the leaders of Wise Use saw the political power of the private property rights argument and adopted it.

The Wise Use Movement

The Wise Use movement is an anti-environment marketing campaign begun by an experienced direct-mail marketer and an activist trained in environmental grassroots strategies. Alan M. Gottlieb of Bellevue, Washington, a direct-mail fund-raiser, started the Center for the Defense of True Enterprise. Thomas Lewis (1992) credited Gottlieb with saying he sought "another evil empire to stimulate giving." Environmentalism was the perfect target for him. Ron Arnold, who joined Gottlieb in 1984, had seen companies "destroyed" by environmental regulations and was determined to stop the environmental movement before it ravaged industry (Lewis 1992). Arnold is a former Sierra Club activist who feels that the best way to fight the opposition is to use their techniques. Intentionally twisting the definition of conservation as coined by Gifford Pinchot, the first the U.S. Forest Service chief—the wise use of resources—Arnold dubbed the organization the Wise Use movement.

Calling the campaign a "movement" was a brilliant marketing tactic and it gave the organization credibility before there was even a fully developed strategy. Gottlieb and Arnold generated financial and popular support by exploiting the emotions in the conflict between environmental regulators and the public. They used emotionally loaded phrases, like "a holy war" and "a cosmic struggle between good and evil" (Lewis 1992), and they collected and redistributed a great deal of anecdotal information, much of it incomplete as presented. It is easy to accept emotional information as reality when it offers a scapegoat for difficult economic times. And Wise Use capitalized on current events.

In Washington, Oregon, and the northern counties of California, timber industry workers lost jobs in the months following the listing of the northern spotted owl. Many blamed the owl's listing for their loss and were highly emotional about it, as shown in this speech prepared by a spokesperson for the American Loggers Solidarity, Barbara Mossman:

> This is not a scientific issue; it is a moral issue. The deprivation and oppression of tens of thousands of timber dependent families cannot be justified by any science known to man. Logging is not a job; it is who we are. . . . You may not know what it is like to see everything you have worked for all your life sacrificed to the god of environmentalism; but I do. You may not know what it is like to go to bed hungry; but I do. The Endangered Species Act is referred to as the "pit bull" of environmental laws for good reason. It is vicious, cruel and unrelenting.

Environmentalists asserted that these jobs would have disappeared anyway because the Pacific Northwest was on the verge of being logged out. The listing, they claimed, merely caused the timber companies to reduce logging sooner rather than later. Supporting that view, Daniel Glick (1995:10) described a community in Douglas County, Oregon, where residents had felt the pinch on the timber industry in the late 1980s. "Automation of lumber mills and logging also cut jobs. By the early 1990s, mill wages had declined and wood-products jobs had been increasingly difficult to find." Clinton's Northwest Forest Plan included funds to retrain workers, and many have taken advantage of that. Fifty-one-year-old Ray Jones went back to school, admitting that he had not expected his job to last to retirement: "My job was a dinosaur. Most of us know they were just cutting the timber too fast" (quoted in Glick 1995:12). New forest industries are surfacing that do not devastate the land. People in Oregon got creative; "the industry has become more efficient and innovative" (Glick 1995:13).

In Riverside, California, victims of a brushfire blamed the kangaroo rat listing for similar trauma. In the fall of 1993, brushfires burned out of control in Riverside County and destroyed several homes in the process. Those homeowners claimed that the ESA and the Fish and Wildlife Service prevented them from protecting their property. They believed that disking, a soil-turning process, would have provided a protective firebreak and allowed the fire to bypass their property. The FWS prohibited disking because of the damage it would do to kangaroo rat habitat. Although a report from the General Accounting Office exonerated the FWS from wrongdoing, the issue still smolders in the area.

At a 1988 conference in Reno, Nevada, Wise Use and two hundred other organizations produced over one hundred papers; these subsequently were published as the *Wise Use Agenda*. The papers called for opening all public lands to oil drilling, logging, and commercial development; for immediate oil and gas development of Alaska's Arctic National Wildlife Refuge; for liquidation of all old growth forests; and for privatization of public rangelands. Wise Use relies on three themes: private property rights, pro-jobs economic development, and multiple use of federal lands. Because these issues are especially sensitive in the western states, the movement gained strength in the West and remains primarily a western phenomenon today.

Wise Use was credited with influencing President Ronald Reagan to issue Executive Order 12630 in 1988, which required all federal agencies to review the effect of regulations on the possibility of a "taking" of private property. While the order may seem reasonable, in practice such a review can dramatically slow the listing and recovery planning process or deter listing consideration completely for an endangered species. Some environmentalists claim that Wise Use helped pack the U.S. Claims Court in the District of Columbia with Wise Use sympathizers. This court is charged with settling land disputes and other compensation claims against the government. It was this court that awarded a New Jersey developer $2.68 million in damages when he was prevented from building on 12.5 acres of wetlands (only 5 percent of the total parcel of land originally purchased for $300,000.) The court also awarded $2 million to a Florida company stopped from mining 98 of its 1,560 acres in order to protect the groundwater, and $150 million to Whitney Benefits, a Wyoming coal company prohibited from strip mining in a protected area (Lewis 1992).

Another effective Wise Use strategy has been calling its member organizations by names that sound like environmental protection groups. For example, the Marine Preservation Association is composed of fifteen oil companies promoting the welfare of petroleum companies, and the National Wetlands Coalition is a leading opponent of preserving wetlands. The members of the American Council on Science and Health are chemical firms arguing that consumers need not worry about the health effects of pesticides and food additives. The National Endangered Species Act Reform Coalition consists of utility companies and municipal governments working to weaken the Endangered Species Act (Lewis 1992).

David Helvarg (1995) indicated that the movement portrays itself as financially strapped and up against a powerful and well-financed "green establishment." Its backers, however, include the National Inholders Association (owners of private property within federal lands), Wilderness Impact Research Foundation, International Association of Shopping Centers, National Association of Realtors, Off-road Vehicle Manufacturers, Western Fuels Association, American Legislative Exchange Council, National Rifle Association, American Farm Bureau, the National Beef Cattleman's Association, and the Heritage Foundation. The People for the West, a grassroots organization with twenty thousand members dedicated to defending the 1872 Mining law, received $1.7 million in start-up funds from companies like Chevron, Pegasus Gold, and the American Mining Congress. Honda, Suzuki, Yamaha, and Kawasaki sponsor the Blue Ribbon Coalition, which advocates opening parks and wilderness to off-road vehicles. The Environmental Conservation Organization (ECO) was created in 1990 by the Land Improvement Contractors Association (Helvarg 1995).

Each of the Wise Use organizations has a unique charter, and interests vary. The National Endangered Species Act Reform Coalition (NESARC), for example, has been effective at getting legislation introduced to modify the Endangered Species Act. The American Farm Bureau Federation, Tri-State Generation and Transmission Association (Denver), and Apache County, Arizona, formed NESARC in December 1991. The coalition represents agriculture, power companies, water utilities, and municipalities. NESARC Executive Director Nancy Macan McNally described its mission in simple terms: "Its purpose is to reform the ESA, which is too rigid" (McNally 1995). The coalition worked with the media and with the public and actively lobbied and developed policy papers to influence Congress. NESARC also ghostwrote S. 191, the ESA reauthorization bill that Senators Slade Gorton (R-Wash.) and Bennett Johnston (D-La.) introduced in May 1995.

To strengthen the image of popular support, grassroots organizations received the credit for leading state and national lobbying efforts for anti-environment legislation and for all the legal actions taken. Inasmuch as Wise Use has access to pro bono legal services with the Pacific Legal Foundation and the Mountain States Legal Foundation, there is no financial impediment tu legal action. Wise Use attacks environmental legislation with takings suits. It defined takings as any limitation on the property owner's intended use of the property as well as any fraction of private land restricted because of environmental regulations.

Private Property Rights Movement: History

The right to own property is an integral part of the value system upon which the United States was founded. "Under the American system, land is owned in a fee simple absolute, just as any other commodity. It can therefore be easily sold and freely mortgaged" (Gray 1993:188). American colonists from England left behind a leaseholder system, in which a citizen could own his own house but the landlord owned the land; the colonists brought with them land grants from the crown when possible. Thus from the 1600s, private land ownership was a simple fact of life in North America and was therefore perceived as a basic human right. For hundreds of years, real property was the primary source of human livelihood and economic sufficiency.

The right to private property was affirmed and codified in the Bill of Rights of the United States. For the delegates to the Constitutional Convention in 1787, "property was not a privilege of the higher orders but a right which a man would fight to defend. Men had indeed died to defend it in the war with England" (Bowen 1986:70). The first slogan of the American Revolution was "Liberty, Property and no stamps!" The Massachusetts Circular Letter of 1768 said property was "an essential, unalterable Right, in nature . . . that what a man has honestly acquired is absolutely his own" (Bowen 1986:71). To the framers of the Constitution, *property* meant both land and acquired items kept on the land. Land was so plentiful then that even the poorest person could claim a spot, build a cabin, and clear and sow the land.

The roots of American belief in the sanctity of private property are deep. The U.S. Constitution, Article IV, Section 2, gives the Congress power over all public land. The Fifth Amendment addresses individual rights to private property in the third and fourth clauses—"nor be deprived of life, liberty, or property, without due process of law; nor shall private property be taken for public use, without just compensation." This is the Constitution's takings clause.

For most of its history, the United States has had a surfeit of land. Nineteenth-century politicians believed in Manifest Destiny, the inevitability of coast-to-coast expansion of the United States. The Homestead Act, passed in 1862, encouraged settlement of the West, and Congress gave free land to railroads to encourage national expansion. "In our guts, we still equate private property with personal freedom" (Stapleton 1993:27). The laws enacted to encourage western development granted special privileges: vast and inexpensive grazing rights, nominal fees for mining and timber extraction on public lands, and guaranteed water rights in country where the scarcity of water makes it the most valuable resource. These privileges became so intrinsic to the culture of the western states that today they are deemed inalienable rights. Easterners, however, believe it is a national burden to have to support—in effect, to subsidize—the western ranching and extraction economies.

Statutory Support of Private Property Rights

In the last few decades of the twentieth century, federal regulations increasingly affected private property owners. In his majority opinion in *Lucas v. South Carolina* (505 U.S. [1991]), conservative Supreme Court Justice Anton Scalia warned that "anyone who purchases property always takes a risk that government regulation will diminish its value." Nevertheless, Doug Harbrecht (1994) pointed out, the private property movement contends that the Fifth Amendment protects landowners from regulations preventing them from doing what they wish with their property. The interpretation that partial loss of property use is as much a constitutional taking as full loss has been stretched further with the western claim that regulatory infringement on grazing rights is a taking because it also diminishes the property value of the rancher's land.

These contemporary takings definitions are radically different from the standard the courts have historically sustained. Constitutional case law supports compensation only for the taking of the full use of property. The contemporary interpretations of the Fifth Amendment have provoked environmentalists to label property rights advocates greedy.

Private property rights advocates believe environmental laws increasingly infringe on their right to full and unimpeded use of their real property. Laws such as the Clean Water Act of 1972 with its Section 404 wetlands regulations, and the Comprehensive Environmental Response, Compensation and Liability Act (CERCLA), commonly referred to as Superfund, have produced more takings cases than the ESA. The Endangered Species Act has created comparatively minor private property offenses.

Lynn Greenwalt, retired vice president of the National Wildlife Federation and former director of the Fish and Wildlife Service, believes it is "an outgrowth of states rights and concern about grazing and managing riparian zones. It wasn't an issue until we found endangered species on non-federal grounds" (1995). He said the Endangered Species Act of 1973 had little effect on private land until the application of Section 9, species takings, and the Fish and Wildlife Service's promulgation of a definition of harm in the early 1980s (Greenwalt, pers. comm., 1995).

Mike Vivoli, a CEI fellow, colorfully asserted, "To those who own private lands they deem critical for their *own* survival, however, it [the ESA] is a Trojan Horse full of bureaucrats trying to effect national land use planning" (Vivoli 1995:10). On the difficulty of taking an ESA case to court, he stated: "Landowners are impaled on the horns of a dilemma: either give up their property rights or violate the ESA outright" (Vivoli 1995:12). "Historically, the purpose of owning land had been to acquire the power to use the land and its resources for personal gain" ("Noss Reports" 1995:23).

There is no doubt that the ESA is challenging the traditional sanctity of private property. The question is: should the public's good take priority over private good? If yes, should the public—that is, the government—compensate the landowner for the loss? If yes, how? On what value basis should compensation be made—current market value of property, purchase price of property, or potential developed value of property? Who assesses the value? As noted in chapter 4, the concepts of property are evolving. Beside the legal tradition that property holders do not own vertebrate wildlife because wildlife is a common good lies the tradition that plants belong to the landowner—protecting plants on private property produces many more cases of perceived invasion of rights. Whereas property rights were created to protect individuals from harm, we now aim to protect individuals from harming species (Rolston 1991).

Endangered Species: A Public Problem

Habitat Conservation Plans, the mechanism for private parties to obtain incidental take permits, are often a disincentive. They require getting a biological assessment of alternatives for the species and developing a conservation and/ or mitigation plan to offset any jeopardy caused by the planned development activity. While developers and local governments have accepted the process, it is expensive and time-consuming. The bigger the territory, the greater the likelihood of multiple species being involved. For small property holders, the expense is prohibitive.

Multiple sources have related instances of developers clearing their property of plants that provide habitat for birds and insects suspected of being endangered. A less overt action, but one that is equally damaging to a species, is changing a logging rotation. Ike Sugg (1995) related this story: Benjamin Cone of Greensboro, North Carolina, was able to harvest trees in only two thousand of his eight thousand acres because of the red-cockaded woodpecker. Cone estimated his loss at $2 million. The woodpeckers build their nests in trees older than seventy years. To keep the birds away, Cone changed his logging rotation so that the trees would be cut before they got old enough to attract the woodpeckers.

In addition to grassroots strategies and corporate and NGO advocacy, the private property rights movement relies on takings litigation to curb the impact of environmental regulations. To Jonathan Adler of CEI, any prohibition of the use of private land, as long as such use does not directly infringe on the rights of others, constitutes a regulatory taking. Furthermore, he maintains that there is a "fundamental difference between preventing a property owner from despoiling the property of his neighbor and enacting land use controls in order to provide public good" (Adler 1995:4). Historically, however, partial loss of land use has been considered a normal, natural risk.

Takings case law is about a century old. The Fifth Amendment clause was first evoked in 1871 in *Pumpelly v. Green Bay Co.* (80 U.S. [13 Wall] 166 [1871]), which addressed a physical government invasion of property. The first case involving regulation of land was in 1922 in *Pennsylvania Coal Co. v. Mahon* (260 U.S. 393 [1922]). In 1978 the Supreme Court established guidelines for information required for takings decisions in *Penn Central Transportation Co. v New York City* (438 U.S. 104 [1978]). Necessary information included an assessment of the economic impact of the action, the extent to which the action interfered with reasonable investment expectations, and the character of the action. Since the Penn Central case, there have been more than two dozen Supreme Court decisions moving toward greater protection of property rights (Meltz 1995).

Holmes Rolston (1991) noted, however, that the courts in general have been reluctant to advance property rights applicable to Fifth Amendment takings when the taking was due to environmental restrictions. In 1978 in the Tellico Dam case, *TVA v. Hill* (436 U.S. [1978]), the court affirmed that Congress

saw danger in the extinction of any species and that "untempered" development impeded conservation. This precedent became a barrier to successful takings litigation for private property owners.

The other side of the issue is the belief that the right to develop one's land is an inalienable American right. In the West, where grazing and water rights convey with the land deed, regulatory restriction of grazing rights or infringement on water access is perceived as an infringement on personal property. The counterargument is that these are privileges, not inalienable rights, and are government subsidized. (Ranchers pay a fee far below market value to graze their cattle on public lands; there is no landowner "fee" for water rights.) Control of water rights conveys control over the land and over other ranchers. Environmental statutes are perceived to threaten that control.

Two suits brought by Nevada ranchers tested this interpretation of regulatory taking. In the first, landowner Wayne Hage sued the U.S. Forest Service for $28 million in damages. He claimed that the Forest Service "ruined his business by introducing elk that competed with his cattle for grass; [by] allowing backpackers and elk to drink from springs used by his livestock and restricting how heavily his cattle could graze stream side vegetation" (Harbrecht 1994:9).

The second suit was filed by Steve and Carol Wilmans, owners of fifteen thousand acres with grazing permits on 2 million acres of public land. They built a pipeline to carry water from the Toiyabe National Forest to their ranch. The Forest Service district required them to get a permit to alter public land, but the Wilmans argued that water rights came with the purchase of the land, as did rights-of-way. The Wilmans also were required to remove their cattle earlier than usual from a wilderness area because of poor stream bank conditions. They contended that "such direct action and conduct by the Forest Service resulted in physical invasion and occupation" and thus constituted a taking.

In *Lucas v. South Carolina Coastal Commission* (505 U.S. [1992]), the Supreme Court added more confusion to the issue. In his analysis of this case, James Joseph (1995:29) noted that property rights advocates expected this decision to galvanize the movement, but "no one is really sure what Lucas gave us." Neither side claimed victory or defeat. In favor of private property rights, the case "dealt environmental regulations a potentially serious blow by saying that a citizen's understanding of his rights does not include the possibility that his property be rendered worthless" (30). (Recall, however, Scalia's words in delivering his opinion in this case that value diminishment may be

expected.) On the other hand, the court was unclear on what amount of value diminishment constitutes a taking. In *Lucas*, the Supreme Court held that the petitioner lost the full economic value of his property.

Robert Meltz of the Congressional Research Service reviewed the takings cases decided between 1990 and 1993 and summarized the results (Meltz 1995). In only 15 percent of the cases involving federal statutes or filed against the United States was a taking found. Moreover, the number of takings found decreased from six in 1991, when there were fourteen cases, to only two in 1993, when there were thirty-one cases.

With so little success in the courts, the private property rights and Wise Use movements targeted state legislatures. Harbrecht indicated that thirty-seven state legislatures introduced takings bills. Most were defeated due to cost or concerns that state authority to protect public safety would be eroded. Legislation incorporating some form of property rights protection is in effect in Arizona, Delaware, Florida, Idaho, Indiana, Kansas, Louisiana, Mississippi, Missouri, Montana, New Mexico, North Carolina, North Dakota, South Dakota, Tennessee, Texas, Utah, Virginia, Washington, West Virginia, and Wyoming.

Meltz describes property bills as falling into two categories: assessment bills and compensation bills. The former require federal agencies to evaluate the takings implications of proposed actions; many require risk assessment and cost-benefit analysis for each project.

Compensation bills tend to establish a statutory threshold for compensation, for example 10 or 20 percent of property value. Congressional debate on compensation bills revolves around the determination of property value and how to quantify adverse impact, or benefit, of government programs on private property (Meltz 1995). One fear has been the potential of such legislation to cause a speculator "gold rush." Should a profit be made because endangered species reside on public land? Are landowners not members of the public and therefore partaking of the value of the species? But compensation based on the amount paid for the land would work only with recent purchases. Land handed down in a family for generations cannot be valued by purchase price.

Several bills were introduced in the 102nd Congress requiring the ESA to consider property rights issues. None was voted on outside of committee. By the 103rd Congress, the movement succeeded in introducing, though not

passing, around two dozen bills, including one specifically addressing compensation for taking property. The 104th Congress, with Republicans dominant for the first time in forty years, introduced a host of bills supporting private property, minimizing the impact of environmental regulation, and establishing guidelines for compensating regulatory takings. Again, none passed. There was also a flurry of attempts to amend bills unrelated to property taking. These amendments would have restricted or temporarily halted environmental regulation to protect property.

While the 105th Congress adopted the environmental purists' emphasis on improved recovery planning, both bills also directly addressed private property issues with incentives for landowners to cooperate and protect endangered species. As Michael Bean pointed out, "Property rights are pervasive and a political fact of life today. It is a message that resonates well and a key American right" (Bean 1995).

The Endangered Species Act should not be blamed for all the ills of society; however, it has created some unanticipated hardship. The regulatory takings approach is not the answer to the private property issue. Nor is the answer to declare all land where endangered species occur to be a public trust and to require federal purchase.

The private property rights advocates have a legitimate concern. Three regulations were promulgated between 1996 and 1998 to provide more equitable treatment of private property and public lands—No Surprises, Safe Harbor, and greater cooperation between the federal government and private and other nonfederal entities. These policies, discussed more fully in chapter 8, address the problems in a reasonable, more equitable manner and do not include any modification to the national takings policy codified in the Constitution and upheld by the U.S. courts. They are imperfect policies, but they represent a general step forward.

The country's fiscal realities will inevitably govern outcomes; both private property advocates and environmentalists would do better to accept these realities. Some landowner incentive to protect species is appropriate and worthwhile. Steps to relieve the financial burden of HCPs on small landowners are also in order. Property owners cannot expect to be relieved of all burden of saving the species, nor should they be asked to shoulder the full burden. The public benefits from saving the species and it makes sense to require a reasonable degree of public contribution to the expense.

Part Three

Conflict

Chapter Six

In the Halls of Congress

Congress has become . . . the most potent institution in
the intricate structure of "checks and balances." . . . [It]
has also become a rich source of delay, confusion, and
waste in both making and implementing environmental
policy. . . . a case of checks and balances gone awry.
—Walter A. Rosenbaum, 1995

T HE POLITICAL ENVIRONMENT has not been friendly to the ESA since
it lapsed in October 1992. The Democratic 102nd Congress (1991–
92), aware of political forces desiring to weaken the law, avoided bringing reauthorization to the floor. Authorizations for environmental laws
have often lapsed for lengthy periods; the ESA survived one earlier long interval between reauthorizations in the 1980s. Congress continued to appropriate funds to implement the statute but evaded major changes to the law
by not bringing reauthorization to a vote. Also, the act lapsed near the beginning of a presidential election year, providing another excuse to delay action.
There was no cause for concern when the 102nd Congress did not reauthorize the ESA.

The 1992 election brought in a Democratic president, Bill Clinton. Clinton
ran on a platform that included strong environmental support, and his running mate, Al Gore, was a well-known proponent of environmental protection. After twelve years of the conservative and environmentally unfriendly
Reagan and Bush administrations, the Enviros were elated over their win and
collectively breathed a major sigh of relief. At last, they had a friend in the
White House!

In spite of greater access to the White House, however, national conservation groups no longer had the political impact they had once enjoyed. Representative George Miller (D-Calif.), chairman of the House Natural

Resources Committee until 1994, observed that conservation organizations had lost some of their competitive edge during Reagan-Bush years and were out-organized by the religious right and groups concerned with private enterprise, private property, and jobs. Votes were needed to pass legislation, he concluded, not just to stop it (Wicker 1994). In fact, throughout the Reagan-Bush years, Enviro pressure was essentially reactive in nature: while successful in stopping damaging bills, Enviros were unable, for the most part, to introduce or pass proactive legislation. Proactive efforts were needed to rally the environmental supporters in Congress, to find and support champions, and to help write bills that would serve the environmental cause.

The combination of a Democratic Congress and president, therefore, did not help the environment in 1992–93. The growing perception that environmental regulation infringed upon private property rights and delayed progress in general continued the unfriendly climate for ESA reauthorization.

The 103rd Congress (1993–1994)

Leading ESA protagonists in the 103rd Congress included George Miller (D-Calif.), Gerry Studds (D-Mass.), and John Dingell (D-Mich.) in the House and Max Baucus (D-Mont.) and John Chafee (R-R.I.) in the Senate. Baucus was chairman of the Senate Environment and Public Works Committee. Chafee was the ranking Republican on the committee.

Anti-ESA House leaders included W. J. (Billy) Tauzin (D-La.) and Jack Fields (R-Tex.); the Senate leaders were Slade Gorton (R-Wash.) and Richard C. Shelby (R-Ala.). Many of the Republicans who became leaders in the 104th Congress dedicated resources during the 102nd and 103rd Congresses to researching and preparing arguments against the ESA. However, under Democratic control, conservative Republicans were continually frustrated. Pressure and resentment mounted.

Several new ESA opponents were elected to the 103rd Congress. Two were elected on anti-ESA platforms and deserve credit for representing their constituencies faithfully even though each made noteworthy efforts to thwart the law. Republican Senator Kay Bailey Hutchison from Texas was elected in 1993 to replace Democrat Lloyd Benson, who moved to a cabinet position. In her reelection in 1994, she won a two-thirds majority vote that was based in part on her pro–property rights and anti-ESA platform, a popular stance in a state that is home to a number of endangered species considered instrumental in slowing economic development. In the House, Republican Representative Richard Pombo, a rancher from the Central Valley of California, near Stockton, was elected in 1992 on a property rights platform and the promise to change environmental laws, such as the Clean Water Act and the ESA. True to their campaign pledges, both introduced anti-ESA bills in Congress that were intended to stop endangered species listings and critical habitat designations, on the one hand, and to eliminate protection for bald eagles, grizzly bears, gray wolves, and Pacific salmon, on the other.

Two parallel movements took root in the 103rd Congress: takings laws and deregulation. The takings legislation, as already discussed, was intended to compensate landowners for loss of the use of a percentage of real property. Deregulation had been a Republican issue for many years, but the private property rights movement gave this old saw a new edge during the 103rd Congress.

Both types of takings bills—assessment bills and compensation bills—were introduced in the 103rd Congress. Proponents of the assessment type argued that it was necessary to codify congressional intent not only to have federal agencies evaluate takings implications (also mandated by Executive Order 12630) but also to add strong incentives for agency compliance. Opponents of the assessment type believed these bills would merely impose another layer of red tape.

Proponents of compensation takings bills asserted that the constitutional remedy (the courts) was too time-consuming, too expensive, and too unpredictable (not winnable). The federal judiciary maintained that a taking could only be assessed *after* determining how an action affected a specific property; that is, after the action was taken. Compensation proponents believed that a single value-loss threshold used as a trigger for compensation would afford greater certainty to both landowners and government agencies and would instill in federal agencies more respect for private property, although they acknowledged that such compensation would be costly and would confound deficit reduction goals. Opponents charged that compensation bills would eviscerate programs. They objected to compensating owners for not putting their land to harmful use and asserted that some moderate level of private property impact was the necessary price for achieving broadly supported collective goals (Meltz 1995).

At least three takings bills were introduced in the 103rd Congress: the Private Property Owners Bill of Rights in both Houses (H.R. 3875 and S. 1915) and the Just Compensation Act of 1993 (H.R. 1388) in the House. None of these passed. Property rights advocates did succeed, however, in adding takings language to the California Desert Protection Act, one of the few environmentally friendly laws passed in the 103rd Congress. The addendum required that the land acquired by the federal government under the act be appraised without regard to the presence of any listed endangered or threatened species. In the second session, the House turned back an effort to include similar language in another bill. Instead, the House adopted provisions to inform property owners about their existing rights under the Constitution. But these provisions were not taken up by the Senate and the bill died.

The bill authorizing the establishment of the National Biological Survey (NBS), H.R. 1845, generated heated debate because deregulation proponents feared survey findings would lead to the creation of new restrictive regulations on economic development. The purpose of establishing the NBS was to catalog America's plant and animal life, much as the U.S. Geological Survey studies and catalogs geological resources. The House approved the measure, but the Senate never took action on it. Both houses, however, included funding for the new agency in the 1994 and 1995 Interior appropriations bills.

Several attempts were made to amend or reauthorize the Endangered Species Act during the 103rd Congress. Many in this Congress sought greater consideration of the economic costs of wildlife protection. At least nine different bills were introduced in the House and four in the Senate.

H.R. 2043 sponsored by Gerry Studds (D-Mass.), John Dingell (D-Mich.), Newt Gingrich (R-Ga.), and Jim Saxton (R-N.J.) was the most notable of the House bills. This bill encouraged more coordinated protection of interrelated species and their habitats. It required greater species recovery efforts with reduced social and economic impacts. It also created incentives for private landowners to conserve species and improved the interaction and cooperation between the federal government and the states. Enviros and property rights advocates alike agreed that these changes were needed, but the degree of change and the methods for its implementation were then and are now sources of contention.

Representatives Jack Fields (R-Tex.) and Billy Tauzin (D-La.) introduced opposing legislation. The Fields-Tauzin bill proposed various procedural amendments to the ESA and required that economic factors and private property rights be given greater consideration in species conservation. Senators Max Baucus (D-Mont.) and John Chafee (R-R.I.) introduced the Senate parallel to the Studds-Dingell bill, S. 931, and Senators Richard Shelby (R-Ala.) and

Slade Gorton (R-Wash.) sponsored the Senate parallel to the Fields-Tauzin bill, S. 1521. Both houses held hearings on these bills and on other issues relating to the act throughout the 103rd Congress, but neither took further action.

Other issues included managing the national wildlife refuge system, reforming wetlands conservation management practices, and protecting Antarctica's environment, the chinook salmon, and the Snake River (Idaho) birds of prey. The only species conservation legislation passed by this Congress was an amendment to the Marine Mammal Protection Act.

Michael Bean (1995) of the Environmental Defense Fund has suggested that Congress has historically responded to controversial topics by avoiding them. This was certainly true of the 103rd Congress in handling the ESA reauthorization. The Studds-Dingell bill had 120 cosponsors, and the opposing Fields-Tauzin bill had an almost equal number. Because all of the introduced bills included the controversial application of a cost-benefit or risk assessment analysis, Congress did not vote on any of them. Although cost-benefit analyses and risk assessments are two standard business tools used for any project of substantial value to a company, the Enviros and many in Congress saw them as a means of clogging up bureaucratic progress.

The 104th Congress (1995–1996)

While the frustration and pressure were building in Congress, the conservative private property rights movement presented 1994 Republican candidates a platform to which they could respond with confidence. On November 8, 1994, the lid blew off the congressional pressure cooker. For the first time in forty years, Republicans won the majority in both houses. Seventy-three new Republican members took seats in the House of Representatives and twenty in the Senate

In its publication *HSUS News*, the Humane Society of the United States provided commentary on the attitudes of some of the new Republican freshman who were strong opponents of the Endangered Species Act. During her campaign, Representative Helen Chenoweth (R-Idaho; now Chenoweth-Hage) was asked whether she believed sockeye salmon deserved to be listed. Her response: "How can I when you can . . . buy a can of salmon off the shelf in the [supermarket]?" Another freshman, Representative Sonny Bono (R-Calif.), said during his campaign, "Give [endangered species] a designated area and then blow it up" ("Saving the Endangered Species Act" 1995).

Veteran congressional Republicans, some of whom had experienced years of frustration in the minority role, assumed leadership roles. They were ready for their turn to control the legislative process. Bolstered by the freshman Republicans, who believed they had a mandate to roll back regulations, the new GOP formed an almost impenetrable block. The Democratic minority did not have the strength to break this block.

No Democratic leader for environmental issues emerged; a defeatist, no-can-do attitude seemed to pervade the party. In time, moderate Republicans, unhappy with the radical nature of the environmental and social changes being pushed through by the conservative freshmen–old guard block, began to speak out. By the end of the first session of the 104th Congress, the moderate block had coalesced and had begun to exercise its will.

In the early part of the decade, the ESA had had a heavy impact in a handful of states, and legislators from these states tended to be its strongest opponents: Louisiana, Texas, Washington, and California. Shrimping is a big industry in Louisiana, and the turtle exclusion devices (TEDs) imposed on shrimpers to protect dolphins and turtles from accidental death in shrimp nets were unpopular. Despite a federal study indicating that the shrimp catch had not declined with the introduction of TEDs, Louisianans disagreed. Senators Bennett Johnston and Slade Gorton coauthored a pro-industry ESA reauthorization bill, and Senator John Breaux signed on as a sponsor. More than 70 percent of the Louisiana House delegation voted anti-environment in the first hundred days; none of them were freshmen.

Concerns in the Texas delegation focused on agricultural issues and building development. Many Texans believed that such endangered species as the golden-cheeked warbler, the black-capped vireo, and the Texas blind salamander had slowed development and decreased property values. More than 80 percent of the House Texas delegation voted against environmental bills in the first hundred days of the session; only five of the thirty representatives were freshman. In fact, Texans held key congressional positions: Dick Armey, who considers the hunting organization Ducks Unlimited leftist, was the House majority leader. Tom DeLay, who stated to the press that DDT is not harmful and need never have been banned, was the majority whip (Bean 1995).

In the forests of California and Washington, listing of the northern spotted owl had greatly affected the timber industry. Although both states had healthy gross products, there were population pockets in the Olympic Peninsula of

Washington and in northern California that suffered from the loss of timber-related jobs. These groups also feared the impact of the potential listing of several salmon subspecies. Most of the Washington delegation in the House voted anti-environment in the first hundred days; two-thirds of that delegation were freshman.

California, however, with two of the largest U.S. metropolitan populations and a diverse industry-agriculture base, is politically mixed on environmental issues. Senator Barbara Boxer was solidly environmental, and Senator Dianne Feinstein, though not solid in her support, leaned toward the pro-environment bills. Twenty of the fifty-two-member House delegation voted favorably on environmental bills during the first hundred days; only six of the fifty-two were freshman.

Oregon legislators have not been at the forefront of the anti-ESA effort, despite the timber industry representing a substantial portion of the gross state product. Although Senator Bob Packwood signed on as a sponsor of the Gorton-Johnston reauthorization bill before he left the Congress, Senator Mark Hatfield did not. A majority of the Oregon representatives actually voted pro-environment in the first hundred days.

There is no strong history of negative ESA impact in Idaho, yet members of Congress from this state became leaders in the anti-ESA movement. Freshman representative Helen Chenoweth was a strong ESA antagonist and Senator Dirk Kempthorne sponsored one of the anti–ESA reauthorization bills introduced in the 104th Congress. By the 105th Congress, however, his antipathy toward the law had moderated.

A succession of laws that significantly reduced federal regulations were passed in the first session of the new House. While the fervor of the new Congress was to right overregulation wrongs and to address private property issues, the effect was a concentration on providing regulatory relief to business and industry and on rolling back environmental protections. The vigor of this anti-environment effort in Congress startled the public and the environmental community. The Enviros were nervous after the election but ill-prepared for the onslaught on existing environmental laws that followed with the new Congress. It took the Enviros and the public well into 1995 to respond to the spectacular nature of the environmental changes proposed by the new Republican House. At first, the average citizen had difficulty accepting that Congress could be doing what it was trying to do to remove human well-being protections. Neither the environment nor the Endangered Species Act had been a national issue during the 1994 campaign, nor were they local election issues, with a few exceptions in western states. To many voters, deregulation meant cleaning up the bureaucracy and perhaps cutting costs and taxes: it had seemed like a good thing to vote for a candidate whose primary focus was government deregulation.

In the *Congressional Quarterly* of June 17, 1995, Bob Benenson confirmed that the Republican majority was "making clear its intention to rewrite many of the nation's major environmental laws to provide regulatory relief to businesses and individuals." Republican strategists believed that the November election "provided a mandate to reduce environmental regulation" (Benenson 1995:1693).

Numerous popular polls refute the congressional perception that there was a mandate to change environmental regulations. Benenson cited two. In 1994, the annual Roper Starch Worldwide Survey indicated that 75 percent of Americans viewed themselves as environmentalists. A Cambridge Reports Survey conducted in September 1994 indicated public willingness to sacrifice economic growth for environmental conservation. Two other public polls substantiated that the majority of United States citizens strongly supported environmental legislation in general and the Endangered Species Act specifically. Both addressed the private property issue. The first was sponsored by the Nature Conservancy and was taken before the 1994 election; the second, sponsored by the National Wildlife Federation, surveyed voters after the election.

The Nature Conservancy poll, commissioned in May 1994, involved eight hundred households across the country (Cheater 1994). Of the respondents, 66 percent said they were *more* concerned about the environment than they had been a few years earlier and only 18 percent were *less* concerned. Similarly, 65 percent indicated that more land should be set aside for conservation, while 25 percent said enough land had been set aside. A full 59 percent of respondents said that some restrictions on landowners are justified to protect plants and animals, while only 30 percent said landowners should be able to do as they wish. The poll thus indicated strong popular commitment to environmental preservation. It also indicated that the gap between absolute property rights and modified rights, though substantial, was narrowing.

After the election, the National Wildlife Federation conducted a nationwide telephone survey of twelve hundred people who had voted on election day. Identical questions were posed to a separate sample of two hundred NWF members to compare the responses of the general public with the views of respondents more likely to be biased toward conservation. The results were foreseeable. Although the margin for error around the estimates on the smaller sample was twice that in the larger poll, the conservationist responses were consistently ten percentage points or more higher than those of the general public. Nevertheless, the responses of the general public demonstrated that a majority was concerned about conservation.

The percentage of respondents who had voted for Republican versus Democratic candidates was even: 51 percent in the larger sample, 52 percent in the small sample. In response to whether Congress should maintain strong ESA requirements or relax them, 57 percent of the large sample replied "maintain" and only 32 percent wanted to relax ESA requirements; in the smaller NWF-member sample, 68 percent favored maintaining and a mere 20 percent favored relaxing ESA requirements. Regarding government compensation to property owners when environmental laws restricted their right to do as they wished with their property, 56 percent of the general public said "no" and 34 percent thought property owners should be compensated; in the NWF sample 66 percent said "no" and only 24 percent favored compensation.

Benenson (1995) also summarized the three basic Republican principles in the 104th Congress: force federal agencies to justify regulations before promulgation, protect private property rights, and relax federal control and privatize responsibility. A fourth precept discussed in the article would become more important in the second session of the 104th Congress—devolution of responsibility to the states. The "current push to scale back environmental regulations is very much in keeping with the overall conservative philosophy of moving policy decisions from the federal government to states, localities" (Benenson 1995:1696).

Under the leadership of Speaker Newt Gingrich (R-Ga.), the House pumped out legislation. The *Contract with America* was published early in the 104th Congress, making commitments to overhauling the federal regulatory structure but not directly addressing environmental issues. The contract was an indicator of the singular drive by this Congress to tackle difficult issues. The speed with which legislation passed through the 104th House of Representatives is further evidence.

The first indication of the plan to attack environmental regulations came in February 1995 when the House passed the Regulatory Transition Act (H.R. 450). This bill placed a government-wide moratorium on developing or implementing new regulations throughout 1995, and it stopped new ESA regulations through 1996. Then H.R. 9, the Job Creation and Wage Enhancement Act, included provisions for compensating property owners. This bill also required federal agencies to perform scientific risk assessments and cost-benefit analyses on most proposed rules. Although the bill addressed a number of federal agencies, many perceived it to target environmental regulations primarily. The Senate saw introduction of companion bills to the Regulatory Transition Act (S. 219) and the Job Creation and Wage Enhancement Act—S. 34 by Bob Dole (R-Kans.), S. 291 by Bill Roth (R-Del.), and S. 333 by Frank Murkowski (R-Alaska). Dirk Kempthorne (R-Idaho) introduced S. 455, which allowed construction to continue in designated critical habitat *while* consultation is taking place. There were many bills addressing private property rights introduced in 1995 in both the House and Senate; none passed.

In March, Senator Kay Bailey Hutchison (R-Tex.), introduced S. 191, the Farm, Ranch, and Homestead Protection Act. Had it passed, this bill would have halted endangered species listings, critical habitat designations, and the obligation of federal agencies to comply with Section 7 of the Endangered Species Act until the ESA could be reauthorized. Later Hutchison introduced S. 503 to impose a moratorium on species listing and critical habitat designation. She failed to get either bill out of committee.

After the first five months of this Congress, environmental organizations began to regain strength. Grassroots networks hummed with news on critical environmental laws such as the ESA and the Clean Water Act. *ESA Today*, a daily Internet-Fax newsletter published by the Endangered Species Coalition, grew tremendously as new funds enabled its expansion. Large membership groups such as the National Wildlife Federation, Sierra Club, National Audubon Society, and others informed their members at least monthly of the environmentally ravaging legislation being proposed in Congress. Telephones started to ring at the White House and in congressional offices.

Moderate Maryland Republican Representative Wayne Gilchrest emerged as an environmental champion in the House. As a member of the strongly anti-ESA House Natural Resources Committee, he fought the Pombo-Young majority on the committee. Representative Don Young of Alaska had taken over as chair and Richard Pombo was his protégé. House action on the Clean Water Act (dubbed the "Dirty Water Act" by Enviros) bothered many other moderate Republicans. By July 1995, six of the more than one hundred names on Representative Bruce Vento's (D-Minn.) letter to the Natural Resources Committee were moderate Republicans, an indication of a weakening in the block. This letter beseeched the committee to preserve the strength of the ESA in its reauthorization (Vento 1995).

The ESA Reauthorization Bills

The first ESA reauthorization bill of the 104th Congress, S. 768, was introduced in the Senate by Slade Gorton (R-Wash.) and Bennett Johnston (R-La.). Enviros quickly responded that it "gutted" the act, and Secretary of the Interior Bruce Babbitt summarized the bill in five words: "The ESA is hereby repealed" (Babbitt 1995). The bill did not even enjoy widespread support among ESA opponents because it omitted compensation for loss of private property value. Gorton was criticized for introducing a bill written by industry organizations; indeed, the National Endangered Species Act Reform Coalition (NESARC) admitted to having formulated much of the bill's language (McNally 1995). This bill was not taken up in committee.

The Gorton-Johnston bill was notable, however, because it set the tone for later ESA reauthorization bills and because it served to spur environmental grassroots activity. It eliminated the goal of species recovery by allowing the secretary of the interior to decide whether saving a species was desirable; by allowing captive-bred populations (e.g., hatchery fish) to be counted in the population count for assessment of endangerment; and by not requiring maintenance of viable populations in the wild. Provisions eliminated much of the protection for marine animals other than fish, made it difficult to designate or protect endangered species habitat, and eliminated protection for distinct populations of species. By requiring more public hearings and scientific peer review for all biological assessments, the bill added time and cost to the process of determining if a species was endangered—and it permitted the consultation process to be waived.

Even so, S. 768 was moderate compared to the later Young-Pombo and Kempthorne bills. Representative Don Young, a multiterm Republican from Alaska, was the new chairman of the House Natural Resources Committee. Early in 1995, he appointed second-term Representative Richard Pombo (R-Calif.) head of the Endangered Species Task Force in the House; Pombo's strategy was to get "a lot of concurrence on the ESA reauthorization bill within the Committee before introducing it" (Pyle 1995). After a summer of debate, the House Natural Resources Committee reported out the Young-Pombo bill, H.R. 2275, the Endangered Species Conservation and Management Act of 1995.

While it incorporated the Gorton measures, this bill went much further. It required federal compensation to property owners when any ESA action diminished the value of any portion of the property or water rights by 20 percent or more; diminution in value greater than 50 percent required federal purchase of the devalued portion of the property. It limited citizens' ability to enjoin federal agencies from violating the law. It eliminated restrictions on harassing species, redefined *harm* to mean only actions that kill or injure a member of the species, and reduced aquatic species protections. It also removed protection for grizzly bears, the gray wolf, and salmon.

The Young-Pombo bill granted broad authority to exempt categories of activities and to issue incidental taking permits. It limited the right of the United States to protect foreign species through import. It granted exemptions on the use of turtle exclusion devices. It required that greater weight be given to empirical scientific data than to modeled projections and that all ESA actions have scientific peer review. Consultation between federal agencies and the FWS became optional and the bill added broad consultation exemptions.

Further, the bill abolished the Endangered Species Committee and allowed the secretary of defense authority to exempt activities for reasons of national security. H.R. 2275 imposed new requirements for public notification and longer public review cycles. Also, it required emphasis on captive breeding as a species protection and recovery device, while allowing hunting, mineral extraction, grazing, and off-road vehicle use on the biological reserve system it created.

This bill created great furor among scientific, religious, and environmental communities. Under the aegis of the American Association for the Advancement of Science, nine leaders of scientific bodies signed a letter to Representative Don Young, stating: "This bill to reauthorize the Endangered Species Act is so riddled with scientific errors and misstatements as to be indefensible." The letter ends: "Unfortunately, H.R. 2275 reflects an almost complete lack of scientific understanding" (AAAS 1995).

In April 1995, freshman Senator Dirk Kempthorne (R-Idaho) declared his intent to modify the ESA in *Roll Call* and states: "We cannot afford to have the entire natural resource management system rest on the back of the

ESA." He expressed concern that "the ESA is being used as a big club to require compliance with the ecosystem management principle" (Kempthorne 1995:8). In October 1995, he introduced a second Senate reauthorization bill, S. 1364. Unlike the Gorton-Johnston bill, it included takings compensation for the value of any property restricted by endangered species regulations, and it was nearly identical to the House bill.

One unanticipated result of the Young-Pombo bill was to strengthen the growing separation of the moderate Republicans from the conservative block in the House. Shortly after the bill was introduced, Representative Wayne Gilchrest introduced another ESA reauthorization bill, H.R. 2374, the Endangered Species Natural Legacy Protection Act of 1995. This bill was ahead of its time: much of what it included was reused in the two ESA reauthorization bills presented in the 105th Congress. But in the 104th, it was defeated in the House Natural Resources Committee by a vote of 28–17. Although the Enviros found little of interest in it for them at that time, they later supported similar elements in the Miller bill of 1997.

The Gilchrest bill emphasized federal coordination with states and authorized voluntary conservation agreements for states, Indian tribes, and local governments. It established a Conservation Planning Fund to assist states, other local parties, and individual property owners in developing Habitat Conservation Plans. For the first time, *biological diversity* and *ecosystem* were defined in a reauthorization bill and proactive conservation of habitats was promoted. In response to the ongoing complaint that species were not delisted promptly, the bill established a delisting criterion; it also required a list of prohibited activities to be published at the time of listing. The secretary of the interior was required to seek "scientific and commercial data" from each affected state prior to making a listing and during the consultation process, but peer review was needed only when evidence of a scientific dispute over the data was present. H.R. 2374 expanded the composition of the recovery planning team to include the affected states, Indian tribes, and local governments, biologists, private landowners, conservation organizations, and industry representatives.

Gilchrest's bill also set an eighteen-month time frame for development of each recovery plan. Furthermore, this bill directed the federal government to work cooperatively with private landowners and to use economic incentives to encourage private owner cooperation and to minimize adverse economic impact on the owner. It also called for the FWS to assist private landowners and local governments in developing conservation plans and established a program to reward property owners for conservation efforts. It encouraged multiple-species Habitat Conservation Plans, which cover listed, candidate, and any other sensitive species and their habitats. Finally, it incorporated some protection against requiring changes to private HCPs when new endangered or threatened species were discovered on the land involved.

None of these bills reached the floor for a vote in the 104th Congress. In fact, by the end of the first session (1995), it was clear that the three extant bills were political hot potatoes. The second session of the 104th saw some rhetoric on the issue but again no action.

Governing by Amendment

Although no ESA reauthorization bill reached the floor of Congress for a vote, the ESA was restricted and effectively hobbled by moratorium amendments on listings and spending. Inasmuch as amendments only require a majority voice vote of the members present in the chamber at the time they are proposed, they are a politically practical way to make changes when debate on issues stymies passage of laws. Many Americans consider amendments a sneaky strategy since they are introduced and passed so quickly that the public cannot comment. The sneakiness is magnified when an amendment unrelated to the bill under discussion is included in it with no public notification and by a simple majority of the members present.

Representative John Boehner of Ohio, chairman of the House Republican Conference, justified the amendment strategy: "It's the only real process available to us this year because we've got a White House that doesn't agree with many of our policy positions" (quoted in Welch and Lee 1995:9A). Welch and Lee (1995:9A) described how congressional spending authority could be used to control policy: "From clean water to affirmative action, congressional Republicans are using their power of the purse to make laws and reverse decades of federal policies. . . . Attaching provisions to spending bills increases GOP leverage with Clinton. . . . The GOP hopes he [Clinton] will be under pressure not to veto them when they are included in must-pass spending bills."

This tactic worked well early in the first session of the 104th Congress. Senator Kay Bailey Hutchison (R-Tex.) used it when she proposed an amendment to the Defense Supplemental Appropriations Bill (which, among other things, covered the expenses of U.S. military initiatives in Haiti) that imposed a hiatus on listings of endangered or threatened species for the balance of fiscal 1995. With little resistance from the members present on the floor, this amendment passed.

In the House, the Rescissions Bill (H.R. 1158) was passed. This bill cut the Fish and Wildlife Service's budget for listing species; cut funds for Department of Energy conservation programs; cut financial assistance to states for monitoring drinking water; and cut funding for land acquisition by the National Park Service, Bureau of Land Management, and Forest Service. It also carried two environmentally damaging riders. A timber salvage rider allowed six billion board feet of "diseased" timber to be removed from public lands and placed the decision to remove the trees in the hands of those in whose interest it was to cut the timber. NEPA and ESA were suspended under these conditions. A clean air rider stopped the Environmental Protection Agency (EPA) from approving state measures to clean up auto emissions.

Congressional freshmen repeated this tactic many times, putting riders on the Interior Appropriations bill and combined Veterans Administration–Housing and Urban Development–Environmental Protection Agency appropriations bill to restrict EPA's environmental regulatory power.

The Senate passed the Supplemental Defense Spending Bill with the ESA moratorium and the Rescissions Bill with the timber salvage and clean air riders. President Clinton signed the Defense Supplemental Spending bill in April 1995 and the Rescissions bill that July.

By August 1995, signs of congressional resistance to dramatic environmental law changes began to appear. The Senate passed an amendment to the Interior appropriations bill that increased funds for ESA listings, prelisting, and conservation land purchase. The Senate also defeated Senator Jesse Helms's (R-N.C.) amendment to stop the reintroduction of red wolves.

The public had become aware of the environmental changes being proposed by this Congress. Environmental organizations had rebuilt their grassroots and lobbying forces and were getting through to moderate Republican legislators, to the president, and to the vice president. Newspapers all over the country decried the attack on environmental regulations and emphasized the importance of saving species, keeping the waters of our country clean, and saving our forests and wildlands.

Moderate Republicans separated themselves from the conservatives on most environmental and some social issues. The size of the moderate block in the House was sufficient to block a majority vote. An Interior appropriations bill reached the floor of the House in September 1995 with cuts in ESA funding and in national park maintenance and with a number of riders calculated to hobble Environmental Protection Agency regulations. Since the large majority of listed species are protected by the Fish and Wildlife Service, which falls under the Department of the Interior, the Interior Appropriations bill was critical to the health of the ESA. However, this bill with all its riders was defeated again and again in the first session of the 104th. The "easy wins" were over for the freshmen.

In October, Speaker Newt Gingrich established a new GOP Environmental Task Force to work out differences among Republicans on ESA legislation before a floor vote (*ESA Today 1995a*). Many believed that Gingrich was the kingpin for the ESA in the House. He was known to love animals, had co-sponsored a pro-ESA bill prior to assuming the leadership, and had testified in favor of the ESA at one of Representative Pombo's ESA Task Force hearings. The establishment of the new Environmental Task Force was as much an acknowledgment that public opinion was going against the Congress on environmental issues as that the ESA needed help. A November 1995 article in *Time* magazine suggested that moderate Republicans feared losing the pro-green suburban voters and began to voice their frustration with the rush to weaken environmental regulations.

November 1995 was a watershed month for the environment. Both Speaker Gingrich and Senator Gorton admitted that no ESA vote was likely in 1995. *ESA Today* (1995b) reported that environmental activists had delivered to Gingrich on November 1 bags of petitions labeled the "Environmental Bill of Rights" and bearing the signatures of approximately 1.2 million American citizens. The petition declared opposition to all Republican proposals that would weaken laws protecting the environment. "These are the most signatures gathered on environmental issues in the history of the environmental movement," said Gene Karpinski, head of the U.S. Public Interest Research Group (USPIRG), a nonprofit consumer and environmental advocacy group.

Another major environmental victory occurred in the House that month when the moderate Republicans coalesced for the first time to defeat a series of riders damaging to the Environmental Protection Agency in the VA-HUD-EPA appropriations bill. This action gave heart to the Enviros and sent another message to the White House to stand firm on environmental issues. In addition, the moderates signed a letter to the House Budget Committee requesting the removal of revenues from oil drilling in the Arctic National

Wildlife Refuge from the Budget Reconciliation Bill. The Interior Appropriations bill failed a second time in the House, and finally, two new environmentally friendly members were added to the House Natural Resources Committee. In retrospect it is clear that the speaker was working behind the scenes to protect the ESA.

The Senate postponed markup on Bob Dole's S. 605 takings bill. Senate Democratic leaders held a press conference at the end of November with Senators Bill Bradley (N.J.), Frank Lautenberg (N.J.), Joe Lieberman (Conn.), Dale Bumpers (Ark.), Barbara Boxer (Calif.), and Paul Wellstone (Minn.). The same day *Greenlines* reported that before the conference Bradley had said the senators would "discuss how, under the guise of balancing the budget and so called 'reform,' the Republican majority in Congress has launched a concerted and sustained attack on environmental laws and the ability of the federal government to protect the environment for future generations." By Thanksgiving, Clinton had publicly promised to veto any budget bill with environmentally damaging riders, such as permitting oil drilling in the Arctic National Wildlife Refuge.

The battle continued. Representative John Doolittle (R-Calif.) proposed H.R. 2542 to "change the focus of species conservation efforts from prevention and recovery to crisis intervention." Senator Pete Domenici (R-N.M.) introduced his Public Rangelands Management Act, S. 852, which treated public rangelands like a private commodity for the livestock industry and waived NEPA. This bill was later replaced by "son of S. 852," S. 1459. Representative Don Young introduced H.R. 1675, which altered the national wildlife refuge system act in a damaging way. The national wildlife refuge system is the network of federal lands established to conserve fish and wildlife and covering more than 91 million acres in all fifty states.

On December 6, President Clinton formally vetoed the Budget Reconciliation bill. Congress, however, kept the anti-environment, anti-ESA measures coming. The next day the Senate passed an appropriations bill for the National Oceanic Atmospheric Administration (NOAA), the home of the National Marine Fisheries Service (NMFS), by a narrow vote of 50–48. This bill included a moratorium on listing species and designating critical habitat by NMFS. About a week later, the Senate passed the Interior Appropriations bill with its anti-environment riders by a vote of 58–40. Then the Senate Judiciary Committee passed out S. 605, Dole's takings bill.

The House Farm Bill, H.R. 1542, passed with a provision that would have crippled wildlife viability requirements in the national forest system. The provision would have permitted a mining or logging project to continue even when it started clogging streams with silt. Another provision prohibited the Forest Service from enforcing laws that require minimum stream flows for fish.

Clinton continued to exercise his veto on bills that rolled back environmental regulations. On December 18, he vetoed the Department of Interior Appropriations bill with riders that increased logging in Alaska's Tongass National Forest, eliminated the National Biological Service, and put moratoriums on listing endangered species, on grazing regulations, and on energy efficiency standards. At the same time he vetoed the appropriations bill for the VA-HUD-EPA, which contained riders that crippled EPA pollution control. The next day, he vetoed the appropriations bill for the Commerce, Justice, and State departments because of another ESA moratorium stopping listings and critical habitat designation.

Also in December, Representative Elizabeth Furse (D-Ore.) introduced a bill to repeal the timber salvage rider enacted in July. At introduction, the bill had thirty-one cosponsors. Many more signed on in subsequent days. Representative Jim Saxton (R-N.J.), with twenty cosponsors, filed a bill to create a National Institute for the Environment. GOP Whip Tom DeLay admitted to the *Wall Street Journal*, "I'll be straight with you, we have lost the debate on the environment. . . . There has not really been a leadership environmental strategy. There was a regulatory reform strategy that deteriorated into an environmental issue, and that cost us" (quoted in *Greenlines* 1995).

During December the federal government went out on its second furlough of 1995. This furlough was the longest one in history and was directly attributable to the inability of the Congress and the president to reach agreement on a budget package and congressional refusal to pass a Continuing Resolution to maintain funding at the previous year's levels. Attempts at talks between congressional Republican leaders and the White House repeatedly failed. The freshmen Republicans were unwilling to compromise on their seven-year balanced budget plan, and Clinton was unwilling to be "blackmailed" by federal furloughs. The two federal agencies with primary responsibility for implementing the ESA were furloughed for over four weeks in the fall and winter of 1995, and no environmental programs administered by the Fish and Wildlife Service, other Interior agencies, or National Marine Fisheries Service were executed.

Throughout most of the budget battle of 1995 and early 1996, the public supported Clinton. In January 1996, the House tried and failed to override the presidential vetoes on the appropriations bills for the Commerce, Justice, State, and Interior departments. The bluff and bluster continued throughout the second session of the 104th Congress in 1996. Several more attempts failed to repeal the moratorium on species listings until Clinton finally revoked it midyear. More riders were attached to more unrelated bills to curtail ESA implementation, but they too were defeated.

One, however, did pass: in October 1996, the Immigration Reform Bill was reported out of the conference committee with waivers of the ESA and NEPA for Immigration and Naturalization Service activities along U.S. borders. Clinton signed that bill.

The 105th Congress (1997–1998)

On January 13, 1997, Jessica Matthews wrote in her *Washington Post* column that "the excess of the 103rd and 104th Congresses produced a startling public backlash," and the environment "for the first time . . . influenced — and sometimes determined — how people voted" in November 1996. "Eighty-five percent of defeated Republican incumbents had been on an environmental hit list (overall, just 6 percent of these incumbents lost)." The 105th Congress, sworn in during January 1997, also had a Republican majority but with less of a margin than the 104th. As Matthews pointed out, not all the freshmen made it back and some long-term members lost. From the lack of activity on environmental legislation in the first session of the 105th, it is clear that this Congress intended to be cautious.

In mid-1996, the Enviros had drafted and sent a bill entitled the Endangered Natural Heritage Act (ENHA) to the Senate Environment and Public Works Committee and to sympathizers George Miller (D-Calif.) and Bruce Vento (D-Minn.) in the House. For the balance of the year and well into 1997, the Enviros kept the pressure on to get their bill endorsed and into committee.

On January 29, 1997, Senators Dirk Kempthorne (R-Idaho) and John Chafee (R-R.I.) floated a draft reauthorization bill for comment. As was reported in *Environment and Energy Weekly*, the immediate reaction of the Democrats, the Clinton Administration, and the Enviros was negative (*E&E*

Weekly 1997a). Nevertheless, this bill was remarkable in being the first since the Republican takeover that was widely circulated to stakeholders for comment and modified based on those comments. It evolved into a bipartisan bill and there followed nine months of collaboration and negotiation to hammer out details acceptable to most parties. For this reason alone Kempthorne and Chafee deserve great credit.

In April and May, there was a flurry of activity spurred by H.R. 478, the Flood Prevention and Family Protection Act of 1997, introduced by Representatives Richard Pombo (R-Calif.) and Wally Herger (R-Calif.). This bill waived ESA requirements during flood disasters. By May, Representative Sherwood Boehlert (R-N.Y.) introduced an amendment that caused Pombo and Herger to withdraw the offensive ESA waivers. In doing so, however, Boehlert earned the wrath of the conservative wing (*Daily War on the Environment* 1997a).

Two other issues engendered heated debate and took some time to resolve. In June, H.R. 1420, the National Wildlife Refuge Improvement Act, passed the House after a year of wrangling. It was the result of a compromise between a bill introduced by Representative Don Young in 1996 and one introduced by Representative George Miller in 1997 (*Daily War on the Environment* 1997b). The bill enacted will be beneficial to the refuge system, which is an important contributor to species conservation.

In July after months of argument, S. 39, the International Dolphin Conservation Program Act, passed. With a compromise suggestion from Senator John Kerry (D-Mass.), the Congress resolved the question of when the "dolphin-safe" label could be used on tuna cans. To improve trade with Mexico and other Pan-American countries, the administration wanted to lift the embargo on tuna caught by the encirclement method, which is believed to entrap and drown dolphins. The compromise included funding for a three-year study of the method's actual impact on dolphins and a mechanism for removing the label should the study confirm that dolphins are negatively impacted (*E&E Weekly* 1997b). It permits use of the label only when fishermen ensure that any dolphins caught are released safely.

Representative George Miller introduced H.R. 2352 in July. This first ESA reauthorization bill of the 105th Congress differed greatly from the Endangered Natural Heritage Act proposed by the Enviros. It addressed the issues of the private property rights movement by providing landowners incentives to cooperate and participate in conserving species. Called the Endangered

Species Recovery Act of 1997, it emphasized improved recovery planning. According to E&E's August report, Miller's bill "puts teeth into the ESA statute by injecting better long-term habitat planning and forcing more expeditious recovery plans." Miller's bill codifies the controversial No Surprises regulation (private landowner protection from the need to update HCPs continually) but allows the federal government to pay landowners if events occur outside the landowner's control that require modifying the plans (*E&E Weekly* 1997c).

After the summer recess, Kempthorne and Chafee introduced their bipartisan compromise bill, joined by their fellow minority committee members Max Baucus (D-Mont.) and Harry Reid (D-Nev.). S. 1180 was also called the Endangered Species Recovery Act of 1997. Secretary of the Interior Babbitt joined them for the introduction. Believing that most of the hard work had been accomplished, the committee scheduled only one hearing, on September 23, and a markup for September 30. In spite of their input into it, Enviros did not support this bill and their grassroots networks were humming in an effort to stop it.

Both the House and Senate bills were vast improvements over anything offered in the 104th Congress. Both focused primarily on improving the recovery planning process. Both provided some incentives for private property owner cooperation, although the incentives were much greater in the House bill. Miller's bill emphasized ecosystem management for species conservation, while the Senate bill did not mention this. The Clinton Administration supported the Senate bill despite concern over whether it could meet the requirements if annual appropriations did not match those proposed in the bill. Unfortunately, little attention was given to the Miller bill because of a general belief that it would not get passed in committee.

The ideal legislation for species would include elements of both of the 1997 bills. For example, the House bill's tax incentives are persuasive, as is the disincentive of the damage liability. However, the Senate bill's public outreach training and acknowledgment of outstanding contributions is a superior public outreach approach. The Senate's inventory of species is also an excellent step toward supporting a national biodiversity policy.

While the Enviros decry the Senate's modifications to the consultation process, the specific requirements reduce the redundancy of efforts between agencies, and that is a positive step. The compromise that allows the FWS to object to any decisions within a stipulated time frame is very reasonable.

Furthermore, implementation agreements between the FWS and other land management agencies are an excellent tool, if kept brief, and would preclude the need for many consultations while still protecting species.

The ecosystem management and planning language of the House bill would vastly improve the Senate bill without making a substantial difference to its context. The House bill is stronger on Habitat Conservation Plans while the Senate bill is stronger on recovery plans. Both strengths belong in the final statute. Neither bill mandates devolving responsibility to the states, a popular approach in the Congresses of the 1990s, but the Senate bill does open the door to greater state responsibility with the possibility of delegating the recovery plan to the states involved. In spite of these improvements, legislators were still not ready to pass an ESA reauthorization and the 105th Congress did not do so.

The 106th Congress (1999–2000)

Miller reintroduced his Endangered Species Recovery Act as H.R. 960 in March 1999. The House Resources Committee (renamed from Natural Resources Committee) did not take it up. In the Senate, a number of bills were introduced to amend the Endangered Species Act of 1973, three of them by the late senator from Rhode Island, John Chafee. In May 1999, Chafee introduced a bill to allow writing recovery plans for non-indigenous species. In June, he introduced a bill to fund conservation of foreign species in foreign countries. In October he floated a bill to require annual reporting to Congress on the state of species conservation. The only threat to the strength of the ESA came from Senator Craig Thomas (R-Wyo.) when he introduced a bill to reform the endangered species listing and delisting process. Max Baucus of Idaho introduced a related bill, which amended the Internal Revenue code to provide tax incentives for voluntary species conservation.

In October 1999, Don Young introduced H.R. 3160, Common Sense Protections for Endangered Species Act. He indicated his determination to get this bill and a related property rights bill marked up for floor presentation by the end of March 2000. The property rights bill did pass the House. By September, H.R. 3160 still had only thirty-one cosponsors, not an auspicious start. This bill was subtler but no less anti-ESA than the Young-Pombo bill of the 104th Congress.

H.R. 3160 provided parity for economic development goals and species protection. Though it added several new layers of reviews—for listings, for recovery plans, for consultation decisions—it did not supply additional funding to accomplish the additional reviews. Those mandated included peer reviews (by a panel of nongovernment experts) for listings and recovery plans and five-year FWS reviews of listings and plans. The bill mandated more intense state participation in species protection but often in ways that made little scientific sense. For example, FWS could delegate species recovery planning to states, but the conditions or circumstances under which this could occur were not clear. Species, especially animals, seldom range within state boundaries. Therefore, single-state authority would not protect the species. In several ESA implementation processes key to the protection of species, economic and social requirements were emphasized over species protection. This bill suggested no new understanding of the value of species diversity to the welfare of human beings.

Despite the significant problems with this bill, there were several recovery components in it that deserved to be incorporated into the next reauthorization. First, it gave species recovery its own section in the statute, Section 5. This would highlight its importance much more clearly than did the 1973 statute, which buried recovery planning in Section 4. Young's bill also created an Office of Species Recovery in the Fish and Wildlife Service. This action would likewise highlight the importance of this function and might assure more regular appropriations for species recovery. Last, the bill required that recovery plans include benchmarks to measure recovery progress. These too are needed.

The components of the bill that would jeopardize species protection were far more numerous. The bill added economic considerations to the determination of whether to list a species and emphasized the importance of using peer-reviewed, published, empirical, and field-tested scientific data for determining whether to list species. Since there are seldom enough field-tested and documented data available on the species concerned, limiting listing and recovery decisions to those supported by such data would exclude a large number of species in jeopardy. There is more guesswork than is desirable with biological assessments on species, but that does not change the reality. We must use limited data and make judgments from modeled and estimated data because of the lack of available empirical data. Otherwise, we write the species off.

The bill required the FWS to seek and include commercial and avocational expertise as well as that of educated and trained professionals. Often dedicated volunteers such as bird-watchers and amateur beetle collectors have an important store of information. Commercial scientists and practitioners similarly have a store of useful knowledge, though it tends to come with a bias. The bill seemed to demand using all resources without adequately testing the validity of each. Also required was advice from governors of the states affected by the species listing. Certainly, there is a bias perspective there.

The bill required peer review panels to include economic and takings experts in addition to scientists and state representatives. The mix of interests represented would likely create conflict and therefore lengthen the process. Yet the bill also included deadlines for species listing that were barely achievable even without a conflict-ridden peer review.

While more public information was required by this bill, with up to five public hearings possible in the states affected, and it would disseminate information more widely, the time needed to make the listing recommendation would need to be extended for that benefit. In addition, the bill required a cost-benefit analysis be done for each listing. Interestingly, while it required more public input in affected states, it permitted the FWS to withhold from the public any information of a "proprietary" nature or about species occurrence on private property if the landowner wanted this kept private. More time would elapse between petitions and listing because this new bill made all listings decisions subject to judicial review and provided any person affected economically with standing to challenge an FWS decision in the courts.

The bill created new loopholes in the federal consultation process. First, Interior was required to conduct all biological assessments. The current law requires the agency *responsible for* the action that might place a species in jeopardy to conduct and pay for the biological assessment. (Again the appropriations in the bill were insufficient to pay for that additional cost.) FWS was prohibited from issuing a jeopardy decision when there was insufficient scientific information available, which would be the case most of the time. Also, the ESA could not supersede the organic authorities under which other agencies operated. This would leave the door open for other agencies to ignore the ESA mandates.

H.R. 3160 limited recovery plans to indigenous species but did not specify the appropriate biological and ecological data required in a recovery plan. Finally, the annual appropriations in the bill represented expenditure increases that fell far short of the expense associated with the new requirements.

There was strong opposition to the bill among Democrats and in the environmental and conservation communities. In her testimony before the House Resources Committee in March 2000, Jaime Clark, director of FWS, said: "H.R. 3160 reverses the essential conservation thrust of the Endangered Species Act and tips the balance from one that errs on the side of protecting the species to one that places economic considerations and development needs first. . . . We believe H.R. 3160 would reverse the progress we've made in species conservation and could lead to the extinction of many species" (E&E Daily 2000b). The Senate did not introduce a companion bill to Young's. However, in October 2000, Sen. Frank Lautenberg (D-N.J.) introduced S. 3156, companion legislation to George Miller's 1999 Endangered Species Recovery Act (H.R. 960). Lautenberg had nine cosponsors upon introduction of his Endangered Species Recovery Act. The bill closed the 106th Congress on a positive note for ESA reauthorization.

One of the biggest problems for the Endangered Species Act is and has been funding. Among the most important improvements that could be made to the ESA is a self-funding mechanism. In the 105th Congress, a proposal called Teaming with Wildlife introduced the concept of funding wildlife conservation with a tax on consumer goods associated with wildlife appreciation products such as birdseed, wildlife guides, and binoculars. While wildlife supporters strongly favored this approach, congressional Republicans refused to consider further taxes of any sort.

Don Young introduced a new funding option in February 1999 in H.R. 701. Called the Conservation and Reinvestment Act (CARA) of 1999, this bill assigned revenues from the oil and natural gas leases on the outer continental shelf to be used to pay for some species recovery efforts as well as many other non-ESA conservation programs. H.R. 701 was passed out of committee by a vote of 37–12 in November 1999. With 315 cosponsors signed on, the bill was assured passage in the House. H.R. 701 passed the House in May and was marked up by the Senate Energy and Natural Resources Committee in July.

Passage in the Senate in the 106th Congress is doubtful. Senator Mary Landrieu (D-La.) introduced S. 25 in January 1999. In March 2000 she introduced a bill identical to H.R. 701, S. 2123. Later in March, Senator Jeff Bingaman (D-N.M.) introduced a third bill, S. 2181, called the Conservation and Stewardship Act. The latter gained the support of Senators Lieberman and Boxer, who had each introduced earlier bills directing OCS revenue expenditures. Opinions in the Senate were clearly divided.

Both H.R. 701 and S. 2123 estimated $2.825 billion in revenue from OCS oil and natural gas leases. These two bills assigned $100 million annually to the secretary of interior (FWS) to support a new conservation easement program that would provide matching grants to entities purchasing easements for conservation. They also assigned $50 million annually to support species recovery plans submitted by nonfederal entities (E&E Daily, 2000a). This funding increased the amount available to FWS for species protection, but it did not increase ESA funding. With the Conservation and Reinvestment Act (CARA) bogged down on the Senate side, and the desire to address President Clinton's request for large amounts to fund his proposed Lands Legacy program, Rep. Norman Dicks (D-Wash.) offered a compromise approach that was passed in the 2001 Department of Interior appropriations bill. A dedicated fund for multiple conservation programs, including the Land and Water Conservation Fund, was established with 12 billion new dollars covering six years.

The gridlock remained unbroken through the 106th Congress, though some signs of a break began to appear.

Chapter Seven

Presidential Power

The Endangered Species Act has been underapplied,
underfunded, undermined and under-enforced.
—Defenders of Wildlife Report, 1993

P RESIDENTIAL POLITICS HAVE significantly influenced the implementation of the Endangered Species Act. Presidential attitudes toward the
ESA have varied from one administration to the next and have often
confounded the bureaucracy's efforts to implement the act effectively. For most
of its years in force, the ESA has been either in disfavor with or ignored by
the president. Except for Richard M. Nixon, the anti-ESA presidents were
Republican. However, the Democrats who have occupied the office since
1973 cannot be deemed actively pro-ESA.

Nixon urged Congress to pass the ESA and he signed it into law. The law
drew little political attention and therefore little presidential attention until
the first controversies arose over the construction of the Tellico and Grayrocks
dams in the late 1970s. Prior to the Tellico crisis, there was no presidential
influence on the ESA's application because there was no political need for
this. It was in the twelve years of Republican administrations from 1980 to 1992
that the ESA suffered the most. Presidential actions, or inaction, in the early
years of the ESA set the stage for today's dilemma. The story of presidential
influence proceeds chronologically.

The ESA's First Presidents: 1973–1993

The president with the most positive impact on U.S. environmental policy
was Nixon. He signed the majority of the major environmental statutes into
law, including the Endangered Species Act of 1973. In the 1970s, however, it
was politically popular to support environmental protection. Environmental

regulation was still too new to have a major impact on growth and development planning; and air, water, and toxic waste pollution problems were too visible to be ignored. Although the TVA–Tellico Dam controversy raged during Jimmy Carter's administration, the setting for the battle was the courts, not the White House. Carter's primary contribution to endangered species was signing the first reauthorization of the act in 1978.

Ronald Reagan entered the White House in 1981 with the belief that environmental regulation impeded economic development. He appointed conservatives with industry backgrounds to the two key environmental positions: James G. Watt as secretary of the interior and Anne Burford as Environmental Protection Agency (EPA) administrator. Reagan viewed the Endangered Species Act as a barrier to progress and undermined it with the budget process. In five years under Reagan, for example, no funds were requested for cooperative agreements with the states (Ernst 1991). Moreover, neither the Fish and Wildlife Service nor the National Marine Fisheries Service received adequate funding even though Congress usually provided more funds than Reagan requested (DOW 1993).

Reagan also imposed Executive Order 12630. This directive required all federal agencies to consider the potential impact of any action, environmental or otherwise, on property takings. Therefore, it raised private property impact to a level almost equal to that of species jeopardy. Under James Watt, Interior emphasized species recovery not "adding to the problem" by listing new species (Fay and Kramer 1995). Watt's overt anti-environmental attitude was one of the primary forces that encouraged the expansion of the environmental movement in the 1980s. After Watt's resignation in 1983, Secretaries William P. Clark and Donald P. Hodel (1985–89) completed Reagan's tenure with less flamboyance, but with no more enthusiasm for conserving species.

Because of the substantial public backlash over Watt's outspoken enmity to "environmental radicalism," both Clark and Hodel took more moderate public positions on environmental issues. In 1986, Secretary Hodel reversed Department of Interior policy and restricted the ESA's Section 7 consultation requirement to domestic activities only. International activities were freed of ESA scrutiny. The Defenders of Wildlife filed suit against DOI to force international activities to be included, but the issue was not taken up by the courts until 1990 (DOW 1993). In 1990, the Eighth Circuit Court of Appeals upheld a lower court ruling that the ESA must be applied to international activies. The Bush Administration appealed to the Supreme Court in December 1991 in *Lujan v. Defenders of Wildlife* (504 U.S. 555 [1992]). In June 1992 the Supreme Court remanded the case back to the district court on the grounds that the DOW did not have standing to bring the suit. Hence the issue remained unresolved.

George Bush exerted environmental leadership by fostering and propelling the 1990 amendments to the Clean Air Act through passage. However, his environmental leadership stopped there. *National Wildlife*'s 1991 annual environmental review charged the Bush Administration with paying stewardship of the environment lip service while undercutting it ("Year of Unfortunate" 1992). Defenders of Wildlife gave Bush a D grade for "proposing and implementing policies which undercut conservation laws . . . and for continuing a double standard of disregard for listed species overseas facing destruction at the hands of the U.S." (DOW 1993:4–5). Bush's opposition to any action to reauthorize the Endangered Species Act effectively stopped its consideration in the 102nd Congress. Under Bush's interior secretary, Manuel Lujan, the Fish and Wildlife Service continued to defer designation of critical habitats. Bush ordered that economics as well as biology be used to guide development of recovery plans ("Year of Unfortunate" 1992).

The case of the Louisiana black bear was typical of the attitude toward the ESA in the Bush Administration. The Fish and Wildlife Service was petitioned to list the animal in 1987. It took until June 1990 for the FWS to propose listing the bear as threatened, not endangered. Deadlines on the bear's case came and went. In late 1991, Lujan finally acted when the Defenders of Wildlife and the Sierra Club Legal Defense Fund (now the Earthjustice Legal Defense Fund) filed suit (DOW 1993).

Public controversy over job losses blamed on the northern spotted owl listing in the Pacific Northwest forests in 1990 slowed the Fish and Wildlife Service development of the owl's recovery plan (see chapter 9). The Bush Administration was not interested in listing or recovering the owl, and foot-dragging was the tacit mandate. Spurred by environmental organizations, the courts stepped in. U.S. District Court Judge William L. Dwyer (Seattle) suspended all timber sales in spotted owl habitat in thirteen U.S. forests until federal obligations to the bird were met. In his decision, Dwyer chastised higher administration authorities for their slowness.

The Endangered Species Committee, the "God Squad," met for the third time in fourteen years in 1993 on the northern spotted owl. The committee denied requests to open up thirty-one parcels of old growth forest in Oregon to logging. However, it overruled the ESA on thirteen tracts of land in the same area that were managed by the Bureau of Land Management. The northern spotted owl became a symbol of the national economy's ill health; environmental regulations and the ESA took the blame for contributing to U.S. economic woes.

Environmental issues were aired during the 1992 elections. George Bush maintained that the country must choose between economics and ecology; he announced that he would make massive changes in the ESA to save jobs and would lift restrictions in the Clean Water Act to help industry. Bill Clinton, by contrast, declared for the environment and chose publicly recognized environmentalist Al Gore as his running mate. The public chose the Clinton/ Gore ticket.

The Clinton Administration, 1993–2001

Within thirty days of assuming office in January 1993, Clinton replaced the badly neglected Council on Environmental Quality (CEQ) with the White House Office on Environmental Policy. The CEQ is mandated by the National Environmental Policy Act (NEPA) for the purpose of advising the president on environmental issues and acting as an oversight office for all federal agencies. During the Reagan-Bush years, funding for this office was continually cut and staffing was reduced to barely functional levels. Clinton's new office was "designed to strengthen the hand of Vice President Al Gore in shaping environmental policy, thus signaling the Clinton administration's intentions to give environmental issues priority in the executive branch" (Smith 1995:50). Between this action and the budget battle that began in November 1995, however, Clinton did little to support the environment.

On the international level, Clinton did take a positive stance on population growth by ordering the resumption of aid to the United Nations for population programs. Within his first months in office, he also signed the Convention on Biological Diversity, which at the end of the 106th Congress remains unratified. At the time he signed the CBD he announced the formation of the National Biological Survey, known today as the BRD. In Washington, he promoted environmental conservation policies within the administration, such as recycling and using recycled paper. But on the national level, Clinton made no major speeches on environmental or conservation issues.

On the whole, the early Clinton Administration disappointed environmental advocates. Initial administration budget proposals included Interior Secretary Bruce Babbitt's suggestions for mining reforms, increased grazing fees, and an energy tax. Enviros had long sought all these reforms. Within two months, however, Clinton surrendered to pressure from western legislators to remove the mining and grazing reforms (Wicker 1994). With that rug pulled out from under him, Babbitt turned his attention elsewhere. He helped conclude the ongoing conflict in southern California between developers and conservationists over the coastal California gnatcatcher's habitat, California's regional habitat conservation plan called the Natural Communities Conservation Plan (NCCP). Babbitt was pleased with the final plan, but both conservationists and developers got less than they wanted.

Clinton's Pacific Northwest Forest Plan also disappointed the Enviros, although it included worker retraining and community investment to create jobs. On another front, many environmental leaders believed that an administration deal with sugar growers in the Florida Everglades allowed growers to elude their fair share of the costs for repairing damage to the ecosystem (Wicker 1994). Clinton established an early image of weakness in environmental matters and continued to reinforce it. Vice President Gore also made no visible early environmental contributions in spite of the new Office on Environmental Policy. He was busy with international affairs and other assignments.

Nor did Bruce Babbitt make the early changes that environmentalists expected from him. He was an environmentally progressive governor of Arizona, where he had directed the development of the nation's most progressive groundwater protection law and had doubled the size of Arizona's state park system (Hamilton 1994). Babbitt entered the Department of the Interior with aggressive plans to change western attitudes and practices, especially about stock grazing and mining, but he lost momentum when Clinton backed down from recommended changes. Babbitt's approach was to negotiate and to encourage cooperation between government branches and interest groups. Republicans and conservative Democrats tried to thwart him at every turn. Probably because of the anti-environment fervor on Capitol Hill, the administration never offered a proposal to reauthorize the ESA, although it did announce support for Senator Kempthorne's reauthorization bill in 1994.

In time, Babbitt began to work actively on improving the administrative policy on the law's implementation. After a tour of the country to discuss environmental and ESA issues with the public, he announced a memorandum of understanding (MOU) in September 1994 among fourteen federal agencies to improve implementation of the ESA. The agencies agreed to coordinate planning efforts for protecting species and for conservation and recovery planning. The fourteen signers were the U.S. Forest Service (Department of Agriculture); the Bureau of Land Management, Bureau of Mines, Bureau of Reclamation, U.S. Fish and Wildlife Service, National Park Service, and Minerals Management Service (Department of Interior); the Army Corps of Engineers (Department of Defense); the National Marine Fisheries Service (Department of Commerce); U.S. Coast Guard, Federal Highway Administration, and Federal Aviation Administration (Department of Transportation); and the Environmental Protection Agency.

On March 6, 1995, the Departments of the Interior and Commerce jointly released "Guideposts for Reform." These ten points of policy addressed the major objections to the ESA. Babbitt proposed procedural changes as well as statutory changes. The press release states: "The list of principles reflects the Administration's commitment to minimize impacts on landowners, grant greater authority to states and local governments, make implementation of the law simpler and more efficient, and improve the recovery rate of species." Undersecretary of Commerce for Oceans and Atmosphere D. James Baker said in the release: "Science would be assured a stronger place in decision-making. Small landowners would encounter more flexibility and less regulation. And all landowners would be encouraged to provide good habitat for listed species and not be penalized for doing so." The list of principles made it policy to apply responsiveness and consideration for the people affected. It affirmed that social and economic impacts would be weighed where mandated and where doing so made sense. It reactivated state, local, and federal government interaction on endangered species issues, a statutory dictate that had fallen into disuse from lack of funding. While the ten guideposts were restatements of elements already required by law, the fourteen-agency MOU reaffirmed the bureaucracy's commitment to uphold the law in a more reasoned, conscientious manner.

One of the guideposts is known as the No Surprises policy. First proposed by FWS and NMFS in August 1994, the policy assured landowners who obtained approval on their Habitat Conservation Plans that there would be no surprise requirements imposed later. In October 1996, the Spirit of the Sage Council, Biodiversity Legal Foundation, and other environmental and activist organizations filed a lawsuit against the two services for violating the ESA. The settlement required the services to issue the policy as a proposed rule for public comment (60 Fed. Reg. 29091).

Clinton's waffling on environmental issues sent the message to Congress that the administration would not work with it to resolve the issues. While Babbitt's ten points directly addressed ESA issues, what resulted from the ten guideposts was that the federal government usurped some local and community decisions. Two months after the publication of the ten points, Tom Pyle of Representative Richard Pombo's staff reflected the feelings of the House Natural Resources Committee when he said: "The best approach is to level the playing field. Give the landowner the same size 'stick' [property takings] as Fish and Wildlife has with species takings. Then negotiations can proceed on a fair footing. Because the law serves as a public benefit, costs should not be born by individual landowners" (Pyle 1995).

In early August, Clinton issued an executive order challenging the congressional curbs on Environmental Protection Agency regulations. At a public meeting in Baltimore on August 8, President Clinton, Vice President Al Gore, and EPA Administrator Carol Browner denounced congressional "bowing to the interests of business lobbyists by writing 18 provisions into an EPA appropriations bill that would undermine the government's ability to control pollution" (McAllister 1995).

For the first time, the president threatened to veto anti-environmental legislation. When Clinton signed the Defense Supplemental Spending Bill in April with the ESA listing moratorium and the Rescissions Bill in July with the Timber Salvage Rider, Enviros lost faith in him. His actions also indicated to Congress that Clinton would approve environmental curbs if they were buried in spending legislation.

By the end of October 1995, however, after a federal court ruling that old growth timber sales in Oregon and Washington must be permitted under the timber salvage provision, Clinton responded to the political pressure and promised to pursue a legislative remedy to the Timber Salvage Rider. He then claimed the salvage-logging rider was intended to facilitate only those sales that did not violate the administration's environmental standards. This signaled that Clinton might begin to honor his election promises on the environment.

Two environmental coalitions worked especially hard to assure that any legislation that rolled back environmental progress stopped at the White House. They were the Alaska Coalition, working to save the Arctic National Wildlife Refuge from oil drilling, and the Endangered Species Coalition, working to assure an ESA reauthorization that retained the intent and muscle of the original act. The grassroots activist networks of these two coalitions were extensive and worked vigorously in the Congress and the White House to stop environmentally damaging legislation. Activists kept the phones ringing at the

White House and in congressional offices. Members of Congress received thousands of empty medicine bottles to drive home the importance of the Endangered Species Act in preserving species that are a source of life-saving pharmaceuticals. Activists wrote letters to the editors of papers all across the country decrying the damage being done to the environment and to endangered species. Others met with newspaper boards to influence editorials that would be read by the Congress and the White House; these efforts resulted in numerous editorials decrying congressional actions attempting to destroy the ESA and the Arctic National Wildlife Refuge.

Environmental coalitions maintained a strong lobby with the White House, and their congressional lobby team began to have renewed impact on the Hill. The White House began to respond to the public pressure, as did moderate Republicans at the Capitol. In a Saturday nationwide radio address in October 1995, Clinton spoke of the importance of protecting our environment and pristine wilderness areas crucial to biological diversity and to Native American cultures. Some wilderness areas include sacred Native American grounds; others support a life stage of wildlife that is essential to the livelihood of tribal groups. For example, the caribou herds that use the Arctic National Wildlife Refuge for calving grounds are pivotal to the culture of the Guichin, a native group in Alaska.

There were many environmentally damaging riders on the 1995 Budget Reconciliation Bill, the legislation that set forth the specifics for the 1995 budget and required balancing the national budget within seven years. There were more damaging riders on the federal department appropriations bills. In October, Clinton informed Congress that he would veto any bill that carried environmentally damaging riders, including the budget bill. When no agreement was reached on the budget, the government was furloughed in November. A continuing resolution brought this furlough to an end. But in December 1995, Clinton made good on his promise to veto any environmentally damaging legislation. He vetoed the Budget Reconciliation Bill and the Interior, VA-HUD-EPA, and Commerce-Justice-State appropriations bills because they contained such riders. The week before Christmas in 1995, many federal agencies were shut down again, this time for three full weeks.

In January 1996, a *Washington Post* editorial conveyed the ambiguity environmentalists felt toward Clinton: "It isn't clear what will happen next. . . . The question now is, how hard will [Clinton] bargain on these issues, and what will he sign? Mr. Clinton has lately become a 'greener' president because he has found the issue works for him in the polls, but the green is still a pretty pale shade" (*Greenlines* 1996a).

The budget battle ended with the exclusion of most of the environmentally damaging riders. Clinton also exercised his new line-item veto to veto several anti-environment riders that did get through. His record was imperfect, but by mid-1996, Clinton was clearly fighting the anti-environmental efforts of the Congress. Though members continued to attach riders that were damaging to the environment throughout the 104th, 105th, and 106th Congresses, few such bills made it to the president's desk after this time.

By his second term, President Clinton found his environmental niche in protecting federal lands. He invoked the Antiquities Act of 1906 several times to protect public lands. In spite of opposition, he declared the Grand Staircase Escalante National Monument, located in Utah, in September 1996. In 1998, Clinton asked Secretary Babbitt to draw up a list of unusual and fragile areas in the United States. He declared three new national monuments (two in Arizona and one in California) and extended the area of a fourth one in California in January 2000. In 1999 he proposed to Congress his Lands Legacy initiative and asked for $1 billion to expand federal protection of critical lands in America, including wild areas, estuarine and coastal areas, several national parks, farmlands, and urban green spaces. While Congress did not grant the full amount requested, the Lands Legacy program is now funded and under way. Thus Clinton has contributed to the protection of biodiversity, indirectly. He also did not interfere with Secretary Babbitt's initiatives to improve species protection.

Historically, the best way to break gridlock has been through united presidential and congressional leadership. In the early 1970s, Nixon asked Congress for strong environmental laws, and several pro-environment leaders in Congress followed through. In 1990, after almost a decade of gridlock over the reauthorization of the Clean Air Act, President Bush exerted leadership and convinced the public of the need to pass a strong reauthorization of the act. However, the Clinton Administration's strategy in the face of bipartisan gridlock differed. It could be called "Let's just do it and deal with political consequences later." For that is the approach Secretary Babbitt took to resolve some of the ESA problems in the face of congressional inability to act to reauthorize the law and minimal direction from the White House. It is also the tactic Clinton used when he declared national monument status for several sensitive wild areas.

Chapter Eight

The Bureaucratic Contribution

The administrator of the act is always conscious of the possibility
of powerful forces effecting a change in the act that may have
shattering future consequences. One is always aware of the need
to strike a balance, to proceed with caution, to accommodate
today in order to prevail tomorrow. — Lynn Greenwalt, 1991

T HE FIRST Fish and Wildlife Service director to have Endangered
Species Act enforcement responsibilities was Lynn Greenwalt. He
summarized the challenge he and his successors have faced: balancing the statute's power to disrupt human plans in order to save species with
the omnipresent fear that its power might speed its revocation. This is one of
the bureaucratic difficulties with the ESA.

The federal bureaucracy has contributed at least four components to the
ESA dilemma. First, implementation standards have varied from one administration to the next. In practice, implementation has been sporadic and un-
reliable. Second, from the outset the bureaucracy separated responsibility
for terrestrial species and marine species: the Department of the Interior's Fish
and Wildlife Service handles terrestrial species, including birds and freshwater species, and the Department of Commerce's National Marine Fisheries
Service (NMFS) handles marine species, including marine mammals. Both
bureaus took on endangered species authority with inadequate organizational
structures for the task of protecting species, inappropriate existing procedures,
and insufficient congressional funding. Add to these difficulties the inherent
deficiency of scientific knowledge about species' requirements, and the task
was a huge challenge.

Third, there have been instances of regulatory mishandling of cases that
have been magnified by interest groups and the media to make the ESA look
unnecessarily harsh. A few FWS biologists, facing the jeopardy of an endan-

gered or threatened species on private property, have overzealously enforced the no-takings clause with minimal effort at public relations. Unfortunately, the actions of a few are the actions most widely publicized.

Fourth, throughout the life of the ESA, the agencies charged with enforcing it have had insufficient funding to do the job adequately. Perforce, all aspects of the effort to save species had to be prioritized and therefore some efforts were not made. Steven L. Yaffee (1991) wrote that annual ESA funding stayed relatively constant while consultation activity quadrupled by 1988. The demand for listing analysis and recovery planning increased daily. All four components are related.

Bureaucracy bashing is a popular pastime. However, every administrative entity—public or private, commercial or nonprofit—has flaws; the U.S. federal bureaucracy is more visible and therefore more vulnerable than others. Federal agencies are political entities and intensely sensitive to political considerations. The views and values of each administration direct the actions, policies, and regulations promulgated by all federal agencies. Congressional pressure has impact. Popular opinion, especially when represented by active interest groups and industry lobbies, also affects the actions of federal agencies. Voter opinions often swing against the bureaucracy. Public hostility cycles back to influence congressional and administrative politics.

While the primary ESA regulators are the U.S. Fish and Wildlife Service and the National Marine Fisheries Service, several other Interior Department agencies have considerable endangered species responsibility. Each handles the charge to protect species based on its own culture. These include the National Park Service, Bureau of Land Management, Bureau of Indian Affairs, and to a lesser extent the Bureau of Reclamation. Department of Agriculture land management agencies include the U.S. Forest Service and the Natural Resources Conservation Service, previously known as the Soil Conservation Service. The Department of Defense, being a large landowner, must often consider endangered species before taking action. Through its regulation of pollutants, the Environmental Protection Agency is also a frequent consultant with FWS.

Tim Clark and Ann Harvey (1991) believe bureaucratization to be the root cause of many ESA problems because the existing organizational structures of the lead agencies did not meet the ESA's needs. The federal government continues to reexamine its hierarchical structure and resources to address today's complex issues. The agencies are aware of their shortcomings. The

1995 report from the Interagency Ecosystem Management Task Force outlined a number of procedural and structural changes to be made within all land management agencies.

Environmental issues involve many participants and demand a range of scientific and social science expertise. Resolving today's environmental issues requires biology, economics, physics, chemistry, earth sciences, technology, and the social sciences to deal with scientific, cultural, and social barriers.

Regulatory mishandling of the ESA occurred when agencies disregarded their own policies in species listing, recovery planning, designation of critical habitat, cooperating with states, and in conducting the full scientific investigation required. As the lead agency for the ESA, the Fish and Wildlife Service has contributed to and in some cases created the problems associated with the ESA. For example, while Section 7 specifies consultations between federal entities, it does not prohibit this process in cases involving private property. Yet the FWS never extended this consideration to private property owners. Why? The impact of this failure has been significant. If FWS had handled the treatment of species protection more equitably with private landowners and used the information sharing and negotiation process inherent in consultation, private owners might not have taken so many self-defensive actions.

Wise Use organizations have capitalized on inadvertent bureaucratic errors and have repeatedly publicized episodes of bureaucratic insensitivity to further their goal of destroying environmental regulatory influence. The result is a public perception, strongest in but not limited to the West, that the ESA is insensitive to people and is a threat to property. "Inevitably the heavy [regulatory] hand leads many Americans to view the ESA as the symbol of everything they dislike about bureaucratic regulations and big government in general" (Chadwick 1995:31).

The Record

Requests for listings mounted rapidly in the first few years after the law's enactment and quickly outpaced the available budget and staff of the Fish and Wildlife Service. In January 1975, the Smithsonian published its required list of endangered plants—there were 3,200 on the list! At that time, processing one listing was estimated to take 240 person hours. Greenwalt told the House Merchant Marine and Fisheries Committee, a forerunner of today's Natural Resources Committee, that he would need to triple his staff over three years, and would need a corresponding budget increase, to implement the program mandated by the law (Greenwalt 1995).

He requested $115 million in 1977 and $89 million in each of the next four years. Congress responded with $41 million for the total five-year period, a mere 9 percent of the request. Thus Capitol Hill provided mixed signals to the bureaucracy from the beginning. The law clearly stated that saving species from extinction was a federal priority, but the dollars to do so were not provided. Greenwalt worried that Congress did not recognize the power of the legislation they had passed in 1973 and decided caution was appropriate in promulgating regulations.

The ESA, Greenwalt (1995) said, was "a blade with two edges." One edge was the temptation to administer the law through political compromise, to decide that a species had little intrinsic merit. (Insufficient data on the function of each species sharpened this edge.) The other edge was the use of the act to stop unpopular projects such as the Tellico Dam. This blade undercut the true intent of the law and its value.

Insufficient appropriations led directly to regulatory short cuts, at best, and at worst to regulatory mishandling. From the outset, the bureaucracy had to deal with the overriding reality of underfunding. For example, while cooperation with states was recognized as an effective means of facilitating the recovery of a listed species, funding was so limited that only about half the requests for assistance from states were accommodated.

To cut corners, the Fish and Wildlife Service gave priority to listings or to recovery as politics permitted. It set standards for prioritizing which species to address. The majority of consultations were handled informally. Yaffee believes informal consultations may have been both a budgetary necessity and a means of downplaying controversy. It has always been and remains impossible to keep political considerations out of the listing, recovery planning, or consultation processes. No matter what course the FWS took, it was criticized. However, Congress and the administration carry a large share of the responsibility.

The 1980s were dominated by a Republican administration hostile to the Endangered Species Act. In spite of the mounting requests for listings, only 246 species were listed from 1981 to 1986. As a result the candidate list, the list of species awaiting listing evaluation, grew by the hundreds. Furthermore, FWS employees admit that many species were listed in those days in Washington without much supporting data, instead of in the field where on-site biological evaluation could occur. When the evaluation occurred in Washington, field agents often had little forewarning of a new listing to be enforced. Public complaints that the FWS struck all of a sudden were often well founded because FWS agents had no time to prepare local residents for the fact that an area species might be considered endangered before the law required people to stop all activities that could jeopardize the species' existence.

The mounting number of listing petitions indicated both an increased awareness of the importance of identifying species in jeopardy, a benefit brought by the ESA, and the continued rise of human activities that modify the land or otherwise jeopardize species survival. Even if the agency had had strong administrative support, underfunding meant that FWS staff would have been unable to address all the petitions in a timely manner.

Delaying listing of species, however, exacerbated their jeopardy because the populations of species that are candidates for listing are often dangerously low at the time of the request. Delay also resulted in high research and management costs and a high risk of failure (Reffalt 1991). Furthermore, recovery planning has always lagged far behind listings.

"Although the FWS must list species shown to be endangered or threatened by biological research, it may do so as agency resources permit. This tremendous loophole has resulted in a list of more than 600 'category one' and 3000 'category 2' candidate species" (DOW 1993). The most urgent candidate list, category one, contained species that had been studied and were known to qualify for listing but for which there were insufficient enforcement and/or recovery planning resources to do so. With a tacit mandate to avoid listing, resources were often directed to other priorities. The category two list contained species awaiting study to determine if they were in danger.

Administration policy could and did focus agency priorities away from listing requests. Jaime Rappaport Clark, then assistant director of the Fish and Wildlife Service, indicated that listings have not been evenly spaced (Clark 1995). In the 1980s, listings slacked off because the administration was not interested in implementing the ESA. However, in 1992, the Fund for Animals sued FWS for failure to reconcile the backlog of listings. After the court ruled that the FWS must catch up on backlogged listings, about one hundred species were listed in 1993 and 1994. While this was a steep increase, it still left too many species unprotected.

Listings were not the only part of the ESA to suffer. A Congressional Research Service (CRS) report said: "As a practical matter, FWS and the NMFS have often failed to designate critical habitat for many species, since the process is very costly, subject to much dispute, and is not the section of the law that offers the greatest protection to listed species anyway" (Corn and Baldwin 1990:18). In June 1994, the FWS published a fact sheet indicating that they had increased the number of species to 468 plants and 423 animals that were threatened or endangered. Another 102 plant and 41 animal species were in the process of being listed. The category one candidate list shrank by May 1994 to 238 plants and 57 animals. Still remaining on the category two list were 1,697 plants and 1,800 animals. Critical habitat, however, had been designated for only 111 species and proposed for 10. The FWS had issued permits for twenty-eight conservation plans and for eleven amendments to existing plans. One hundred plans were in the development process at that time, and only 483 species had approved recovery plans.

One frequent criticism of the ESA was that it slowed or stopped development. FWS statistics on Section 7 (consultations relating to public land projects) do not support this contention. When a determination is made that a planned project will jeopardize the survival of an endangered species, alternatives are examined in hope that both the project and the species can be protected. In an undated fact sheet published sometime in 1993, "Fish and Wildlife Service Facts: Questions and Answers on the Endangered Species Act," FWS reported that there were 86,000 informal and 2,412 formal consultations conducted from 1988 to 1992. Only 341 (14 percent) of the formal consultations resulted in jeopardy opinions. In only 18 cases (0.1 percent) did the biological opinion find no reasonable and prudent alternatives to the plan and stop development. By definition, planned actions that go through informal consultation do not result in species jeopardy. Informal consultation includes all communication between the FWS and the project applicant to design the project so that there will be no adverse effects on the species if it does occur in the action area. It is true enough that on public and private lands where endangered species occur, more delay occurs than if no listed species is found.

During the Reagan and Bush administrations (1981–92), all agencies tended to delay taking action on species listing, critical habitat designation, and recovery planning. The 1993 Defenders of Wildlife report asserts that the Reagan and Bush administrations practiced sting operations to convict direct takers and to uncover trade in endangered species. Indirect takings through the destruction or degradation of listed species' habitat—the primary source of species endangerment—were not curtailed.

In *Northern Spotted Owl v. Hodel* (716 F. Supp. 479 [D. Wash. 1988]),

conservation groups sued the secretary of the interior for not listing the northern spotted owl after being petitioned to do so. The court found that the FWS
"disregarded all the expert opinion on population viability, including that of
its own expert, that the owl is facing extinction." It called the actions of the
service arbitrary, capricious, and contrary to the law.

The 1993 Defenders of Wildlife report stated that the FWS listed the
Tombigbee River freshwater mussel *after* the Tombigbee Waterway was completed, too late to stop the damage to the mussel's habitat. Listing of the Alabama flattened musk turtle was delayed beyond deadlines specified by the law
while FWS assured the state that its listing would not clamp down on coal
industry water pollution. Under congressional pressure, FWS Washington
headquarters reversed a regional determination that construction of Stacey
Dam in Texas would jeopardize the survival of the Concho water snake. These
are just three examples of the pressure applied during the Reagan-Bush years.

To compound the political pressure, the FWS suffered from insufficient
scientific information, a problem that is ubiquitous, as discussed in chapter
3, and that continues today. Knowledge of the habitat, nutritional, and general ecological requirements of many of the species at issue was and remains
limited. Biological research takes time, and the funds have always been inadequate to pay for the work to determine a species' needs so as to develop a
recovery plan.

FWS western regional biologist Joe Dowhan related the case of the San Diego Mesa mint plant. As part of the conservation plan prepared by a California developer who proposed to build in the plant's habitat, Dowhan and other
local conservationists were requested to mark off key sites to be protected. They
had to select the "best" sites from hundreds of vernal pools the plant occupied on the construction site—a near impossible decision. They selected the
biggest and the best mesa tops. At that time, in the late 1970s, this area was
wild habitat on the outskirts of San Diego. Just ten years later, he returned to
the area to find the chosen mesa sites completely enclosed by chain-link fence
located within a dense cluster of homes.

Both nonscientists and scientists criticize the FWS for its lack of scientific
knowledge. Scientists, however, are more sympathetic because they share the
frustration on the dearth of data available on species. In March 1995, the
Senate Environment and Public Works Committee's Drinking Water, Fisheries and Wildlife Subcommittee held a hearing on S. 191, Senator Slade
Gorton's ESA reauthorization bill. The testimony of Robert E. Gordon before this committee exemplifies the nonsympathetic view. Gordon identified

himself as executive director of the National Wilderness Institute and NWI as a private conservation organization "dedicated to the use of sound, objective science for the wise management of natural resources." He testified that there were statements in the species recovery plans indicating that insufficient information was available about population size and/or distribution and/or habitat needs. From this, he concluded that the law could not do the intended job. He also asserted that listing mistakes are costly—approximately $60,000 to list, and $37,000 to delist. In short, he concluded, we should not try to recover species since we do not know enough. NWI is a Wise Use organization.

Gordon's information about recovery plans is correct. A study of 314 approved recovery plans (Tear et al. 1995) shows that 81 percent of the plans had inadequate biological information to guide decision making. ESA opponents believe that inadequate scientific information is a deficiency in the statute. It is not. It is a deficiency in society's knowledge base. That fact aside, the study indicates that there is much more information available that the FWS recovery plans could include to bring the plans closer to workable recovery goals.

There are dozens of stories in circulation on the mishandling of endangered species protection by the Fish and Wildlife Service; most suffer from the human tendency to overemphasize the dramatic, and the stories change to fit the telling occasion. In his testimony at the March 1995 Senate hearing, Richard Perry, commissioner for the Texas Department of Agriculture, described several incidents of FWS mishandling of ESA regulations in Texas. Perry said Texas had been hit harder than other states because 95 percent of the state is private property and it has a high diversity of wildlife and habitat. (The state had sixty-seven species federally listed as endangered or threatened at the time.) "Each listing brings more regulations and restrictions on what a person can do with the property he or she owns" (Perry 1995:2).

He related the story of a seventy-four-year-old woman who bought land in central Texas as an investment for her retirement. Because the land was home to golden-cheeked warblers, an endangered bird, restrictions on what could be done on the land devalued it from $1 million to only $30,000. In another story, an eighty-seven-year-old widow cut a fence line across her property and she received a letter from the regional FWS office threatening a fine of $50,000 or imprisonment for compromising endangered species habitat. FWS later admitted they had overreacted.

Attempts to protect four endangered species, including the Texas blind salamander and the San Marcos salamander, created a furor over the use of groundwater drawn from the Edwards Aquifer. This aquifer supplies the irrigation and drinking water of the city of San Antonio and several military bases in the area. Perry indicated in his testimony that the Sierra Club threatened to sue to cut off the water to the bases and to have federal funds to farmers in the area cut off to protect the species. These stories are clearly not complete; however, they indicate why public reaction was so strongly against the ESA.

Perry further stated that the FWS sent unclear directions to landholders. These letters were perceived as threatening and were often released before site inspection. Between the lines of hyperbole emerges evidence of poor public communication by the FWS and of insufficient investigation.

By contrast, Bob Holmes presents a very different account of FWS actions with private property owners in Florida. The Preston family bought property to build a house in Malibar, Florida. After the purchase, they discovered that the endangered Florida scrub jay lived there. Within two months they worked out a solution that allowed them to protect the jay and build their home. They received the permit to build. The solution was not onerous: part of the lot was left in vegetation, more oak trees were planted, and the family maintained a bird feeder (Holmes 1995). The criticisms involving heavy-handedness by the FWS and other federal agencies come most vehemently from the Wise Use organizations and those politicians who buy their arguments.

Information published by Senator Slade Gorton's office in 1995 refers to the weaknesses of the FWS in managing Section 7 consultations. "Deadlines [for consultation resolution] are routinely ignored by FWS. . . . Permit or license applicants are subject to endless delays and extensions" (*Point-Counterpoint* 1995). The document goes on to accuse the FWS of using the consultation process to restrict third party activities unrelated to the consultation process and of failing to follow their own recovery plans.

The politicians neglect to connect the delay tactic of the federal bureaucracy with the pressures politicians themselves exert upon the bureaucracy. The necessity to accommodate political pressure is an ongoing concern of all federal agencies. If concessions to politics are made too often, the agency is charged with abandoning its basic duties; in turn, that produces even more pressure.

Mollie Beattie, first Clinton Administration director of Fish and Wildlife Service, addressed the "myths and realities" of the ESA in a May 1995 speech (*ESA Action* 1996a). She called endangered species "warning flags and smoke alarms of ecological stress, the red-line on the tachometer of the engine of growth that runs on land and water." She cited the example of fruit growers on Guam who were overwhelmed by fruit flies that used to be kept in check by a now endangered bat. In response to the accusation that FWS was listing-happy, she noted that in the past five years, the service had turned down 75 percent of the petitions it had received for listing. Countering the allegation that the ESA stopped economic progress, she cited a 1994 agency study revealing that more than 99.9 percent of permit applications under ESA between 1988 and 1993 were approved.

One change the U.S. Fish and Wildlife Service has made is perhaps sensible, if slightly suspicious in its suddenness. In July 1996, the FWS announced that it had reduced the list of potential endangered species candidates from 4,000 to 182. Only top-tier candidates for which the FWS had sufficient information to support final listings remained on the candidate list. According to FWS spokesperson Meg Durham, "this was a scientific scrubbing of the candidate list that was long overdue" (ESA Action 1996b).

Habitat Conservation Plans

Under Bruce Babbitt and his ten-point program, FWS has made strides to improve support of the habitat conservation planning process. Until 1994, the service did not consult with the plan developers or provide them any data on species or species recovery. Habitat conservation plans are costly in time, expense, and the trouble it takes to produce them. Joe Dowhan (1995) described the FWS rationale for restricting its role. He said that the service did not involve itself in HCPs because these result in species takings; the service's role is to stop takes. Because HCPs were a private sector mechanism, the FWS was required to work under the Section 9 rules. The ESA required FWS to consult with other federal agencies on actions on public lands, and it could have adopted similar consultation procedures with private owners but chose not to do so.

On the other hand, lack of funding limited the service's ability to contribute to the HCP process. Developing an HCP is a trial-and-error process for the private citizen or corporation and therefore is expensive, frustrating, and time-consuming. In too few cases did the service function in an advisory role for these landowners.

Thus for private property owners, HCPs became the proverbial straw that broke the camel's back. Before the 1982 amendments created the HCP process, fear of federal regulation caused many private landholders to take measures to avoid attracting species to their property. Worse, owners sometimes drove species from their property to protect themselves. HCPs created a further disincentive causing private landholders to avoid endangered species at all costs. The case of southern California's Natural Communities Conservation Plan (NCCP) is an excellent example of development of an HCP that never seemed to end because new species were continually discovered. Understandably, developers wanted guarantees that the process would not go on interminably and continue to drain their financial resources. They sought what has become known as a No Surprises clause. Bob Holmes (1995:14) wrote: "No matter how quick or easy habitat conservation plans become, the extra paperwork and the risk—however slight—of government interference are not likely to encourage landowners to attract endangered species onto their property."

A look at the history of the first Habitat Conservation Plans shows that they created as many problems as they solved. This explains why policies such Safe Harbor and No Surprises are needed, as is better cooperative interaction between agencies and private citizens. Charles Mann and Mark Plummer documented the stories of two representative HCPs: the Balcones Canyonlands Conservation Plan (BCCP) in Texas (Mann and Plummer 1995b) and southern California's Natural Communities Conservation Plan (NCCP) (Mann and Plummer 1995a).

The BCCP was the fourth HCP submitted to the FWS. It differed from its predecessors because it covered multiple development sites and was regional in scope. The Texas plan addressed seven endangered species, including the black-capped vireo. Over thirty-six other endangered, threatened, or candidate species occupied the area in question. The Nature Conservancy assumed leadership of the plan's development. The parties began meeting in July 1988. They included the Texas Parks and Wildlife Department, Sierra Club, Lower Colorado River Authority, Hughes Interests (the developer), Texas General Land Office, Travis Audubon Society, Texas Department of Transportation, the City of Austin, Travis County commissioners, Texas Capital Area Builders Association, and Earth First! (Mann and Plummer 1995b).

After a biological assessment was conducted, the team designed a system of preserves. They determined how to pay for the preserves with taxpayer and developer fees and how to construct countywide processes for working with the property and species. Two of the endangered birds required a great deal of territory. While this assessment was under way, the Hillwood Development

Company began clearing hundreds of acres of juniper—the nesting habitat of the golden-cheeked warbler. Hillwood was eventually stopped, but its actions illustrate the steps private owners would take to avoid potential economic loss.

The parties discussed, argued, and negotiated for four years until a plan was hammered out and approved in June 1992. Then it went to the Fish and Wildlife Service for approval. The local governments (city and county) were ready to move ahead. The City of Austin approved a bond issue before FWS approval. Travis County, on the other hand, lost its bond issue vote. "Austin had all the ingredients for a successful regional habitat conservation plan: sophisticated models from top scientists; ideological opponents who nevertheless wanted the project to succeed; a general wish to be proactive; and the full support of the Interior Secretary Bruce Babbitt. None of these were enough, though, to avoid a hostile stalemate" (Mann and Plummer 1995b:204). Nat Williams of the Nature Conservancy (Williams 1995) and Secretary Bruce Babbitt viewed the BCCP as a success. Mann and Plummer believe that "the BCCP ran aground because the latitude for politics was too *little*, not too great . . . federal biologists have been transformed into ecological mandarins with the power to govern projects" (1995b:208).

The story of California's Natural Communities Conservation Plan began with the Fieldstone Company's purchase of 2,300 acres in San Diego County in 1988. Shortly thereafter, the company learned that the property's abundant sage scrub vegetation was the habitat of the coastal California gnatcatcher, a species likely to be listed as endangered. The species had been identified by biologist Jonathan Atwood, who requested that it be listed as endangered about the same time he described it (Mann and Plummer 1995a).

John Barone, project manager for Fieldstone, hired Lindell Marsh to address the anticipated gnatcatcher problem. Marsh was the creator of the San Bruno Mountain plan developed in northern California long before the concept of habitat conservation planning became law. Marsh suggested that Barone create the HCP before any listing occurred. The NCCP would be the sixth HCP to be submitted.

In fall 1991, Barone found a piece of land to serve as a reserve for the gnatcatchers. The Fish and Wildlife Service did not approve it. He tried again. Working with California's Endangered Habitat League, Atwood, and the City of Carlsbad, Barone developed a new proposal in which Fieldstone would set aside half of the eastern portion of its parcel in return for permission to develop the western portion, at a cost of $12 million to Fieldstone. The parties agreed to this in May 1992. In the meantime, Barone learned that the western portion of his property was full of Del Mar manzanita, an endangered plant. So the plan had to be modified again. By this time, Barone learned that there were thirty-six potentially listable species on the property (Mann and Plummer 1995a).

During this period, Monica Florian of the Irvine Company, a developer with huge holdings in Orange County, recognized the need to develop a co-ordinated plan for the entire southern California area. Her goal was to avoid a "nightmare" of HCP proposals being generated simultaneously for the same area by multiple developers. She contacted the Resources Agency of California, the state's environmental agency, and asked its head, Doug Wheeler, to coordinate an HCP for the entire scrub sage ecosystem. She also asked that the state and federal governments postpone the gnatcatcher listing until that HCP was complete. Wheeler agreed to the large-scale HCP; but the federal government did not agree to postpone the listing.

California Governor Pete Wilson announced plans to create the NCCP publicly on Earth Day 1991. To lay out guidelines, the Resources Agency appointed a panel of five scientists led by Dennis Murphy, director of the Center for Conservation Biology at Stanford University. The NCCP was to cover six thousand square miles, including San Diego, Orange, Los Angeles, Riverside, and San Bernardino counties. Fieldstone's existing plan would merge into the larger plan. The planners also worked with the diverse conservation efforts already under way in these areas.

Some local developers were unwilling or unable to cooperate, complicating the development of the plan. One source of ill will was the refusal of the Natural Resources Defense Council (NRDC) to support delay of the gnatcatcher's listing. The state of California listed the bird in August 1991. The NCCP became part of California law in October 1991, long before it was completed. Soon afterward, it met the opposition of the Endangered Habitat League.

When the bird was finally listed federally as endangered in March 1993, the listing required that landowners who participated in the NCCP avoid gnatcatcher problems and permitted them to develop 5 percent of the coastal scrub sage area while NCCP arrangements were in progress. During the extended period, more and more developers joined the NCCP. Three more plans in San Diego County merged under the NCCP umbrella. Fieldstone established another plan in October 1994. Bruce Babbitt called the NCCP a "once-in-a-century opportunity to preserve the landscape."

While many deemed the plan a success, the process was long and arduous. Its development included state and local governments as well as private landowners. Notably absent from the list of participants in the development of either the NCCP or the Balcones plan is the U.S. Fish and Wildlife Service. They were at worst obstructing and at best delaying the process by withholding information and guidelines.

Development in southern California is proceeding; and gnatcatcher habitat is being conserved. Nevertheless, all the issues are not fully resolved. The environmental community was divided on the final approval of the NCCP. David Wilcove of the Environmental Defense Fund called the agreement a step "to try to figure out ways to protect species without incurring the ceaseless wrath of the development community." Bill Snape of Defenders of Wildlife believed the government gave away too much: "We're locking in land management and species protection policies for 50 to 75 years" (*Greenlines* 1996b).

Changes to the ESA to facilitate HCPs are still needed. However, recently introduced regulations go a long way toward reversing the trend toward destruction of privately owned species habitats, encouraging the owners to sanction and protect endangered and threatened species habitat while maintaining the economic value of their property.

No Surprises and Safe Harbor

In 1995, the Department of the Interior issued for public comment two policies that provide incentives for private and other nonfederal landowners to protect the lands on which endangered, threatened, or potentially threatened species are found and even to attract species to those lands: No Surprises and Safe Harbor. These two policies are controversial because they include some risk for endangered species. However, they address the barriers to private landowner cooperation that had been growing for years. Both address species protection on nonfederal lands.

Many private landholders had indicated an interest in protecting the species on their lands, but they feared that in doing so they might attract populations of an endangered species. When that happens, either the full power of the ESA's no taking provision (Section 9) is applied or the long, expensive

HCP process must happen. Landowners often end up changing some or all of the planned use of their land.

Michael Bean of the Environmental Defense Fund conceived the concept of Safe Harbor agreements as an encouragement to landowners to take proactive conservation measures to protect species on their lands. Bean believed that the ESA's existing incentive for forestland owners in the Southeast was "to be the first to liquidate their share of the available habitat before the Fish and Wildlife Service's minimum threshold of remaining habitat is reached." He said these actions were not malicious; "rather, they're fairly rational decisions motivated by a desire to avoid potentially significant economic constraints . . . a predictable response to the familiar perverse incentives that sometimes accompany regulatory programs" (Bean 1994). Under the new policy, however, in return for their voluntary agreement to conserve habitat, the property owners receive some confidence that if species migrate to the improved land, the FWS and state and local wildlife agencies will not apply future restrictions on its use.

For FWS approval of a Safe Harbor agreement, at least one endangered or threatened species must be known to reside on the land in question. Another policy, Candidate Conservation Agreements, also fully voluntary, covers habitats of species that are proposed for listing. Like Safe Harbor, Candidate Conservation Agreements include managing the land for species stewardship, and they protect the landowner from future land use restrictions should the species be listed. These policies remove the disincentives to protecting species on nonfederal lands—a huge step forward toward resolving the conflicts between private landowners and the ESA and toward protecting species habitat to avoid endangerment.

The No Surprises policy is implemented as part of the Habitat Conservation Plan process. When an incidental take permit is issued to the holders of an approved HCP, the landowners are assured that no further land use restrictions or financial contribution above that specified in the HCP will be required regardless of whether unforeseen circumstances (such as another endangered species) arise. The risk to species with this policy is greater than with Safe Harbor or Candidate Conservation Agreements because science continues to uncover new information on species daily, which could change known needs or add requirements for protecting the species. The administration does not deny the risk but accepts it as a reasonable one.

The largest issue arising from these new policies is how long the protection from any new requirements or expenditures should last—ten, twenty, fifty, one hundred years? The one-hundred-year figure has been proposed and is hotly contested by Enviros. One hopes that the potential long-term risk to species under the No Surprises policy will be offset by the short-term benefit to species in the removal of one of the greatest objections to the ESA and one of the greatest disincentives to landowners to protect species.

The two new policies are radically different from historical ESA regulations and are long overdue improvements. They indicate a sincere desire to work with nonfederal landowners and to encourage them to protect species and species habitats.

The Bureaucratic Culture

The Nature Conservancy conducted a 1995 survey of property owners affected by the ESA. While not based on a random sample, the information they derived was enlightening. The owners believe that the science being used to determine whether a species is endangered is suspect—it is not enough and appears slanted. They also believe that the Fish and Wildlife Service is too far removed from most local situations to deal effectively with them. The Nature Conservancy suggests that better public education is needed to create awareness of the act, why it exists, and what it is intended to do. The Conservancy also recommends training FWS operatives in public dealings and education (Nature Conservancy 1995).

To a substantial extent, these political and economic pressures have always existed and will continue in a democratic system. What can and ought to change to handle today's issues is the inappropriate organizational structure of the bureaucracy and its antiquated internal culture. Clark and Harvey proposed the need in 1991 for organizational change. Although they did not recommend specific ideas for change, the indication was that less hierarchy and more of a matrix organization would be more effective. The Interagency Ecosystem Management Task Force (1995) emphasized regional planning and interagency implementation teams rather than the more typical top-down approach of sending instructions from headquarters. In addition, the task force recommended coordinated ecosystem budgets in which all collaborating agencies would coordinate their budget proposals at the local level, and each would request funds from its parent agency for its portion of the planned effort. The task force also encouraged short-term exchanges of personnel among collaborating agencies.

In general, the task force indicated that adaptability in organizational arrangements was as important as the recommended adaptive approach (defined in simple terms as using trial and error and adapting the plan based on what was learned) for on-the-ground ecosystem management. Each federal land management agency has developed its own ecosystem management program to accommodate the task force recommendations, and there is clearly a strong effort to work in interagency teams. The effectiveness of changes made in individual agency organizational structures remains to be determined.

Change in the federal culture is an equally important innovation needed to do away with the syndromes of "we've always done it that way" and "we carry out the letter of the law." Cultural myopia often prohibits creative bureaucrats from trying new approaches. Furthermore, the existing reward system discourages experimentation. Regulations, by tradition, attempt to address all possible scenarios. Yet it is impossible for one person, or one agency, at one point in time to address all possible situations.

The poor public communications on the ESA and its requirements is a good example of cultural myopia. The FWS generated many attractive full-color brochures, posters, and other information vehicles, but their distribution channels fell far short of informing the public. Instead, the public received curt, threatening letters informing them of liabilities they had no idea existed. Although heavy-handed tactics were not widespread, the actions of a few tainted the credibility and effectiveness of the whole.

The federal culture needs to reward experimentation and creative problem solving. Regional adaptation is important in implementing laws like the ESA where different situations require different methods to reach solutions. New skills and methods need to be added to the existing scientific-administrative mix in the Fish and Wildlife Service as well as the other agencies enforcing the ESA. Needed skills include marketing to determine better information distribution channels, individual communication and conflict management skills to enable more effective public interface, and scientific and decision-making models to facilitate planning and decision making in the real world of insufficient information.

The Fish and Wildlife Service is staffed largely with biologists trained in skills very different from those needed for public interaction and information dissemination. It may be unrealistic to ask people with critical and, by definition, narrowly focused scientific skills to become generalists with multiple expertise. It takes a team of people, each with different skills, working together to solve the complex problems of simultaneously protecting species and economic health. To be effective, that team must include all the stakeholders, not just bureaucrats at the local, state, and federal levels.

Reorganizational needs include eliminating less important job descriptions to add more appropriate skills and retraining of those whose skills are phased out. Allowing individual flexibility and creativity requires reducing long, hierarchical management chains. Such changes may be difficult. Since the June 1995 report of the Task Force on Ecosystem Management, the FWS has adopted an ecosystem team approach to decision making and as the base of budget formulation. Fifty-two ecosystem teams establish priorities and develop three-year ecosystem plans with field-level input (FWS 1997b).

Commonly, established bureaucrats and politicians avoid big risks, preferring the status quo when there is no statutory or executive mandate. Trying new and controversial policies without a mandate is risky in the political arena. Bruce Babbitt deserves high marks for his courage in putting personal comfort aside and promulgating No Surprises, Safe Harbor, and other innovative but contentious approaches to gain the support of private property owners in protecting species. FWS directors under him, Mollie Beattie and Jaime Rappaport Clark, also deserve credit. FWS is now taking a collaborative approach with private landowners to develop HCPs. The communication barriers that fostered ESA difficulties are dissolving under the initiative of bureaucracy.

Rather than take the defensive, Babbitt recognized and acknowledged the internal and external problems. Then he promulgated the ten guideposts to correct them and adopted some contentious new policies. No Surprises and Safe Harbor carry some risk to species, but these policies have extended to private interests an understanding, collaborative approach and have given those landowners incentives to cooperate. The risk may be well worth the gains in cooperation in the long run. Under Babbitt's tenure the FWS has done much to repair its earlier mistakes with the ESA.

Chapter Nine

Species Economics

Unless we can discover ways of living that integrate the
competitive imperatives of economic opportunity and
environmental protection, we will never be able to reverse
the alarming decline of species and natural habitats.
—John C. Sawhill, 1995

N	O DISCUSSION OF ENVIRONMENTAL POLICY would be complete
	without looking at the economic factors. The economics of endan
	gered species is a complex topic. Some claim the ESA has put thou-
sands of people out of jobs in the Pacific Northwest; others claim it robs property owners of their intrinsic and constitutional right to use their property to
their economic advantage.

Economic theory views the environment, and especially endangered species, as an "externality" and therefore outside the control of the marketplace.
Because biodiversity includes the resources upon which the human race relies for its survival (Watson and Heywood 1995), many scientists believe that
loss of biodiversity has significant economic and social impact. Some economists proclaim that if the market value of species were defined, the free market economy would take care of the problems of biodepletion and species extinction. But how does one place a value on species? Should species be saved
if their rescue infringes on the human right to economic development and
growth? How has the ESA affected the economy of the United States? How
much have annual congressional appropriations for ESA implementation
contributed to the problems with the act?

Economic Impact

Opponents of the ESA frequently cite stories of the lost jobs, infringement
on private property use, restriction of inalienable citizen rights to progress and

economic development, and excessive additional costs of doing business under the law for endangered species protection. Proponents cite the benefits of species protection requirements to their industries; the economic wealth derived by such industries as ecotourism, sport fishing and hunting equipment manufacturing, and pharmaceuticals; and the protection of jobs afforded by the application of more sustainable extraction techniques and the prohibition of overharvesting.

In their 1993 book *Trashing the Economy*, Wise Use founders Ron Arnold and Alan Gottlieb declared the ESA to be an "economy-trasher"; they deemed it very economically damaging. Stephen Meyer of the Massachusetts Institute of Technology offers a different perspective. In a working paper released in 1995, Meyer provided key data on the impact of endangered species on the economies of states. He looked at the period from 1975 to 1990 and at 48 states. "The data show that endangered species listings have not depressed state economic development activity as measured by growth in construction employment and gross state product. . . . In fact a state by state comparative analysis across three consecutive five year periods reveals the converse to be true: higher numbers of listed endangered species are associated with higher rates of economic growth and corresponding population pressures" (Meyer 1995:1).

Meyer examined two economic indicators: growth in construction employment and growth in gross state product. The number of listings per state was used to measure the endangered species burden. This number was intended to be a relative measure and did not take into account the species range, which in some cases spanned multiple states. He found no evidence of a decrease in growth of construction employment or a decrease in growth of gross state product (GSP) based on number of species listings either in 1975 or in 1985.

To determine if the effect of species listings might be subtler, Meyer included three more variables: land area of the state, size of the state's economy (measured in GSP), and percentage of GSP derived from extractive industries, excluding ranching. With these factors, Meyer notes that "state experiences during the period 1975–1990 do not conform to the notion that the Endangered Species Act has hurt economic performance. . . . All three time periods now show a statistically significant relationship between species listings and growth in gross state product" (Meyer 1995:8). In the analysis, he found that as the number of species listings increased, state economic growth rates did not decelerate and in some cases accelerated. Meyer concluded that "the economic effects of endangered species listings are so highly localized,

of such small scale, and short duration that they do not substantially affect state economic performance in the aggregate" (Meyer 1995:15).

The case of the regulated reduction of timber harvest in the forests of the Pacific Northwest due to the listing of the northern spotted owl demonstrates some of the myths and realities of the economic impact of the ESA. Environmentalists openly used the ESA to fight the continued clear-cutting of the old growth Douglas fir forests in Oregon and Washington. Since the northern spotted owl relies on old growth trees for its subsistence, its population has been declining precipitously for some time. The media played up the jobs-versus-owl aspect of the conflict between logging and species protection and highlighted many of the sadder stories of the impact on individual loggers and their families.

Bill Morrisette, mayor of Springfield, Oregon, told the *New York Times*: "Owls versus jobs was just plain false. What we've got here is quality of life. And as long as we don't screw that up, we'll always be able to attract people and business" (quoted by Egan 1994:1). In his article, Egan noted that "economic calamity has never looked so good. Three years into a dramatic curtailment of logging in Federal forests, Oregon, the top timber-producing state, has posted its lowest unemployment rate in a generation, just over 5 percent" (Egan 1994:1). Oregon mills took their annual 5 billion board feet of timber from tree farms, not old growth federal forests. Furthermore, the state sought new employment opportunities by attracting the technology industry. The nearly 15,000 jobs in forest products lost since 1989 were replaced by 20,000 jobs in high technology. Workers took advantage of retraining opportunities. Graphs accompanying the *New York Times* article show Oregon's unemployment rate dipping below the national rate after 1985 and its employment in high-technology manufacturing climbing steadily from 1979 to 1994.

Ironically, the plight of the northern spotted owl was known as early as 1973, the year the ESA was passed. The history of efforts to resolve the problem dates back just as far. Charles Meslow (1993) provides a thumbnail sketch. In 1973, the Oregon Endangered Species Task Force was formed to address the needs of the owl. It recommended that 300 acres of old growth habitat be retained around each spotted owl location until statewide guidelines could be adopted. The U.S. Forest Service (USFS) and Bureau of Land Management (BLM) rejected this recommendation until a statewide population management goal was established for the owl. The National Forest Management Act of 1976 directed the Forest Service to maintain well-distributed, viable popu-

lations of all native species in national forests. Later, the task force recommended that at least 400 pairs of spotted owls be protected on Oregon public lands.

Not until 1977 did the USFS and BLM agreed to protect spotted owl habitat in accordance with these recommendations. In late 1977, the Oregon Spotted Owl Management Plan was released, calling for habitat management areas for clusters of owl pairs and a minimum of 1,200 acres of contiguous habitat for each pair.

In 1984, the USFS directed forest managers in the Pacific Northwest to analyze the effect of protecting at least 375 pairs of owls in Oregon and Washington (Meslow 1993). In 1985, an advisory panel for the National Audubon Society recommended that a minimum of 1,500 pairs be maintained in three states, adding the northern California habitat. In 1987, the Fish and Wildlife Service received a petition to list the owl as endangered. In December of that year, the agency announced that a listing was not warranted. The decision not to list was appealed in federal court; the court determined that the decision was not biologically based and ordered the FWS to readdress the petition.

Late in 1988, the Forest Service's Record of Decision on the Supplemental Environmental Impact Statement for the northern spotted owl directed the thirteen national forests in Washington and Oregon to establish a spotted owl habitat network. This decision was unpopular with environmental and timber groups. The appeal to the USDA assistant secretary was denied.

In October 1989, a group called the Interagency Spotted Owl Scientific Committee (ISC) was formed to develop a scientifically credible conservation strategy. Meslow (1993) said the committee suggested a system of habitat conservation areas on public lands with no further timber harvests within these areas. The strategy further called for reservation of 5.8 million acres of federal land not previously reserved from timber cutting. In June 1990, the FWS listed the owl as threatened. A recovery planning team began to meet in 1991 and delivered a draft plan to Interior Secretary Manuel Lujan in mid-December 1991. The plan closely resembled the ISC strategy and was released in May 1992. Concurrently, Lujan released his own "Owl Preservation Plan," which though similar to the recovery plan cut the owl's range by 50 percent.

In 1991, the U.S. House of Representatives requested options from four forest experts with scientific credentials. The Scientific Panel on Late Successional Forest Ecosystems, as this group was called, presented an array of options to Congress. The options ranged from high timber yield at one end of the spectrum to high forest maintenance for spotted owls, marbled murrelets, and other forest species. Their report described the trade-offs.

Clearly, there was nothing sudden or unexpected about the impact of the listing of the northern spotted owl. For years scientific and environmental coalitions had been making recommendations to protect the bird, and for years the federal agencies and timber companies had resisted implementing the recommendations. Political, bureaucratic, and industry resistance to the warnings and early suggestions of how to protect the forests exacerbated the economic impact of the owl's listing in the Pacific Northwest. The media exploited the emotions of the loggers and their families. It took presidential intervention by Bill Clinton to devise a working plan to resolve the problems in the Northwest.

Another major industry in the Pacific Northwest is salmon fishing. Representatives of this industry tend to favor the ESA because it protects them from overharvesting. Responding to the introduction of the Gorton ESA reauthorization bill (see chapter 6), Glen Spain, Northwest director of the Pacific Coast Federation of Fishermen's Associations (PCFFA), presented industry views in a May 1995 letter to the U.S. Senate: "PCFFA is the largest trade association of commercial fishermen on the west coast, with many thousands of members coast wide. Commercial fishing is this nation's oldest industry. The food production, the jobs, the health of coastal economies, the commerce and exports it represents depends on the protection of this nation's basic biological heritage. Fishing contributes $111 billion annually to this country's economy and provides jobs for *one and a half million Americans*" (Spain 1995; Spain's emphasis).

Spain continued: "The fishing industry is highly regulated under the ESA. This is why we want an ESA that actually works! In spite of its problems, we believe the Endangered Species Act is instrumental in guaranteeing and protecting the basic biological heritage which supports our economy." Zeke Grader, also of PCFFA, and Liz Hamilton, executive director of the Northwest Sportfishing Industry Association, had written to Representative Don Young, chairman of the House Resources Committee, in January 1995. In the letter they said that the two organizations represented several billion dollars annually to the economy of the area, more than 5,000 sportfishing-related businesses, and 100,000 jobs. They told Young: "We are utterly opposed to the current efforts . . . to immediately suspend all actions under (and rescind all funding for) the ESA. . . . ESA is the only thing . . . driving recovery of the multitude of salmon species in the Northwest which have been devastated by decades of on-shore habitat loss and poorly planned hydropower development."

The 1993 Defenders of Wildlife report on endangered species indicated that there had been a 70 percent increase in employment in the twenty counties around Yellowstone National Park in the two decades since the passage of the ESA. "Only one of every 25 of the new jobs came from logging, mining or agriculture. Eight of every ten new jobs and 65 percent of the increased income came from the service sector." Recreation now generates the majority of direct jobs in six of seven national forests (DOW 1993:16).

While many industries see value in the ESA and in preserving natural systems, there is some evidence of short-term depression of property values on private lands where endangered species have been located. This was true in several areas in Texas. However, there is no evidence of long-term value depression. There is also some short-term expense associated with species protection, as in the case of turtle exclusion devices. Shrimpers must invest in these new nets to assure that turtles can escape the shrimping nets. Industries that resist can spend large sums of money fighting the change.

Economic Theory

Today there is a growing subdiscipline called environmental or green economics with a sizable cadre of adherents. Even within this group, however, few dispute the need for better theory with which to work. Current economic theory still permits the "tragedy of the commons" impact and all too often, long-term environmental damage from an economic activity is still considered an "externality." Species regularly harvested and forming an intricate part of a local economy, such as trees, fish, and domestic plants, often fall prey to the tragedy of the commons—that is, overexploitation because it is economically more sensible for individual users to overharvest than to employ a sustainable extraction method. Species that are not harvested for economic support also fall under the heading of externality and simply slip through the cracks in the theory.

"The greatest part of the literature on the economics of renewable resources is concerned with fisheries and forests. . . . Any resource [species] with a significant minimum critical size faces a real prospect of extinction, particularly if the resource is subject to 'open-access' harvesting. . . . Any resource will risk extinction if the 'steady-state' condition is not met—that is, if the rate of harvest exceeds the rate of reproduction" (Pearce and Turner 1990:262). In fact, there is not much literature on the economics of species other than fin fish, shellfish, and trees. The reason for this is that economists have yet to develop a workable approach for valuing nonfood, nontimber species. Part of the problem is the lack of biological information on the services provided by species, and part of the problem is in the concept of intrinsic value. However, the lack of economic theory is not due to lack of interest. At any forum on biodiversity the economic community will be represented and ready and willing to discuss the problems of species economics.

For example, at an October 1997 workshop on biodiversity presented at the World Bank's Fifth Annual Conference on Environmentally and Socially Sustainable Development, British economist Charles Perrings expressed deep concern over the deficiency of economics in relation to biodiversity. "Economists," he said, "are fixated with species diversity and especially those that have some value in the market." One villain is that prices, the economic signals to users, do not tell the users that the use is socially wrong. He said that everything has a use, direct or indirect. Non-use is really an indirect use. However existing prices do not adequately reflect direct or indirect values of most species. Ecosystem services are indirect. Their value is often in the insurance they provide against future problems, or the service may be essentially unknown, such as the service invertebrates provide in fertilizing and stabilizing soil. A recent estimate of the value of the loss of biodiversity, $33 trillion, was published in *Nature* magazine. No one can disprove such an estimate; many will argue it is too high or too low. The real benefit of publishing such a number is that it gets everyone thinking about the issue.

According to Herman E. Daly, the worldview underlying standard economics is that economics is a system isolated from the natural world. Standard economics fails to make the distinction between growth, a quantitative change, and development, a qualitative change. Economic growth is limited by the complementary relation between manufactured and natural capital (Meffe and Carroll 1997).

If we could measure the value of biodiversity lost because of pesticide use (currently considered an externality), and add this to the cost of producing food, it would increase the price of food that farmers produce. This in turn would shift the demand curve and the quantity of food supplied (Meffe and Carroll 1997). Such an approach would internalize the cost and provide more appropriate signals to consumer. Another component of the economic feedback might be the diminished use of pesticides to produce the food, which would reduce production costs.

"Biodiversity is the natural capital of the Earth, and presents important opportunities for all nations" (Watson and Heywood 1995:1). The United Nations Environmental Programme commissioned the *Global Biodiversity Assessment* (GBA) after the Convention on Biological Diversity went into effect in 1993. The purpose was to mobilize the international scientific community to evaluate the existing knowledge base and to make recommendations to move toward a more complete body of knowledge (Watson and Heywood 1995). The GBA declared that biodiversity provides the goods and services essential to human livelihoods and enables societies to adapt to changing needs and circumstances. Losing the diversity of genes within species, species within ecosystems, and ecosystems within regions makes it likely that future environmental disturbance will result in serious reductions in the goods and services provided by the earth's ecosystems. The rate at which humans are altering the environment and the extent of alterations pose substantial threats to sustainable economic development and to quality of life. These events threaten food supplies; sources of wood, medicines, and energy; opportunities for recreation and tourism; and ecological functions such as the regulation of storm water runoff, control of soil erosion, assimilation of wastes and purification of water, the cycling of carbon and nutrients, and climate control.

The GBA called for all nations to adopt ecologically based management systems that take into account the effects on biodiversity of extracting goods and using services and that balance human socioeconomic and long-term ecological considerations with current demands. "Conservation and sustainable use of biodiversity needs to become an integral component of economic development by correcting policy and market failures" (Watson and Heywood 1995:4).

The GBA recommendations are valid and desirable but much easier to write than to implement. As Holmes Rolston III suggests, developing the value of natural things and a concern for conservation requires an "unprecedented mix of politics, biology and ethics." It raises such issues as balancing natural values versus economic values, the need to evolve concepts of private property in relation to biodiversity, and the capability to distinguish moral concern for species in total from that for species individuals (Rolston 1991:44).

Conservation management decisions are made by comparing the costs of planning and implementation with ecological trade-offs; costs are measured in money or time and effort and ecological trades in biological units. This makes the comparison very difficult.

There is a dichotomy of opinion on setting species values. Economists tend to favor the approach because it enables use of current economic theory. Some conservation biologists favor it; others are opposed. For example, Stanwyn Shetler fears that attempting to place a monetary value on species makes them commodities instead of elements of a natural system. This tends to foster a "biotechnological fix-it" reaction. It could also imply that it is viable to transplant an endangered species or to bring it under perpetual managed care (Shetler 1991). Shetler asserts that artificial maintenance, propagation, rehabilitation, and restoration of species do not save natural systems and confuse public understanding. Also, valuing individual species diverts attention away from preserving whole habitats.

Robert Costanza of the University of Maryland believes that society can make choices more easily if it is clear on valuation. New and better ways to make good decisions in the face of value uncertainties are required (Meffe and Carroll 1997). He suggests a two-tiered approach combining public discussion and consensus building on sustainability and equity goals at the community level with methods for modifying prices and preferences at the individual level. He identifies three types of valuation that need to be incorporated: efficiency-based values, where humans act in their own self interest; fairness-based values, where individuals vote their preferences as members of the community; and sustainability-based values, which require assessing any decision's contribution to ecological sustainability.

Costanza suggests: "Rather than trying to avoid the difficult questions raised by the valuation of ecological systems, we need to acknowledge the broad range of goals being served as well as the technical difficulties involved and get on with the process of value formation in as participatory and democratic a way as possible" (quoted in Meffe and Carroll 1997:525).

Many biologists believe that there is immense functional redundancy among species and that ecological processes would still function well if a species were lost because other plants and animals would fill in. The consensus is that ecosystem function depends on the interactions among relatively few species. But we simply do not have enough data yet to verify that hypothesis. Furthermore, it is difficult to determine the mix of species that is appropriate for an ecosystem's health, resilience, and integrity (Meffe and Carroll 1997). Therefore, another reason to protect species in their habitats must be added to the moral, cultural, and spiritual list: we do not know *which species losses* will result in the collapse of the entire ecosystem or in the loss of a critical natural service.

Among the direct benefits of species, Pearce and Turner (1990) list the membership in ornithological societies, nature trusts, and wildlife organizations. The sale of such products as birdseed, binoculars, field guides, and other birding and wildlife watching gear are more direct benefits with monetary values. Indirect benefits of species include the spiritual and moral values but also include "option values"—economic parlance for unmeasurable values. Option values involve such unknowns as the number of potential medicines still unidentified that are present in plants or animals and the contributions that wild plant genes can make to domestic plants, for example in resistance to disease and drought. Other option values include life support functions such as climate control, natural air and water pollution removal, and flood control. These option values correspond closely to what scientists refer to as ecosystem services. We have not placed a value on natural services, either because they were not recognized or because it is difficult to arrive at a consensus on the value of each service. That value would vary from location to location and ecosystem to ecosystem.

Open Access: The Tragedy of the Commons

Open access to a species (on public lands, in navigable waters, in the air) significantly increases the risk of species extinction by resulting in lower stocks than would occur under private ownership. However, even in a sole owner situation, there is risk. Where the owner seeks to maximize present value of profits, and where such externalities such as nonmarket values are not a factor, extinction can be the economically and socially optimal alternative (Pearce and Turner 1990). In this case a species is driven to extinction *because* it is a capital asset.

As regards problems of overexploitation associated with open access resources, historical examples abound. In describing the history of the whaling industry, Andrew Dobson provides an excellent example. With some variation, this example is also the story of birds captured for the pet trade and large cats killed for the fur trade.

Whaling became an industry with the "golden age of Yankee whaling" in the early eighteenth century. Sperm whales provided lubricant oil, lamp oil, and candle wax. When the sperm whale population collapsed, whalers killed right, humpback, and gray whales. The industry continued to expand through the mid-1800s. At first, the process consisted of small catch boats carrying men with harpoons, the smaller boats launched from larger sailing ships. Modern whaling began in the 1860s when Norway launched the first steam-powered whaler equipped with a harpoon gun. By this time the stocks of right, humpback, and gray whales were waning. Nevertheless, the new technology enabled whalers to pursue the faster blue, fin, and sei whales into deeper water. By the early 1900s, stocks of all hunted whales were low in the North Atlantic, so whaling shifted south.

Because of depleted supplies, the British imposed restrictions on harvesting females with calves and taxed barrels of whale oil produced on whaling stations. These stations evolved on islands close to the whaling grounds for processing efficiency. To circumvent these restrictions, the Norwegians developed factory ships that could process the whales. This technology furthered the growth of the industry. In 1930, quotas were imposed on the number of whales that could be caught in southern oceans when a banner catch year created a glut on the whale oil market. By 1946, the newly formed International Whaling Commission set a formal system of quotas and a limit on the total weight of whales caught in a single year. Because the commission's system worked by closing the whaling season once the year's quota was caught, intense competition flared. Between 1946 and 1951 the number of whaling boats grew from 15 factory boats serviced by 129 catch boats to 19 factory boats serviced by 263 catchers. The season contracted from 112 to 64 days, but stocks of whales continued to decline (Dobson 1996).

The commission established national quotas in 1961 and the season expanded back to 115 days. Whaling became economically unrewarding by the 1970s, and publicly unpopular.

Demand outpaces supply and prices rise when resources become scarce. Rising prices increase the incentive to exploit the stock further. These are typical patterns of market forces, and they are clearly inadequate to ensure sustainable supply. The competition for unprotected resources is compounded by the capital investments made by the participants; in the case of the whalers, they have purchased a vessel. Return on investment requires a continuous source of income. To maximize their profit, it may be better to exploit stock to extinction and invest the short-term profit elsewhere.

Dobson provides a simple example: Assume there are 200,000 blue whales in the Antarctic. A sustainable harvest would be to catch 5 percent of the whales annually. If each is worth $7,000, the annual yield from harvest would be $70,000,000. On the other hand, if all 200,000 whales are harvested in just one year, the value of the catch is $140 billion. If this were invested at 10 percent, the annual income would be $140 million—double that of sustainable extraction (Dobson 1996). Thus capitalization often encourages overexploitation.

As a result, the free market cannot sustain biodiversity on its own. The logical conclusion is that government intervention with laws and policy is needed. However, most biological resources are exploited so fast that needed legislation is proposed only when the resource is almost beyond recovery, when its rarity is increasing its commodity value, and when it is most expensive to save (Dobson 1996).

Economists are working on developing new models to incorporate the environment and biodiversity adequately. However, it is a challenging task given the amount of disagreement on how to set values on species, on biodiversity, and on ecosystem (natural) services. Utility is currently defined as personal satisfaction of some economic desire. While economic theory allows for the satisfaction of some future needs, it does so in a flawed way. Today's models do not adequately address intergenerational equity—the question of benefits to present versus future generations. The goal must be to bring both future human generations and other species to the decision-making table.

One method often discussed is "green accounting." This form of accounting includes deductions in gross domestic product calculations for reductions in natural resource quantities and for degradations in natural resource quality (e.g., soil fertility, riparian erosion, water and air pollution). Several countries have started to use this approach, including Costa Rica, France, Norway, Canada, and the Netherlands.

In Costa Rica, for example, after its GDP was adjusted for natural resources losses, growth was estimated at 7 percent less than without the adjustment. In Indonesia, the average growth in GDP is 7.1 percent, but with natural resources accounting it is 4 percent. In the United States, conventional GDP was 2.04 percent per capita between 1970 and 1980. When these numbers were adjusted for environmental problems, the GDP became 0.14 percent per capita (Siwolop 1994).

Paul Hawken of the Natural Step–U.S., a consulting firm for industry on biodiversity, suggests: "We need to try a natural capitalistic system; put nature on the balance sheet." But, he cautions, "trying to monetize ecosystem services doesn't work" (Hawken 1997). The Natural Step is an international movement that began in Sweden in 1989. It is devoted to reducing society's impact on the environment and to promoting a sustainable future (CESD 1999). Hawken also points out that nature is not a commodity but a flow, a process, a cycling.

Hawken identifies the disconnect between industry and nature and between the economic and natural systems as the traditional need to overcome whatever is in short supply, whatever is a limiting factor. Economic philosophy requires that we invest in reducing limiting factors.

Dobson defines three ways to assign value to biodiversity:

1. commodity value (value of a product where one is evident)
2. amenity value (value of species existence in improving our lives)
3. moral, or intrinsic, value (value because it exists)

A currently popular method for assessing amenity value is called contingent evaluation. Economists survey people and ask how much they would be willing to pay to protect species, independent of any use. One problem with this approach is that values decrease by type of species, plunging to almost nothing for invertebrates. Another approach is to calculate the value of the world market for commodities and services provided by biodiversity—for example, those deriving from tropical rain forests, temperate forests, fisheries, mineral mining, pharmacological plants and animals, and ecotourism.

There are likely to be significant unexplored values of species as commodities. Given that we have only described about 20 percent of the existing species, using Robert May's conservative estimate of 7 million species, what values exist that we do not even know about yet? Pharmacological value provides a good example. Less than 1 percent of known species of plants have been examined for medicinal properties. So far one out of every 125 plant species studied has produced a major drug at an estimated U.S. market value of around $200 million a year (Dobson 1996). The overwhelming majority of prescription drugs used at present in the United States are based on natural products. This number could be higher outside the United States, because U.S. Food and Drug Administration regulations restrict the entry of new drugs.

Biological prospecting is an emerging industry. Merck and Company, a large pharmaceutical firm, has signed an agreement with the government of

Costa Rica to encourage biological prospecting for drugs in the country's forests. With biological prospecting, however, comes the problem of compensation to the host country and its indigenous peoples for any new products discovered.

This is the reason the international Convention on Biological Diversity put such emphasis on the equitable distribution of the benefits of "bioprospecting." Since most pharmaceutical companies synthesize the plant or animal properties that can be used as drugs, rather than harvesting the actual plants, there is no system for sharing the profits. Dobson suggests granting intellectual property rights to indigenous people so that they would receive royalties on sales. Drug companies obviously are not enthusiastic about that suggestion.

Ecotourism is a powerful way to make biodiversity pay. The United States sends 5 million ecotourists overseas each year, who spend $2,000–3,000 each (Dobson 1996). The industry is not problem-free; many parks still undervalue their resource, and there are costs associated with such tourism—damage done by vehicle and foot traffic and hidden costs to the wildlife itself. Nevertheless, many countries are enjoying significant national income from their wildlife resources, and several rely heavily on this type of income.

Another biodiversity benefit comes in the form of relief from national debt. Debt-for-nature swaps were conceived by Tom Lovejoy, then of the World Wildlife Fund, later with the Smithsonian Institution and World Bank. The idea provides a way of buying land to be set aside as nature reserves, and the swaps were designed to relax the stranglehold of debt on developing countries and to reverse the unsustainable use of tropical forests. The first debt-for-nature swap occurred in July 1987 in Bolivia, when Conservation International purchased $650,000 of Bolivia's debt for $100,000. In exchange, Bolivia agreed to set aside an additional 3.7 million acres of tropical forest, extending the existing Beni Biosphere Reserve, and to commit $250,000 in local currency to manage it (Dobson 1996). Other swaps have occurred around the world since then.

The flip side of value in the economic world is cost. One frequent complaint about protecting species is the cost of doing so. There is a public perception that it is extremely costly to protect endangered species. Perhaps exacerbating that perception is the fact that the longer it takes to identify and list an endangered species, the more it will cost to save that species, . However, congressional appropriations tell the real story about species protection expenditures.

Appropriations

There is almost unanimous concurrence that the Endangered Species Act has always been underfunded. It is easy to complain that insufficient research is done on prelisting, listing, critical habitat, and recovery planning research; but the reality is that there has never been enough funding to support sufficient research. The FWS and NMFS have had to set priorities on species from the onset of their task of protecting them because of low funding. Simultaneously, the number of species in need of protection has increased at a far more rapid rate than has the funding to support protection.

Dobson cites a total cumulative congressional appropriation for the Endangered Species Act between 1973 and 1995 of $337 million (the cost of a single jet fighter). The Office of the Inspector General of the United States has estimated the cost to achieve full recovery of all species to be $4.6 billion over a ten-year period. With annual appropriations to the Fish and Wildlife Service running less than $92 million, it would take fifty years to recover all species, *if* no other species were identified as threatened or endangered and *if* appropriations continued at the same pace. Political pressure on annual federal expenditures with the appropriations also has produced odd results. For example, in 1990, more than 50 percent of allotted funding was spent on eleven species; at the same time, there were no expenditures for 114 listed species.

In 1990, the estimated cost to research a candidate species for listing was $60,000. At that time there were 700 species on the category one candidate list awaiting listing. To research them all would have cost $36 million. The Fish and Wildlife Service's total budget that year to research listings, list, consult with other agencies, enforce the law, compensate states for their contributions, develop recovery plans, and so forth was $55 million (Adler and Hager 1992).

This is not to claim that there have not been instances when a significant amount of money has been spent. Dobson cites a one-time expenditure of $64 million to purchase conservation land for the red-cockaded woodpecker. The cumulative amount of money spent on the northern spotted owl probably exceeds the one-time expense on the red-cockaded woodpecker. However, much of that expense can be attributed to refusal to work with the recommendations of the various task forces appointed to study the situation. A General Accounting Office (GAO) report released by Representative Don Young in late December 1996 found that costs of species recovery, based on fifty-eight complete species recovery plans, ranged from $145,000 for the White River spindace fish to $153.8 million for the green sea and loggerhead turtles. The GAO cautioned that the estimates were assembled from only eighty-eight species in fifty-eight recovery plans, out of roughly four hundred recovery plans, and were focused on those species facing greater threats and having the best chances for recovery. The GAO noted that costs would likely be lower for the "lower-priority" species not studied. Furthermore, the cost estimates were "highly subjective, based usually on the 'best guesses' of the plans' authors and not on rigorous analysis" (*ESA Action* 1996b). The GAO also noted that it is important to remember that dollars spent on recovery return more than species survival.

According to Campbell (1991:135), congressional appropriations for the ESA climbed from $4.6 million in 1974 to $22.2 million in 1981. In 1982 appropriations plunged to $17.8 million then moved up to $33.6 million by 1989. Recalling Lynn Greenwalt's 1977 request to Congress for $115 million, and considering the continued increase in demand for listings and recovery of species, funding has been completely inadequate. The Reagan Administration viewed the ESA as an impediment to progress and used the budget process to undermine it (Ernst 1991). The huge drop in funding (minus 22 percent) in 1982, the first budget year of that administration, illustrates this attitude.

Funding for the National Marine Fisheries Service for ESA implementation is combined with that for implementing the Marine Mammal Protection Act. Hence these appropriations are not directly comparable to those for FWS. Average annual appropriations for NMFS have hovered around $4 million.

Other agencies involved in protecting species include the Forest Service, Bureau of Land Management, and National Park Service. None has been adequately funded to protect species on the lands under its management (Campbell 1991), yet the 1987 record, to use one year as an example, was 153 listed species on USFS lands and 140 on BLM lands. Campbell also noted that while FWS spending on the ESA, excluding land acquisition, increased three times faster than the rate of inflation in the 1970s and 1980s, the rise in listings outpaced the spending.

Land acquisition expenditures are funded from the Land and Water Conservation Fund. Annual acquisitions grew in the 1970s and at a slower rate in the 1980s. Congress often funded this program over the objections of the administration (Campbell 1991). Land management was another problem: there continued to be insufficient funds to manage the lands acquired.

A *Seattle Times* editorial in April 1995 sums up the appropriations situation: "Congress tends to set lofty goals without providing the dollars needed to achieve them. Better science, ecosystem management, incentives and takings compensation will be costly. If the Republicans balk . . ., their reforms ring hollow."

Not surprisingly, appropriations continued to decline with the 104th Congress. As already described, the battle of the budget lasted well into the 1996 fiscal year before a settlement was reached. FWS and NMFS had been unable to list any species because of the moratorium passed early in 1995. The 1996 appropriations bills made the listing moratorium worse by eliminating prelisting research to determine whether a species should be placed on the endangered and/or threatened species list. The final 1996 budget did contain some prelisting allocation. Overall, the FY 1997 endangered species budget was 23 percent lower than that of the previous year. Fortunately, the Congress did not continue the downward trend with allocations for endangered species for FY 1998 and ensuing years, in spite of ongoing antipathy toward the law.

Variations in annual budgets and the political activities that swirled around each year's appropriation in the 1990s created a chaotic environment for the lead ESA agencies. It is frankly amazing and largely due to the strength of Interior Secretary Bruce Babbitt and Directors Mollie Beattie and Jaime Rappaport Clark that FWS accomplished for species in this decade as much as it did. The total FY 1995 species budget, for example, was $77.9 million. It sank to $60.3 million in FY 1996, with drops in all categories—for prelisting, listing, consultation, and Section 6 (cooperative agreements with states). The budget roller-coaster moved upward in FY 1997 and 1998 with $81.6 and $91.2 million appropriated, respectively. Nevertheless, the total allocated funds were still a small portion of the need for the task.

The economics of biodiversity and endangered species is a hard spot, beset with many opinions but equipped with little effective methodology to account for the value of biodiversity to society or to protect it from continued destruction. It would seem feasible to develop reasonable valuations for ecosystem services such as flood control and pollution cleanup. There are non-natural equivalencies with associated costs. Other ecosystem services, like plant pollination and climate control, are more difficult to value. However, there are again some equivalencies—emissions control expense might provide a surrogate set of costs for climate control, and fertilizer manufacturer and seed company costs might offer surrogates for valuing pollination services. It is harder yet to assign value to individual species. Most scientists shy away from the concept of intrinsic valuation. Nevertheless, each species has an intrinsic value that probably cannot be captured in terms of monetary units. Perhaps what is needed are two equivalent value systems, one biological and life sustaining and the other economic and subject to cost-benefit analyses. It will take a societal consensus on values to prioritize the ultimate comparison of biological values versus economic values.

As Stan Shetler (1991:41) said, "Focus on species as commodities, rather than as elements of a natural system and process . . . tends to foster a biotechnological fix-it-approach of *ex-situ* conservation and propagation." It will also take societal consensus to convince Congress to provide adequate appropriations to do the job called for by the ESA and to pass more comprehensive legislation to protect habitats. Again, Shetler (1991:41) summed the issue up succinctly: "We need an ethic that gives ecological value a competitive edge or at least parity with economic values."

Part Four

Resolution

Chapter Ten

Ecosystem Management

Given the current condition of the forests, there is no way the
agencies could comply with the environmental laws without
planning on an ecosystem basis. —Judge William L. Dwyer, 1994

IN 1987, THE OFFICE of Technology Assessment estimated that at least twenty-eight federal laws address the maintenance of biodiversity in some form. These authorities are enforced by a multitude of federal agencies with little or no interagency coordination (Norse 1993). The ESA fosters single-species management practices that are implemented only when the species is declared threatened or endangered. We cannot adequately protect species without managing them in the context of their larger ecosystems, and that requires a collaborative practice called ecosystem management.

In 1991 Congress asked the National Research Council (NRC) to review the scientific aspects of the ESA and whether the act is scientifically capable of protecting species and their habitats. The NRC is the principal operating agency of the National Academy of Sciences and the National Academy of Engineering, providing services to government, the public, and the scientific and engineering communities. Fifty-six scientists and engineers on three committees are listed as participants in the ESA evaluation, along with the committee staffs.

According to the NRCs 1995 report to Congress on the validity of the science on which the ESA is based, species are members of communities that are in turn part of an ecosystem. Species are an intrinsic part of such ecological processes as community succession, the rhythm of natural disturbance, the waxing and waning of predator and prey populations, and the cycling of soil nutrients (NRC 1995).

Single-species management is useful as a crisis discipline. Ecosystem management, on the other hand, is a conservation discipline. As noted by J. Stan

Rowe, professor emeritus of the University of Saskatchewan, "Organisms do not stand on their own; they evolve and exist in the context of ecological systems that confer those properties called life" (quoted in Barnes 1993:17). Ecosystem management focuses on the landscape and all its resident species of all biological kingdoms. It is a process that can prevent species from becoming threatened or endangered and that can protect species in population sizes that secure a measure of genetic diversity. It protects against the loss of all components of biodiversity.

"The goal of an ecosystem-based approach to managing natural resources is to maintain biological diversity by recognizing the value of protecting an array of biological communities and habitat types within a larger landscape context" (Hunter 1990, as cited in NRC 1995:160). Ecosystem-focused programs are probably most useful when implemented before individual elements of biological communities are in dire trouble. Among the many advantages to the approach is that species are viewed in the context of surrounding land uses.

For some species, such as the grizzly bear, habitat and ecosystem are almost identical because of the huge range of the animal. For other species, habitat could be as small as a snag where birds, small mammals, and insects nest, breed, and find shelter. A small pond in a meadow often functions as the habitat of numerous aquatic and amphibian life forms. A vernal pool is a temporal habitat that teems with life few only for a few months in the spring.

While more and more ESA recovery plans are written for multiple species protection, most still focus on single-species management. Habitat Conservation Plans often cover more than one species and are evolving into a modified form of ecosystem planning.

Federal land management agencies have adopted and are beginning to implement the ecosystem approach. The Interagency Ecosystem Management Task Force, established in 1993, recommended this change in federal land management strategy in 1995. Now, environmental and land management statutes must be updated to reflect the more advanced practices. The ecosystem approach provides a holistic ecological framework for conserving and managing natural segments of the planet. At its best, it conserves rare and endangered species, preserves and maintains ecological and biological diversity, and in time may restore natural landscapes. In ecosystem management the focus shifts from animals, plants, and soils to four-dimensional landscape and waterscape ecosystems (Barnes 1993). The fourth dimension is time. Furthermore, "By protecting and managing representative ecosystems, we can maintain habitat for as yet undescribed or inadequately inventoried species" (Albert 1993:23).

Edward LaRoe (1993) provides three practical management reasons to support the ecosystem approach:

The increasing complexity of resource management today requires new tools, new concepts, and new ideas.

The ecosystem approach encourages land managers to operate in context of land uses.

The approach offers improved cost effectiveness in management activities. With single-species management, huge sums are spent on a few species (LaRoe cites $9 million spent on the northern spotted owl in 1990 alone), and little or nothing is expended on the vast majority

While ecosystem management has many benefits and it is a critical practice for protecting biodiversity, conversion to it will not be easy. Significant barriers include current federal agency practices and weak public communication and the lack of sufficient scientific knowledge about the nature of the ecosystems and their constituents. The barriers are surmountable, but it will require dedication and persistence to achieve this.

The ESA has afforded some protection to endangered ecosystems from the beginning. To protect the highly endangered old growth forests in the Pacific Northwest from clear-cut logging, environmentalists used the northern spotted owl as the flagship species and as a surrogate for old growth trees and requested its listing. The owl population was in fact declining dramatically, so the species truly needed protection. However, the timber industry, which had its logging activities curtailed, and the loggers, who lost work, criticized the use of the owl as a surrogate for the old growth trees. The ESA does not distinguish between life stages of a species even though life stages such as tree saplings or old growth trees contribute different services to their ecosystems. If it did distinguish, then the old growth Douglas firs would have been listed in addition to the owl, and the impact would have been the same for the timber industry.

The Single-Species Management Approach: ESA Recovery Plans

Listed species recovery plans are "the process by which the decline of a threatened or endangered species is arrested or reversed and threats to its survival are neutralized" (NRC 1995:63). Single-species management has existed for centuries in agriculture, forestry, and some fisheries. Monoculture farming is a form of single-species management. Planting the same crop year after year has proven costly in terms of soil fertility and crop productivity. Meffe and Carroll (1997) note that the common private forest management practice in the Southeast is conversion of mixed-age hardwoods and pine to a pine monoculture. While this practice may improve economic return on the forest, it changes the biological composition of the forest. Managing for a single species can lead to maximizing the production of a few species without regard to the health of the community or ecosystem in which they reside. High densities of one species may cause serious habitat degradation. Species introductions can also be very damaging to an ecosystem. When the western rainbow trout was brought into eastern hatcheries, this new fish devastated eastern brook trout populations with western pathogens unknown in the east.

Recovery plans for endangered and threatened species are narrowly focused on the target species. Without a broader, ecosystem perspective, two different species plans can conflict when the targeted species are linked to one another in ecosystems. However, the NRC evaluation found that "few well-documented cases [existed] where management practices focusing on particular species . . . result in direct conflict with the needs of another" (NRC 1995:90).

Therefore, under current policies the greatest potential for conflicts arises when habitat reductions themselves are the reason for endangerment and when the habitats of listed species are overlapping. Avoiding this problem requires that protected areas be large enough to allow the existence of habitat mosaics (interconnected patches of usable habitat) and dynamic processes of change within these areas. Multispecies plans should be devised to ensure that appropriate habitat mosaics and ecological networks are protected.

The findings of the Tear study (Tear et al. 1995), which was based on 314 approved recovery plans representing 344 species as of August 1991, were disturbing. To assess the type and extent of biological information in the recovery plans, the Tear group used the four major biological guidelines: species distribution, species abundance, population demography, and population dynamics. The study also looked at the time between species listing and approval of a recovery plan. It compared the differences, if any, between plans for threatened and endangered species. Finally, the study compared the quality of the plans for three different groupings of taxa: plants and animals; invertebrates and vertebrates; and among vertebrates, mammals, birds, fish, and reptiles and amphibians.

The Tear team found that the plans generally contained inadequate biological information to guide decision making: 81 percent were missing some critical information. No appreciable distinction was found between recovery plans for threatened and endangered species. The average time between listing and recovery plan approval was 6.4 years. If plans are not implemented expeditiously, endangered and threatened species are further jeopardized, and human activities are also disrupted because individuals' plans are put on hold (NRC 1995).

Tear and colleagues also found that the stipulated recovery goals were too low to achieve viable populations of the listed species. They found lack of biological knowledge a barrier to effective recovery. Available data suggested that species with recovery plans were still at risk of extinction. The scientists found that depending on the choice of minimum criteria of endangerment, the population-based recovery goals in recovery plans would not achieve recovery for 60 to 73 percent of vertebrate species. Less than 20 percent of the species' recovery plans included specific time periods for downlisting or delisting; only 9 percent of species had target recovery dates. Although 92 percent of the plans mentioned public education, only 18 percent reported that public education programs were conducted, and less than 2 percent recommended that public attitude assessment be conducted.

The National Research Council found that there was a large backlog of recovery plans. In 1988, ten years after these plans became law, only 56 percent of listed species had plans and another 18 percent were in preparation. In 1992, 61 percent of species had approved plans, but by 1993 that number dropped to 53 percent because of the acceleration in listing actions. By the end of March 1995, there were 411 approved plans covering 513 species, 54 percent of the 956 U.S. species listed at the time (NRC 1995). By late 1999, 77 percent of the 1,197 U.S. species listed had recovery plans.

The Tear study further found a bias favoring animals over plants, vertebrates over invertebrates, and birds and mammals over fish, reptiles, and amphibians. Yet the average time lapse between listing and approval of a recovery plan was shorter for plants (4.1 years) than for animals (11.3 years) and shorter for invertebrates (6.3 years) than for vertebrates (9.4 years). The Tear team did not indicate why the time lapse difference, but it certainly begs the question of whether the recovery plans for plants and invertebrates were done with less care.

Based on these disturbing findings, the National Research Council (NRC) recommended that the Fish and Wildlife Service convene a working group to develop guidelines for recovery objectives and criteria. The guidelines needed to identify activities that were consistent with a habitat-based approach to recovery. Other guidance requirements were a logical approach to analyzing ecological and genetic data; use of demographic modeling; and the specification of further research needs for the species. Determination of the target species' position in the food web—in networks of interaction that include prey, potential mates, consumers, competitors, pollinators, dispersers, and so forth—also were required in developing recovery plans and goals. (Congress demonstrated that it took note of these recommendations in the ESA reauthorization bills offered in the 105th and 106th Congresses.)

The NRC recommended using estimates of the probabilities of achieving goals over specified periods, expressed both in years and in number of generations of the organism, and that these be included in every recovery plan. Monitoring is key for evaluating plan success and for adaptive management. Evaluation of the long-term and irreversible impacts of each management alternative should be conducted to evaluate effectively the potential for species recovery. The NRC also emphasized the need for prioritizing recovery activities defined in each plan.

These findings clearly demonstrate that recovery plans, the formal embodiment of single-species management, are not working well. The primary problem is lack of agency resources compounded by political foot-dragging. Only congressional appropriation can ensure sufficient resources. Even then, the FWS will need to update its biological, ecological, and risk management skills.

Critical Habitat Designation

The Endangered Species Act calls for the designation of critical habitat, "the specific areas within the geographical area occupied by the species, . . . on which are found those physical or biological features (I) essential to the conservation of the species and (II) which may require special management considerations or protection" (16 U.S.C.A. §1532). In practice, critical habitat has seldom been defined. The NRC found that critical habitat had been designated for less than 20 percent of all species listed in the United States. Once an area is declared to be critical habitat for an endangered species, it is excluded from almost all human activities.

Most scientists believe that some immediate habitat protection step must be taken upon listing of a species because the minimum delay before a recovery plan delineates the management steps necessary for recovery is a year, and the average found by Tear and colleagues was over six years. The NRC concluded that "some core amount of essential habitat should be designated for protection at the time of listing a species as endangered as an emergency, stop-gap measure" (NRC 1995:61). It suggested using the designation "survival habitat" to convey more clearly that such habitat is absolutely necessary to protect the listed species from harm during the time it takes to research and develop a recovery plan. Further, the NRC recommended that no economic evaluation should be involved in the designation of survival habitat. This designation would automatically expire with the adoption of a recovery plan in which the formal designation of critical habitat would occur (NRC 1995).

The Habitat Conservation Plan

When an endangered species is present on their land, private landowners wishing to develop or use the land are required by law to conduct a biological assessment to determine what activities can take place and where without jeopardizing the species. The assessment must include alternatives considered and the impacts of each alternative. Few HCPs were drafted before 1994. In fact, from 1982 to July 1994, the FWS issued only thirty-three incidental take permits and twelve permit amendments (the results of an approved HCP). Many of these were for very small projects rather than full-scale HCPs (NRC 1995). By September 1995, there were more than 100 approved HCPs. By January 1999, 236 HCPs were approved and another 200 were in development.

In spite of controversial elements and valid concerns over how HCPs affect endangered species, they are a significant step in the direction of broadscale planning. They move toward ecosystem planning and some, like southern California's NCCP, are ecosystem based. Since about 59 percent of U.S. land is privately owned and the ESA provides the framework to encourage creative partnerships between the private sector and governments for species and habitat protection, HCPs are important to species conservation.

The NRC endorsed developing regional habitat conservation plans. The committee declared that the plans should address multiple species across multiple habitats, where possible. However, more Fish and Wildlife Service guidance on what HCPs contain was necessary, as was advice on developing biological data, demographic and genetic analyses, habitat requirements of the species, and reserve design, and on monitoring over time the impact of assumptions made in the plan.

The NRC said better guidelines were needed to describe a scientific program for HCPs that would be specific, efficient, and cost-effective. HCPs should not replace a recovery plan; they should be evaluated using the existing FWS/NMFS recovery plan. If the recovery plan were not yet done, the information from the HCP could be incorporated into the planning process. The NRC recommended specific areas where guidance was needed — for development of a reserve design with explicit management goals and objectives; for identification of techniques and data needed to perform population-viability analyses; and for assessing the likelihood of persistence of the species. They recommended guidance for describing management options and for discussing the use of research and monitoring activities to adjust management in response to changes in population sizes and environmental variables. They said guidance was needed for the application of risk analyses in consideration of plan alternatives and for describing how these exercises should be applied in the land use planning process.

The Ecosystem Management Approach

The ecosystem is the biotic, or living, community and its abiotic, or non-living, environment. There are many types of ecosystems, and often several interact in a landscape. The word *ecosystem* describes the intimate linkage of organisms with their habitats and the physical conditions, nonliving resources, and other interacting organisms in those habitats. For example, wetlands, upland forest, and riparian areas are ecosystems. There can be multiple habitats within an ecosystem or just one. However, in everyday usage *habitat* and *ecosystem* are often used interchangeably.

The *landscape* is usually a larger physical area and may include all of these ecosystem types linked by biotic and ecological processes. A desert is a landscape that may have a riparian ecosystem along a river going through the desert or a vernal pool habitat during monsoon season. Linking ecological processes include migration, plant-pollinator interactions, gene sharing among meta-populations (divided populations of the same species), and ecosystem services such as natural pest control and removal of water pollution.

Meffe and Carroll describe four principles of good conservation management. First, critical ecological processes and biodiversity composition are maintained. Second, external threats are minimized and benefits are maximized. Third, evolutionary processes are conserved—species cannot be managed as if they are static over time. Fourth, management is adaptive and minimally intrusive.

An ecosystem is four-dimensional: it includes the land (length, width, depth) or water area and depth, the surrounding atmosphere, and time. An ecosystem has different forms or functions at different times in its life span. It may be cyclical by season; and/or it may be dependent on disturbance regimes such as periodic fires, floods, or landslides that change the ecological successional patterns. It also may be home to both diurnal and nocturnal species that change its functions between night and day. An ecosystem may support specific life stages of animals. For example, many sea turtles deposit their eggs on sandy beaches; the females then return to the sea. The hatchlings go to the sea as soon as they hatch. Sea turtles would go extinct without beach ecosystems to support their reproduction.

"An ecosystem approach conserves and manages the structure and function of an entire ecosystem rather than individually managing the organisms of interest" (Lapin and Barnes 1995:1149). The ecosystem management approach conserves biodiversity in all its forms.

The Clinton Administration established the Interagency Ecosystem Management Task Force (cited as Task Force) to adopt "a proactive approach ensuring a sustainable economy and a sustainable environment through ecosystem management" (Task Force 1995:1). In its 1995 report entitled *The Ecosystem Approach: Healthy Ecosystems and Sustainable Economies*, the task force stated that ecosystem management "is goal driven, and it is based on a *collaboratively developed vision* of desired future conditions that integrates ecological, economic, and social factors [emphasis mine]. It is applied within a geographic framework defined primarily by ecological boundaries. The goal of the ecosystem approach is to restore and sustain the health, productivity, and biological diversity of ecosystems and the overall quality of life through a natural resource management approach that is fully integrated with social and economic goals" (1995:3).

There are many definitions of ecosystem management. All include some measure of the following elements: a team environment composed of representatives of all the key stakeholders, the balancing of socioeconomic and environmental requirements, perpetuation of the basic and endemic ecosystem processes, maintenance of viable populations of all native species, and maintenance of natural disturbance regimes. Meffe and Carroll (1997:367) summarize it well: "Ecosystem management is an approach to maintaining or restoring the composition, structure, and function of natural and modified ecosystems for the goal of long-term sustainability. It is based on a collaboratively developed vision of desired future conditions that integrates ecological, socioeconomic, and institutional perspectives, applied within a geographic framework defined primarily by natural ecological boundaries."

Single-species management may be a component of the broader ecosystem management of any given area, but it is not a substitute. It is also important to note that ecosystems tend to remain in nonequilibrium and many systems rely on disturbances for survival. For example, in some ecosystems periodic fires remove excess fuel and create open space for new herbaceous plants to seed and sprout.

One of the benefits of ecosystem management is that the necessary research can be easier and less costly than single-species research. Albert (1993) shows how scientists in Michigan, for example, found a good deal of information about the ecosystem of Kirtland's warbler and the Karner blue butterfly from land records at the General Land Office. From these records, they found studies of glacial landforms, county soil surveys, and early vegetation and forest stand cover information. These records also shed light on disturbance regimes and on how the land and the hydrologic system had changed.

Ecosystem management cares for all species. It is generally easier to save a species before it has become endangered. Most endangered species are in small populations and are therefore subject to a host of variable factors as well as demographic and genetic problems. It is a continuing challenge to protect endangered and threatened plants and invertebrates. With single-species management, closing the defined critical habitat (if is defined) is the only way truly to protect these species. That is impossible to do on private lands and extremely difficult and unrealistic on public lands. With ecosystem management, a coalition of stakeholders determines the ecological importance of the species and gets the local public to support the protection methods chosen.

Quigley and McDonald (1993) noted that managing ecosystems requires knowledge of the relationships, interdependencies, structures, and functions of the component biotic and abiotic parts. Layered on top of these are government needs to meet the objectives stipulated by legislative and executive mandates. Societal objectives must be met through a complex process of scientific, economic, and political credibility tests. Nevertheless, the question of sustainability must be a major component of discussions for setting ecosystem management goals.

The task force (1995:8) concluded that the ecosystem management approach was right for federal land management in spite of some considerable hurdles that had to be overcome. "As a matter of policy, the federal government should provide leadership in and cooperate with activities that foster the ecosystem approach to natural resource management, regulation, and assistance. Federal agencies should ensure that they utilize their authorities in a way that facilitates, and does not pose barriers to, the ecosystem approach."

The task force said that managed ecosystems should be defined on natural boundaries. However, a political consensus definition based on natural boundaries is also workable. In almost every situation, a practical management area definition can be determined. It does not have to be based on precise, scientifically valid delineation; the stakeholders may determine it, but it should be broad enough to encompass the natural factors necessary to the health of the natural system and to solve the problems.

The task force defined the ecosystem approach as a *process*, not a mapping exercise. It detailed the following necessary functions:

1. consideration of all relevant and identifiable ecological consequences

2. improved coordination among federal agencies

3. formation of partnerships among all appropriate federal, state, and local governments, tribes, landowners, and other stakeholders, such as evironmental, agricultural, and industry groups

4. communication and education of the general public on the issues, goals, and strategies

5. efficient and cost-effective implementation of federal responsibilities

6. use of the best available science and ongoing interaction with the scientific community

7. improvement of information and data management

8. employment of adaptive management, including the flexibility and willingness to use failure as a learning tool

In brief, the ecosystem management approach requires coordination, cooperation, and communication—the three Cs of collaboration.

Long-term monitoring is a critical scientific tool for conserving ecosystems. It helps distinguish natural and anthropogenic fluctuations within the ecosystem. It also is the primary means of evaluating management assumptions and modifying them if they are inaccurate. It is a key source of ongoing research on species interactions, species requirements, and temporal fluctuations. The *Global Biodiversity Assessment* (Watson and Heywood 1995) recommended monitoring in three-year cycles. Fifteen long-term ecological research sites are currently being monitored in the United States, including terrestrial, lake, stream, and wetland ecosystems. Studies include species inventorying, nutrient cycling, plant productivity, population dynamics, and changes in plant distribution. Biodiversity studies link with population, community, ecosystem, and landscape-level ecological studies. The data are being collected in five core areas: primary (plant) production, disturbance regimes, population and community ecology, biogeochemical cycling, and organic matter accumulation. The purpose of these studies is to produce guidelines by ecosystem type for ecosystem management groups to use. However, the guidelines will not replace the need for ongoing monitoring to assess the success of the local effort.

Quigley and McDonald (1993) described the elements of the Forest Service's ecosystem management strategic plan: public involvement, communications, and partnerships; ecosystem characterization, mapping, and analysis; information management and decision support; implementation; monitoring, evaluation, and accountability; research and development; technology transfer, training, and education; and organization, program development, and budgeting.

The ecosystem approach was a significant change in federal government land management. The hurdles that needed to be cleared were substantial and remain so. The task force identified as significant hurdles the disparate missions, planning requirements, regional office structures, budgeting structures, and procedural requirements between agencies. Among them the Bureau of Land Management, Fish and Wildlife Service, and National Park Service (all agencies within the Department of the Interior) and the U.S. Forest Service (in the Department of Agriculture) manage 90 percent of public lands. The Department of Defense also manages a sizable amount of land and that management is divided among military branches. Even within the Department of the Interior, agencies have vastly different missions and management guidelines.

Other hurdles identified by the task force included the inconsistency and insufficiency of data and the lack of common access to the data that do exist. (This hurdle is not exclusive to government.) Agencies had not previously used the holistic approach, nor were their personnel trained in working with public and private stakeholders. The Federal Advisory Committee Act (FACA) is another impediment to stakeholder partnerships. This law procedurally restricts how federal agencies establish nonfederal partnerships and how they can receive outside advice. Public outreach has traditionally been a secondary or tertiary component of management, and when there was a budget crunch, that was the first budget item to go. Finally, there has often been a disconnect between scientists and policy decision makers. Scientists tend to state possibilities and findings without drawing conclusions that might be contradicted by ongoing research. Policy makers seek short, concise facts on which to make decisions and recommendations.

The picture was not totally bleak. The task force also identified activities that work well, such as creating interagency offices separate from but responsible to their parent agencies; regular communication and cost sharing between agencies; use of easements; and grant programs for working with other stakeholders.

Working Ecosystem Management Programs

A number of management projects have begun to use the ecosystem management approach. Some ecosystem management plans have been in existence for decades, such as the one for the Everglades system. However, until recently the Everglades system was managed to control the natural processes not to permit them. Some of the following examples started more or less spontaneously to address local problems and others were mandated from the top down. The success achieved in all these examples can be attributed to the three Cs of collaboration: coordination, cooperation, and communication.

Top-down Mandate: The Pacific Northwest Forest Plan

This plan was developed to resolve the bitter, high-visibility struggle under way in the Pacific Northwest involving the timber industry, its employees, the Forest Service, the BLM, the Fish and Wildlife Service, and environmentalists. The situation was so volatile that President Clinton stepped in to specify the resolution.

The plan is flexible and includes different management strategies for northern California than for western Oregon and Washington, where different logging practices were in place. The California spotted owl is a threatened species; the northern spotted owl and marbled murrelet indigenous to Oregon and Washington are endangered. There are often different recovery tactics applied for threatened and endangered species.

The five principles of the Pacific Northwest plan were:

Protect the long-term sustainability of forests, wildlife, and waterways.

Remember the human and economic dimensions of the problem.

Ensure that all efforts are scientifically sound, ecologically credible, and legally responsible.

Produce a predictable and sustainable level of timber sales and nontimber resources that will not degrade or destroy the environment.

Make sure the federal government works for and with the people.

These principles resulted in a new way of doing business in the Pacific Northwest. The plan created ecosystem-based management of 25 million acres of federal land, an economic assistance plan for displaced loggers and their families, and a blueprint for improved agency coordination (Task Force 1995). The top-down approach broke a difficult impasse. The team that created the plan created the solutions.

Private Initiative–Multiple Ownership: The Applegate Partnership

Inspired by two collaborators with opposite perspectives, Jack Shipley, an environmentalist, and Jim Neal, a logger, this partnership was formed in 1992 to manage a half-million-acre watershed in southwestern Oregon and northern California known as the Applegate Watershed. The BLM and the Forest Service owned roughly 70 percent of the area. Most of the balance was privately owned. Its twelve thousand residents desired "'healthy forests and healthy critters' as well as healthy humans" (Rolle, quoted in Meffe and Carroll 1997:612).

The two collaborators formed a board of directors that formulated and adopted a vision and goals for the watershed. The board included community residents, people affiliated with environmental groups, and representatives from timber, farming, and ranching interests as well as schools and natural resource agencies. Their motto was: "Practice trust—them is us!"

One of the board's first actions was to develop a set of meeting rules. Rules directed that personal agendas be checked at the door and that stakeholders must listen to each other and take all perspectives into consideration. Using a Geographic Information System (GIS) tool, a computer mapping program that overlays multiple data geographically and pictorially, the partnership merged maps of the area. Community residents were then trained to use the system and computers were made accessible to students and residents. The partnership focused on restoring the entire watershed while creating opportunities for local employment. It helped to repair and replant riparian areas on private property, installed fish screens, fenced off streams, and took out roads. It also helped a local feedlot owner restore riparian areas that the cattle had destroyed. The feedlot owner did not have sufficient funds to restore the area himself, so to keep him and the jobs he represented in business, the partnership stepped in to help rather than to shut him down.

"By opening up the bureaucratic processes, . . . agency personnel are gaining local knowledge, challenging traditional ways of doing business, generating more ideas and innovations, reaching better decisions, and shifting the 'we/they' mentality toward an 'us' perspective. . . . The partnership can be called a success simply because it has moved beyond the deeply entrenched animosity and polarity around the issues that had been so pervasive" (Rolle, in Meffe and Carroll 1997:616).

State Initiative: Mack Lake Basin, Michigan

At Mack Lake, studying an ecosystem provided critical information about an endangered species and how to protect it. Mack Lake Basin is in the north-central part of lower Michigan. The endangered Kirtland's warbler inhabited the jack pine and oak forest in a sandy outwash plain. Warbler populations had declined from 1,000 birds in 1961 to about 460 in 1981. These birds nest in stands of jack pine that are from eight to twenty years old. Dense patches of pines interspersed with numerous small openings characterize the ecosystem. The warblers colonize an area when the pines are from six to nine feet tall, and they leave the area when the trees grow tall enough to create a canopy that shades the openings.

In May 1980, a prescribed fire went out of control. This unplanned event provided an opportunity to study the landscape and the warblers' response to its diversity. The fires covered about twenty-four thousand acres surrounding Mack Lake in Oscoda County. A study of the landscape ecosystems within the burn area began in 1986 to determine what physiography, microclimate, soil, and vegetation might favor Kirtland's warbler colonization. The study goal was to determine which biological and physical ecosystems within the larger landscape were best suited to the warblers.

Scientists distinguished two major landscapes, a high-level outwash terrain and a low-level outwash area surrounding the lake itself. Warblers first returned to the area in 1986 when trees grown from seed were about seven years old. They recolonized the high-level terrain first. It was warmer and had more fertile soil. Gradually, over the six-year span of the study, the birds colonized the lower terrain in equal numbers. Fire has proven a good way to create appropriate habitat for this species. "The approach provides the understanding of whole landscapes such that the best areas for warbler management could be selected to maintain a high warbler population" (Barnes 1993:19).

Private Owner Initiative–Federal Participation:
Malpai Borderlands Group

The Malpai Borderlands span a million acres in southeastern Arizona and southwestern New Mexico. The area includes the Animas Valley and mountain range and a small population of about one hundred people. Most of the land is privately owned (59 percent). The federal government (BLM and Forest Service) owns about 34 percent of it, and the balance is state-owned. The predominant land use is cattle ranching. To avoid federally mandated land use practices, the area landowners formed the Malpai Borderlands Group. In addition to the ranchers, the group included scientists, federal and state agency personnel, and other interested stakeholders. Their goal is "to restore and maintain the natural processes that create and protect a healthy, unfragmented landscape to support a diverse, flourishing community of human, plant, and animal life in our Borderlands Region" (McDonald, quoted in Meffe and Carroll 1995:21).

The group identified two major threats to the ecosystem: suppression of fire, and development. The first threat required the most adjustment. Historically, the landowners had tried to avoid fires. The group completed the first prescribed burn in the area's history. The burn required a wilderness area study and coordination among four private landowners, five government agencies in two states and in Mexico, while adhering to NEPA regulations.

The Malpai Borderlands Group also tried to protect a population of Chiricahuan leopard frogs in a joint effort with the states and began a program of

"grass banking." Through the grass bank, ranchers can access grass on another member's land in exchange for conservation action of equal value on their own. "Most important of all," writes Bill McDonald, area rancher and group member, "we are working together, creating as we go a structure of support for actions that promote the biological diversity of our area and the long-term sustainability of our ranching livelihoods" (in Meffe and Carroll 1997:22).

This effort has not been problem-free. In a speech to the National Academy of Science's October 1997 Conference on Nature and Human Society, McDonald reported a hitch in the progress made to protect the Malpai ecosystem. In spite of local efforts to protect the Chiricahuan leopard frog, environmental groups pushed for it to be listed as endangered. The private landowners feared that a declaration of critical habitat for the frog would shut off all human land use. When the Enviros succeeded in getting the frog listed under the ESA, members of the Malpai Borderlands Group were angered. The group's ecosystem management activity halted. McDonald expressed faith that they would get past the hurdle, but the reaction to the listing demonstrates the attitude of private landowners toward the ESA and any federal regulations restricting land use or imposing controls on private owners.

McDonald stated that "a tendency to use big government, in the mistaken belief that government alone can tackle massive issues such as biodiversity loss, will add conservation biology to the growing list of buzzwords abhorred by many rural landowners and thus make it an impediment to the very effort it represents" (in Meffe and Carroll 1995:21). It was creative collaboration with federal participation but without federal control that worked for the Malpai Group.

Ecosystem Management and the ESA

Individual species can best be protected by managing them in the context of their larger ecosystems. Ecosystem management protects species from *becoming* threatened or endangered. Current federal practices use the ecosystem approach for managing public lands. The ESA must be modified to reflect that reality and to integrate the ecosystem management approach into the protection of endangered and threatened species.

Because of the geographic and bureaucratic scope of the ecosystem management approach, statutory affirmation or codification of the current administration's policy most appropriately belongs in a statute that codifies and pre-

scribes a national biodiversity protection policy. Nevertheless, changes to the current Endangered Species Act to incorporate ecosystem management would improve its effectiveness.

Ecosystem management benefits endangered and threatened species by protecting them in the context of their habitats and by safeguarding other species from the need to be listed for protection. Ecosystem management can also be applied to marine ecosystems. While federal agencies are in the process of adopting the ecosystem approach for management of the public lands under their control, state and private ecosystem management groups are forming around the country. Most groups include federal, state, and local government participation as well as private landowners involved in ranching and agriculture; perhaps in time they will include industry. The Department of Defense has also developed an ecosystem management approach, bringing military activity into the equation as well. Major habitat conservation plans such as California's NCCP and Texas's BCCP are early ecosystem management plans created primarily by developers and municipalities. Thus all walks of life are becoming involved. Ecosystem management represents a huge change from past land management practices and the hurdles are significant. The major complicating factor is cooperation among multiple owners (Quigley and McDonald 1993). Of almost equal importance is the cultural difference between private and public landowners. Other barriers include the initial expenses to acquire the necessary tools, such as research, data, mapping, conflict management skills, and more.

The Federal Advisory Committee Act poses difficulties for establishing nonfederal partnerships for federal agencies (Task Force 1995). Multiple federal, state, and local agencies have disparate missions and planning requirements. Each has a separate budget that does not lend itself to interagency coordination. These are large but not insurmountable hurdles. Another is the lack of sufficient scientific data on ecosystems and their constituents. Tough as they may be, all of these difficulties can be overcome, and there are ecosystem management coalitions operating today. Not the least of the benefits of ecosystem management is the potential evolution of human land use practices into what Aldo Leopold called a "land ethic." With a land ethic, people respect the land and treat it as the limited and valuable resource it is. Other ecosystem management benefits include realizing economic efficiencies in joint federal actions that minimize or eliminate duplicated effort and expense. Ecosystem management will also increase the bank of ecological, biological,

geological, and other scientific data and prevent further species endangerment because it includes all species in the ecosystem (vertebrates, invertebrates, plants, fungi, algae, and bacteria). Ecosystem management facilitates protecting the less charismatic species such as plants, invertebrates, and other kingdoms of life. Finally, collaboration between all land use endeavors and human perspectives avoids time-consuming controversy and fosters the ultimate goal of consensus for saving biodiversity and human quality of life.

Chapter Eleven

Antidote

> We have learned to our cost that development which destroys the
> environment eventually destroys development itself. And we have
> learned to our benefit that development that conserves the
> environment conserves also the fruits of development. There is,
> thus, no fundamental dichotomy between conservation and
> growth. —Rajiv Gandhi, at the United Nations, 1987

FROM SMALL AND HOMELY SPECIES to large and majestic ones, from tropical rain forests to desert scrublands to Arctic tundra, all life forms and ecosystems have bearing on the survival of the earth and therefore on the survival of humankind. Nature is and has always been in constant flux—always evolving. The earth has survived single catastrophic events in the past, some of considerable duration.

Can the earth survive the onslaught of systematic and continuous species loss that it faces today? The answer is up to humankind and will depend on concerted and collaborative effort to work at the conservation process.

It will also require giving up short-term territorial protection, overcoming competitive behavior and fragmented interests, and working with too little information (Yaffee 1997). The process must now involve the collaboration of diverse interests to set broad-based goals with the long-term interest of humans and the earth as the ultimate objective. Conservation is a process and there are no quick fixes. Stakeholders representing private property owners, developers, industry, all levels of government, academia, nongovernmental organizations, and the public must work together to develop adaptive management strategies that will benefit the environment, biodiversity, and ultimately humankind.

As the Applegate Watershed and Malpai Borderlands Group partnerships have demonstrated, the process can be difficult at first, but it gets easier with time and experience. The process is most effective in natural geographic and ecological units such as a watershed or an ecosystem. The issues must be addressed "on the ground" where they occur, and the answers will differ for each area based on the ecosystem, the species, and the human needs of the locality. Stewardship cannot be limited to public lands; some sacrifices from private property owners will be necessary. However, it is not reasonable for a public trust like biodiversity to be inequitably shouldered by private landholders. Incentive policies will be part of any workable long-term solution. While the local processes are under way, broad-scope policies can be set at the national and international levels that enable, reinforce, and support the local decisions.

The win-win approach entails concessions by all. No one should be denied the necessities of life, as many are today. To continue to allow large numbers of people to live in subhuman conditions would defeat any effort to reverse the decline of biodiversity and environmental quality. Today's "have-nots" must be guaranteed a comfortable and supportive standard of living in order to protect biodiversity, even if the "haves" must live less extravagantly to share their abundance.

Change is a process, not a one-time solution. Life has evolved over eons in a trial-and-error process called natural selection. What does not work well does not survive over time. What works well does survive. Constructive ideas like policies of safe harbor and no surprises are valuable to the process. Which ideas are unworkable will become clear in time, and these will be discarded. The workable ones will be improved. Looking for *the* single right answer is a futile exercise—none exists. Furthermore, most of the time, we will need to make difficult decisions based on insufficient information.

To avoid the continued environmental damage that jeopardizes human and nonhuman health and welfare, changes to traditional industry approaches are in order. Obviously, changes to social mores (focus on material wealth, definition of prosperity, pressure to have children), lifestyles, and patterns of consumption are also in order. National policy must reflect the scientific realities, but it cannot wait for all the scientific answers to be in place. The evidence of biodepletion is too strong for us to continue to ignore it.

The U.S. Fish and Wildlife Service has unintentionally fostered some of the current problems with the ESA through its handling of listings and of landowners. Unfortunately, a few mishandled cases mushroomed into the perception that all situations are administered with a heavy hand. They are not. The

FWS is a bureaucracy; it has been using time-tested and time-honored ways of doing things, which worked successfully in the past. They are not working today, and the agency knows it and is changing.

While it is true that industry is a significant source of depletion of natural resources and of pollution, industry will justifiably argue that consumers condone their behavior with the continued purchase of products. As a rule, consumers do not research the manufacturers or the manufacturing process of the products they buy, and industry knows this. Hence this argument is somewhat specious. Nevertheless, consumers have a responsibility to act appropriately when they know a damaging process exists or a company has a history of negligence.

Traditional competitive behaviors exhibited by the factions for and against change exacerbate the problem and cause the average citizen to avoid the matter out of confusion over the issues or distrust of the more outspoken proponents. The emotion-mongering statements used by both sides continue the polarization and stalemate and foster public confusion. Both sides wear suits and ties, heels and hose. Neither side burns flags. Both sides are part of the respected nongovernmental-organization world. The extreme groups appear to be mainstream organizations. So how does the average person determine who is right?

The behavioral changes needed to solve the problems demand cooperation, coordination, and communication.

Knowledge sharing must replace withholding and misrepresenting information. Interagency teams must replace the single-agency planning that results in duplication of effort and conflicting priorities. Integrated ecosystem, watershed, or landscape-level goals must supersede those of single forests or single species or a single industry. Multi-year prosperity milestones should replace quarterly profit focus in commerce and industry. Community and individual action must replace isolation, dependence on the consumption system, and individual inertia. Most importantly, the understanding that healthy natural systems protect and support human survival must replace the paradigm that we cannot survive without growth and development. The ultimate goal is to ensure that a healthy earth is passed along to future generations of all species. The war on the environment would be drawing to a close if more of us were committed to the concept of sustainability.

One of the key stakeholders in any collaborative effort is future generations. How can they be represented? One way is to include indigenous peoples whose cultures consider future generations. Another is to appoint a team member to act as the agent of future generations. The role of that member is to think seven generations into the future (or some other agreed upon number greater than seven).

Because of the current polarization, gridlock, and inertia, it may take powerful intervention to move the country in the right direction, just as it took presidential intervention in the case of the Pacific Northwest forests.

Public Education

The public is aware of the loss of our natural resources and the disappearance of animals and plants from the face of the earth. Some are confused by conflicting claims on the health of the environment, and only a small number of people today have more than a rudimentary understanding of the human dependence on natural systems or of the strong linkages among all natural elements and between humans and nature. The knowledge has fallen out of our folklore, our religions, and our prescribed educational curricula.

Most indigenous peoples understand the close link between nature and humanity. Unfortunately, these peoples are scattered in small pockets around the world. Furthermore, "civilized" humans scorn such cultures as "primitive." Civilizations over the past ten thousand years have promoted and believed the idea that we can and should control nature. Today many still believe we need only synthesize the natural elements we require to prosper, and this belief fosters the continuation of the paradigm of human dominance over nature.

Western history also demonstrates a growing human awareness of disappearing species. Since the late nineteenth century, American awareness of species' extinctions has grown more acute. There were ecologically farsighted Americans in the nineteenth century who foresaw the problem. These include transcendentalist Henry David Thoreau and conservationists John Muir and John James Audubon. Each celebrated the beauty of nature and provoked fascination with wildlife and natural settings. Their voices were heard, and they developed constituencies.

At the turn of the twentieth century, President Theodore Roosevelt established the first wildlife refuges, and the first Forest Service head, Gifford Pinchot, instituted land management practices in the national forests designed to conserve the resources. In 1949 in *A Sand County Almanac*, Aldo Leopold introduced to a wider public the importance of ecological balance, of biological diversity for natural stability, and of the ecological impact of losing species. Then in 1962, Rachel Carson published *Silent Spring*. This single book brought about radical changes in U.S. government policy and helped launch the environmental movement.

The 1960s and 1970s were banner decades for passing environmental legislation to protect air, land, water, and wildlife. The Endangered Species Act remains one of the most powerful of these laws. Unfortunately, the 1980s and 1990s were decades of environmental retrenchment.

The intentional confusion tactics of industry, finance, commerce, politicians, and sometimes even scientists interfere with this growing concern for environmental damage and biodepletion. Cleverly phrased questions such as "How can an animal be more important than a human?" divert public attention and put a negative spin on the real issues. Such statements are intended to foster business as usual.

With minimal education in natural sciences, most people do not understand basic ecological concepts or the link between a healthy environment and a healthy human, or the connection between biodiversity and a healthy human habitat. People are easily confused on the issues and distracted by social mores. Public education of children *and* adults must be a part of any change and of any national policy that purports to address protection of biodiversity.

Natural sciences should be added to all public and private school curricula starting in grade schools. While our children's education is critical to any long-term reform, we cannot neglect the education of the adults who manage society today. Adults need to understand the value of biodiversity and the importance of protecting it if change is to occur now and continue into the future.

Several nonprofit organizations devoted to educating the public on environmental issues have sprung up, as have associations that support the individuals dedicated to environmental education. For example, the North American Association for Environmental Education (NAAEE) sponsors a program called Environmental Issues Forums (EIF). One forum focuses on biodiversity.

The National Environmental Education and Training Foundation (NEETF) publishes an annual survey measuring environmental knowledge and attitudes among American adults. Through magazines, action alert networks, and other educational programs, organizations like the National Wildlife Federation, the World Wildlife Fund, the Wilderness Society, Sierra Club, and Audubon do an excellent job of educating their members. But these groups are preaching to the choir. Museum and recreational programs help but are often restrained by narrow historical or recreational objectives.

Additional means of reawakening appropriate attitudes toward the environment need to be explored. There are many opportunities—for example, public meetings on local environmental problems, town hall meetings for dialog on issues of community concern, and public participation on watershed and ecosystem management teams. Legislative and regulatory bodies have opportunities to foster change by passing legislation providing tax credits or other economic incentives for individual and/or corporate conservation efforts or for volunteering. Legislation requiring product labeling that specifies the environmental impact of the growing or canning or preserving process would help consumers make better decisions. The media can provide public service advertising opportunities to make a difference and more news coverage of environmental problems and community activities to solve them. Educational avenues are legion, both in formal school settings and through informal channels like museums, parks, and entertainment media. Continuing education credits can be (and have been) specifically designed for professionals such as realtors, planners, and medical practitioners. There is an unending list of potential educational opportunities, and a key one is through television programming that treats the state of the environmental as a life issue. Imagine how many more people would become aware of the need for solutions if conservation and environmental problems were regularly treated in prime time sitcoms, dramas, and daytime soap operas.

National Biodiversity Protection Policy

There is a critical need for a national policy on biodiversity, *in addition to* the Endangered Species Act. It is a national embarrassment that the United States is the only industrialized nation that has not ratified the Convention on Biological Diversity, the expression of global commitment to conserving biodiversity. The new policy could be the powerful intervention we so badly need. It should function as an umbrella for existing environmental policy, including the statutes which are the authorities of the U.S. Forest Service, National Park Service, Bureau of Land Management, U.S. Fish and Wildlife Service, and National Marine Fisheries Service. A national biodiversity policy should be a statement of (changing) national values and must emphasize the importance of biodiversity to human survival.

One way to start would be with the appointment of a presidential commission or a bipartisan congressional task force on biodiversity and land stewardship to develop policy. The latter would be the more powerful because of being bipartisan. The commission would include leading scientists, responsible representatives of the land management institutions (the Departments of Interior, Agriculture, and Defense), scientific organizations such as the Smithsonian, the National Academy of Sciences or its arm the National Research Council, and the National Science Foundation. Major nongovernment organization (NGO) stakeholders such as the Nature Conservancy, Conservation International, World Wildlife Fund, Natural Resources Defense Council, and Environmental Defense and representatives from other Enviro organizations should also be involved. Representatives of corporate private landowners including timber, mining, chemicals, and agricultural conglomerates (e.g., Georgia Pacific, Monsanto, and the Inholders Association) and independent farmers and ranchers also should be participants, as should representatives from each state's natural resources agency.

Bruce Babbitt provided an excellent model for this commission in the late 1970s when he was governor of Arizona. Arizona was annually withdrawing more groundwater than nature replenished. The water table continued to drop each year, bringing with it land subsidence, serious water quality problems, increasing expense to pump the water up, and costly disputes between major water users. Compounding overwithdrawal, Arizona's population exploded in the 1970s, placing even greater strain on the beleaguered water supply. In 1976, the state Supreme Court acknowledged that it was unable to settle groundwater conflicts satisfactorily because of lack of legislation. Governor Babbitt assembled a group of water users, including representatives from the major cities, agriculture, mining, and the water companies, and charged them with hammering out a workable groundwater solution for the state as quickly as possible. The result was a long, sometimes acrimonious debate; but out of that collaboration came Arizona's Groundwater Management Act of 1980. It was created by consensus and has been praised as one of the most far-reaching laws for managing groundwater (Ferris 1983).

Enacting a national biodiversity policy that requires strong land management stewardship demands a similar sense of urgency and high-level stakeholders, albeit at the national level, to collaborate on a solution. Ideally the following six components would be incorporated into the national biodiversity policy act (NBPA).

1. It would declare and define of the value and contribution of the natural world and biodiversity to human well-being and would make a new land and water stew-

ardship ethic that protects biodiversity and assures sustainable use of the earth's resources the law of the land. Like the National Environmental Policy Act, it would be a statement of national policy and national values and it would not require re-authorization. However, because there is so much to be learned about our natural systems, a mandatory five-year review of the biodiversity policy would be beneficial to enable Congress to make appropriate changes. This section would do the following:

a. Define the elements of biodiversity—genes, species, and ecosystems and sub-elements within each.

b. Define the elements of stewardship.

c. Define industry and commercial practices that would support a sustainable natural community and give a time line for phase-in of these changes.

d. Modify the authorities of each federal land management agency, including the Department of Defense, or direct these to be modified, to meet the new policy requirements and to stimulate cross-agency interaction and cooperation.

2. It would ratify of the UN Convention on Biological Diversity if this were not done before then. The authority for carrying out U.S. responsibilities under the CBD would be assigned to the Biological Resources Division of the U.S. Geological Survey. The BRD would be elevated to full agency status similar to the USGS but with regulatory power. The goals and responsibilities of the strengthened organization would include surveying and generating a national inventory of our natural biological resources: genes, subspecies, species, populations, and ecosystems. Second, the agency would implement a national monitoring system to collect data and to measure the continued viability of the biological systems. (Including a network of volunteer monitors nationwide would reinforce the public's role in carrying out the policy.) Third, the agency would establish and maintain a national biological information database and make this accessible to science, education, policy makers, and the public. Fourth, the agency would advise all land management entities on land management decisions.

3. NBPA would codify the multi-stakeholder, cooperative ecosystem management approach as the basis for all land management, tailored appropriately to each area. Goal setting and management oversight by cross-ownership teams that include all appropriate local stakeholders would be mandatory. The national policy should set clear standards for federal, state, and local land and biodiversity stewardship. This section would:

a. Expand wildlife reserves, national monuments and wilderness areas, and other areas protected under the Clinton Lands Legacy policy and reaffirm and broaden protection for all life within these systems. The new policy would require strong sustainable-use management for the surrounding landscape of each of these protected areas.

b. Reaffirm or physically list all the land areas currently protected as national monuments, wilderness, national parks, or national forests and require assurance that each has the protection status appropriate to protect it.

c. Encourage all local and regional multi-stakeholder ecosystem and watershed protection efforts and assure that any that exist are included in the national process. No existing regulations or statutes should thwart successful efforts.

4. NBPA would promulgate or commission of the formulation of an economic methodology that would account for the intrinsic and life support value of biodiversity. Upon enactment of NBPA, this methodology would immediately be applied to all accounting of the economic status of the nation. This system must support and advance the sustainable use of the earth and its resources. It must measure natural resource depletion and acknowledge the value and principles of sustainable development. It would direct socioeconomic focus to improved lifestyle quality, away from creating more quantity and current volume of consumption. It would emphasize and promote urban renewal programs, mass transit, alternative working strategies such as telecommuting, and alternative transportation strategies such as bicycle paths and working within walking distance of home.

5. The new land policy would establish an equitable program for private landowners to promote their cooperation and contribution to the evolution of the new land stewardship ethic. Incentives also should be included in appropriate statutes such as the ESA, the Clean Water Act, Superfund, and other statutes addressing the use of private lands. Tax incentives should be included not only in this statute but also in the U.S. tax code. Care should be taken in developing incentives so that they do not turn into subsidies. Congress also needs to provide appropriate funding.

6. The NBPA would establish a formal public education/awareness program to assure the ongoing effectiveness of this policy. This would include requiring that ecology, biology, and other earth science studies quickly become part of all elementary, secondary, and public colleges' curricula. Educational programs would clearly indicate the value of the land and all species on and within it to its inhabitants and would promote the concept and value of stewardship. Adult education should also be required. Other information and educational activities include:

a. Conduct periodic national surveys of public attitudes, perhaps as part of the decennial census, to determine the success of the policy and new practices that derive from it.

b. Require all new and existing ecosystem management teams to include a public education element in their planning and to seek funding for this. (Educational programs are currently recommended for most endangered species and ecosystem management programs; however, they are frequently not implemented due to insufficient funding.) The commission needs to recommend a way to assure that public education efforts are not neglected.

c. Require an environmental impact label on all goods regulated by the Food and Drug Administration and establishing a labeling system for durable goods to do the same would help raise public awareness of the reason for the policy

All existing land management and wildlife protection agency budgets should be increased sufficiently to support this national policy, and a program should be included that will make this law self-funded, so that it does not rely on annual congressional appropriations.

During the time the special commission is convened, a professionally directed public awareness effort should be conducted to determine public opinion and awareness levels and to gain public acceptance for the likely recommendations prior to proposal to Congress. Without this step, it is highly unlikely that any Congress would accept or vote on the policy as expeditiously as is needed. History has clearly shown that the public must be a strong advocate of such innovative policy for Congress to pass it.

Can the Endangered Species Act Be Fixed?

Today the ESA is used haphazardly to protect an ecosystem here, to stop or slow a project there, or to change land management practices somewhere else. It has even been used to curtail groundwater withdrawals. To those affected negatively by it, it seems ubiquitous, popping up everywhere and disrupting "progress." The Endangered Species Act has proven to be a good tool to accomplish a variety of ends because of its power.

The drawback of the ESA is that its power has been abused and applied inequitably. Because it is unpopular among some very vocal interests, its enforcement is patchy—heavy-handed in one area, absent in another. It is not adequately protecting endangered species now in part because every required step takes too long to activate, be it listing, declaring critical habitat, developing and implementing a recovery plan, or delisting. However, it fails because it is improperly and sporadically implemented, not because it is inherently deficient. In fact, it is inherently deficient only in one area—funding. It does not contain a self-funding mechanism.

It is past time to resolve the inequities in the law. The ESA is reviewed regularly because the statute requires reauthorization. Is it really necessary to reauthorize the law? The time lapse between reauthorizations averaged five years until the 1990s. All laws can be amended as needed. Why not make that true for the ESA as well as the proposed national biodiversity policy?

All perspectives must be taken into account to resolve the problems. Leaders from both the environmental and private property rights movements must meet and work out solutions, as Michael Bean did in the early 1990s. He worked with the FWS to find better ways to administer the law. The result of this collaboration was the Safe Harbor policy implemented in 1996 by the FWS. While Enviros believe No Surprises gives too much, especially in exempting the landowner from new requirements for a one-hundred-year period, it is a forward step in working with private landowners to protect ecosystems and species. Because of the accumulated public distrust of the ESA, only a dramatic governmental commitment can begin to dissolve the barrier.

Every few hundred years, humankind has experienced major upheaval: from the Dark Ages to the Middle Ages, from the Middle Ages to the Renaissance. Then came the Industrial Revolution that brought quantum change. Today we face new upheavals born of runaway consumption, resource depletion, and the widening divide between rich and poor. It is time to move away from what Hal Salwasser (1991) calls the "Siege Mentality"—that sense of being under siege from the current environmental laws, especially the ESA. Environmental laws were enacted to solve serious national problems. The problems remain and new approaches are in order. The ecosystem management approach is a broad-based conservation tool that includes all stakeholders and considers both human and nonhuman needs.

By the late 1990s, there was evidence of the siege breaking. The signs are good that the factional polarization is yielding. The Enviros sent the Endangered Natural Heritage Act to Capitol Hill and began a concerted campaign to get it adopted. While the proposed bill fell short of what was needed and what could be passed, it served as the base for Representative George Miller's

(D-Calif.) bill in the 105th Congress. In the Senate, Dirk Kempthorne and John Chafee broke the stalemate by circulating a proposed reauthorization bill throughout the private property and environmental communities early in January 1997. Though the bill as introduced in fall 1997 was weighted toward private property protection, Kempthorne and his committee asked for, received, and listened to feedback from all sides. The bill was an evident compromise but one that had practical value in spite of Enviro opposition.

Unfortunately, while the communications door had opened a little between the Enviros and property rights advocates, the congressional stalemate continued through the 106th Congress and the year 2000. With the moderate Republican block tending to side with the Democrats, there was no clear majority for passing what the Republicans and private property rights proponents considered favorable ESA legislation. Nor have Democrats and environmental advocates wished to force a risky vote on less than perfect legislation.

Recommended Changes for a Reauthorized ESA

Equal protection must be provided for vertebrate, plant, and invertebrate species. There is no scientific reason for lesser protection of plants and invertebrates. Nor is there a biological reason for different standards for determination of jeopardy, survival, or recovery on public versus private lands. Enforcing prohibitions against taking or jeopardizing the continued viability of plants and invertebrates is more difficult than for larger animals, not only because of ownership traditions but also because of the vast numbers and small size of these species.

The 1974 Smithsonian list of plants contained 2,832 endangered and threatened taxa and 355 plants that were presumed to be extinct. The listed plants included only ferns, gymnosperms (evergreens), and angiosperms (flowering plants). In 1976, the FWS proposed that 1,726 of the plants be listed, but they were withdrawn from consideration in 1979. By that time, 47 plants had been listed, and as of January 31, 1995, 516 plant taxa were listed. By October 1999, 716 plants were listed as endangered or threatened.

In 1978, Congress restricted use of distinct population segments to vertebrate animals only. As a result, invertebrate species such as insects, arachnids, and mollusks have less protection than vertebrates. In many cases, these species are a greater loss to humanity than losses of larger, more charismatic animals. Many invertebrates provide highly important ecosystem services. Eco-system management will help protect plants and invertebrates. However, ESA Section 4, addressing species listing, must be modified to require equal atten-tion to plants, fungi, bacteria, and invertebrates. This section also must specify that when a priority call is necessary, priority is given to the species with the greatest impact on or contribution to the health of its ecosystem.

Regulatory treatment of species on public and private lands must be equal. Habitat Conservation Plans were created to address listed species on private property, but they have not solved the problem. The Enviros fear that HCPs will replace recovery plans. HCPs may offer excellent research information not previously available to the FWS when it wrote a recovery plan or, if no recovery plan is in place, may provide a useful base for the formal federal plan. Any new and useful information from an HCP should be incorporated into federal recovery plans. Defining more specific requirements for and elements of a recovery plan, and shortening the lag time between listing and the prepa-ration and enforcement of a recovery plan, are necessary. A dedicated recov-ery planning section within the reauthorizing statute is a good idea, as is es-tablishing a separate division within the FWS for recovery planning and implementation.

Better and more thorough requirements for recovery plans need to be defined. This can be accomplished within the reauthorization statute or with language in the statute requiring better regulatory definitions. Existing single-species recovery plans should be merged with any existing and appro-priate ecosystem management plans. Recovery plans also must include cur-rent species population size, number of populations, and probabilities of persistence over specific time periods based on Population Viability Analyses for long-term recovery goals and recovery population size. They should in-clude a description of the political, social, and economic components that affect biological recovery goals and the extinction risk associated with each and should be written and approved within three years of species listing. Re-covery plans should recommend procurement and protection of suitable habi-tat for listed species and should emphasize multispecies and ecosystem management.

Future Habitat Conservation Plans should also acknowledge and incorpo-rate the elements of any ecosystem management plans in place. Recent pro-posed reauthorization bills have included exempting "low effect" private projects from the takings prohibition and from developing an HCP. This is a good way to ameliorate the rigid "no takings" restrictions; however, the definition of low effect should be "any project, once evaluated, that is determined to have an insignificant impact on a listed species." If private property is located in an area where a written ecosystem management plan and an active collaboration of stakeholders exist, and that plan protects endangered species, HCPs should not be required. The landowner should instead be required to abide by the existing management plan in order to receive the incidental take permit to proceed with development.

Though the FWS now provides guidance to private landowners on researching and writing conservation plans, the reauthorization should codify that practice. Guidance should include advice on developing biological data, demographic and genetic analyses, habitat requirements of the species, reserve design, and monitoring impact of assumptions, as well as descriptions of management options and the risks of each. The section of the act on civil penalties should be modified to include a fine for any violations of approved HCPs.

Adequate ESA funding is a must to ensure appropriate planning and protection of endangered species as well as community education on the issues to remove time-consuming resistance to recovery actions. The annual appropriation process has kept the ESA going for almost a decade without reauthorization. On the other hand, the amount of funding appropriated each year has always fallen well short of the need. As long as ESA funding depends on annual appropriations, politics will control and curtail meeting the species' needs. A self-funding mechanism is needed. If the Conservation and Reinvestment Act of 1999 (see chapter 6) is passed, the outer continental shelf oil and gas revenue will help, but that revenue is directed to specific needs. A tax on goods and services enjoyed by wildlife enthusiasts seems the most effective approach.

Currently the Section 9 stipulations on takings foreclose on any activity that could jeopardize an individual of a listed species. There is no current acknowledgment of or provision for collaborative community efforts to protect a listed species, yet collaborative conservation management strategies are clearly the way to assure species conservation.

The Clinton Administration's ecosystem management policies should be included in the reauthorized ESA. All species conservation and management plans, recovery plans, HCPs, and cooperative agreements should be required to establish and/or recognize ecosystem management coalitions to develop plans for sustainable land management to protect species. The public and appropriate stakeholder organizations that will be affected by a recovery plan should be involved in the development of the management plans.

Current public involvement and public education in species recovery and the value of species diversity are insufficient. Though the ESA requires public notification on any species listing, how many citizens regularly read the *Federal Register*? Declaration of critical habitat and notification of new recovery plans do not require public input or public education on the issues. A statutory requirement to increase public awareness of the issues and to require public involvement in all management planning should be incorporated into a reauthorization bill.

Federal-state cooperative agreements need to be better funded and enforced. Because the ESA section on cooperative agreements with states has often been ignored, state contributions to and cooperation with the federal law have been spotty. Most states have passed their own ESAs, but species ranges seldom stay within state boundaries. Cooperative agreements between states and the FWS and among states are a useful management and recovery tool. The self-funding mechanism in the reauthorized statute must include sufficient funds to support cooperative agreements. States are key stakeholders for all recovery, listing, and management planning. Where most of the planning, protection, and enforcement effort applies to a single state, or to several contiguous states, delegation of the federal responsibility is appropriate and must be accompanied by sufficient funds to support that delegation.

The actual listing of species, determination of critical habitat (or whatever term is used for that part of the species' range that is critical to its survival), and development of protective recovery plans take much longer than is mandated in the current statute. Delay exacerbates species jeopardy. More stringent and enforceable guidelines for recovery planning are essential for species recovery. Increased funding to address the requests for listings, to develop recovery plans, and to enforce the law promptly is a must, as is funding to contract the scientific studies necessary to support implementation. Science and ecosystem planning must take precedence over economic gains. Economic impact assessment should only come into the picture with land management planning.

The distinction between threatened and endangered may be impractical. Scientists question whether there is sufficient information to distinguish between these two levels. Furthermore, it would be easier for regulators and more understandable to the affected public to have one set of regulations instead of many. Whether listed species are called "threatened," "vulnerable," "endangered," or by some other term, the same approach should be applied to their protection and recovery.

Section 9 on takings was written to stop the overharvesting, overhunting, and overcollecting of species. It has, for the most part, achieved that goal. To assure that this achievement is not reversed, the section must remain. However, it is important to distinguish between land use controls for the protection of a species' survival and damage control to stop the loss of individual members of the species. This must be clearly delineated in the reauthorization statute.

A Self-Funding Alternative

A self-funding mechanism was proposed informally during the 105th Congress. Revenue under this program, called Teaming with Wildlife, would derive from a tax on expenditures for such products as birdseed, binoculars, and field guides and other merchandise used to enjoy and appreciate wildlife. The plan proposed that these funds would go to state wildlife conservation efforts. However, given the potential magnitude of the revenues and the passage of CARA, which directs outer continental shelf oil revenues to states, I believe these revenues should be used to fund ESA implementation.

Since 1937, a statute called the Pittman-Robertson Act has supported conservation of game species and their habitats through a tax on hunting gear (guns and ammunition and archery equipment). The 1950 Dingell-Johnson Act (later subsumed by the Wallop-Breaux Act) was passed to support aquatic species through taxes on fishing equipment. Most hunters and fishermen are proud of their contribution to the protection of their preferred species and of their role in protecting other nongame species that benefit from their tax dollars. The strides made in species conservation in each of the fifty states are due in large part to the revenues earned from local sports licenses and from federal excise taxes on sports equipment. With both of these statutes, the tax revenue is apportioned to the states based on a formula that considers total area of the state and the number of licenses (fishing or hunting, as appropriate to the revenue source) in the state. With Dingell-Johnson, there are some requirements for state matching funds.

Revenue and apportionment history for both Pittman-Robertson and

Dingell-Johnson is available on the Internet from Fish and Wildlife Service (FWS 2000). In 1939, the amount apportioned to states from Pittman-Robertson (listed under its formal title Wildlife Restoration) was $890,000. By contrast, the total amount apportioned to states in 2000 was $193,168,232. The same data are available, at the same Internet site, for Dingell-Johnson (Sport Fish Restoration). In its first year, 1962, $2,694,911 was apportioned back to states. In 2000 to total was $240,938,312. Both revenue streams have exceeded $3 billion in their lifetime. Were similar revenues collected on wild-life appreciation products and services and used at the federal level, they would make the ESA self-funding and provide revenues for biodiversity conservation. Major outdoor equipment manufacturers, outdoor recreationists, and enthusiasts such as birding groups currently support Teaming with Wildlife. It is a relatively painless way for the public to contribute and to assure funding for conservation activities geared to protecting and conserving biodiversity as well as for educating citizens on diversity and its value.

Individual Responsibility

The most powerful force for world change is individual change. Since most of us today feel powerless to make a difference, that statement requires some explanation. There is a point of convergence (proven, but unpredictable) when the individual efforts of many become the culture of all. This spiritual concept has been scientifically demonstrated in quantum physics (Hartmann 1998–99). Thom Hartmann describes several experiments in the chapter called "The New Science" in *The Last Hours of Ancient Sunlight.*

Ideally our national policy should reflect the convergence. However, our practice of democracy has taken us off the ideal course, and current conditions demand that we initiate national policy and individual responsibility simultaneously. Each of us can make a difference. We are each accountable for the destruction of our natural systems and we can each make choices that will help the repair process. There are many ways to do this.

Here are just a few examples. Stop eating beef to reduce the demand for beef cattle. Reduced demand will in turn reduce the need for deforestation to produce grazing lands. Do not purchase new wood products. Purchasing antiques or previously owned furniture and using only recycled paper are just two ways to reduce timber consumption. Printing and copying written material on both sides of the paper is another. Buy products packaged in recycled or recyclable packaging (glass, steel or tin, recycled or recyclable plastics, paper). Buying organically grown food tells the agricultural community which practices are acceptable to you. Most meat today comes from factory-like farms or feed lots. Not only are poultry and hog factories potentially inhumane, they are significant sources of air and water pollution due to the heavy concentration of waste products. Buy shade-grown coffee only; sun-grown coffee, which is what most grocery stores carry, requires deforestation and heavy use of fertilizer and pesticides. Buying shade-grown coffee supports wildlife dependent on trees and supports individual farms and farmers.

Reduce consumption and reduce discards. Do we really need multiple automobiles? Do we really need gas-guzzling sport utility vehicles? Do we need more and bigger TVs? Rather than sending old appliances to the landfill (by putting them out for trash pickup), why not donate them to charity, hold a yard sale, or give them to someone you know could use them? Many schools, for example, are anxious to get older computers that are still in working order.

Respect all life—including insects, worms, and the plants in your yard. Teach children to do the same. Remember each life form has a role; maintaining the abundance of species depends on our actions.

Have fewer children. The estimated replacement rate in the United States is 2.1 children per household, and a lower-than-replacement rate is desirable to sustain life on earth. Support those who decide not to have children and those who adopt children. Each life on this earth, human or other, is precious, and it is our individual and communal responsibility to care for the life that is here. But it is arrogant, insane, and cruel to the new arrivals to keep adding more lives that the earth cannot support.

It is true that third world birth rate is largely driving the earth's overpopulation, and we can help by supporting the equality and education of women around the world. Women who understand that there are alternatives to the lifestyle of annual birth and motherhood will usually adopt an alternative.

Each of us can review our definition of prosperity. In the United States we believe we have an inalienable right to prosperity. Does this not apply to everyone? Why should that right be limited to the United States? But what is the definition of prosperity? Does it mean how much we own? Does it need to mean we lose our freedom to the monthly mortgage, car payments, and credit card debt? Does it mean working long hours in electricity-consuming buildings, seldom seeing our families or enjoying the activities that really make life worthwhile, so that we can support the consumption paradigm of more is better? These are questions worth pondering. More and more people are answering: no. More and more people are redefining what prosperity means to them. For many, prosperity means fewer material goods to support and more time available to spend in family and community endeavors.

The gridlock of the 1990s started to break up in 1997, but progress halted because there are many who still fight any effort to restrict business as usual, and who continue to resist any restrictions to growth and development. Any regulation that appears to interfere with employment is anathema. The public remains enthusiastic about protecting species but unclear on exactly what it means to do so. The 104th Congress learned that it could not tamper with endangered species and succeed. The 105th proceeded with a great deal more caution. It considered legislation that was more acceptable but it too failed to protect species. Two reauthorization bills introduced in the 106th Congress likewise faltered. George Miller's bill was not taken up in committee and Don Young's bill offered little to merit new congressional consideration.

There is more communication between factions today than at any time in the 1990s. That is progress. The door is only partially open, but it is open. It has been a difficult period for endangered species, but during this time, scientists and conservation organizations have been learning more and more about biodiversity and its life-supporting role. We have also learned the importance of communicating information to the public. If there is a silver lining to the cloud of endless wrangling and delay of ESA reauthorization, it is that we have a clearer awareness of the need to protect all biodiversity and natural systems, not just species in imminent danger. There is a huge amount to be done, and every day lost is a nail in the coffin of future generations. But there is hope as well as challenge ahead. It is a huge challenge, but not an impossible one. Public awareness is rising; children are becoming environmentally savvy. What continues to be absent is full understanding of our natural world and the support it provides humankind.

Without a doubt, biodepletion is a global issue. The hotspots of biodiversity are mainly outside the United States. Nevertheless, here at home, we are seeing the results of biodepletion and it is not a comforting sight. Two U.S. states have very high numbers of listed (endangered and threatened) species: Hawaii with 224 and California with 160. Not far behind them are Florida with 97, Alabama with 89, and Tennessee with 79. Fifteen more states have between

26 and 78 listed species, and thirty states have 25 or fewer. No state has zero listed species.

In growth, material wealth, and individual prosperity, the United States is a leader. Where once we also led in species protection, today the United States is the laggard. If we do not work collaboratively and quickly, domestically and with other nations to change that, we will be left behind in the new world order as the age of the environment takes hold.

References

Adler, Jerry, and Mary Hager. 1992. How much is a species worth? *National Wildlife* (April–May).

Adler, Jonathan A. 1995. Greens vs. property rights: The environmental backlash. In *Property Rights Reader*. Washington, D.C.: Competitive Enterprise Institute. 23–25.

Albert, Dennis A. 1993. Use of landscape ecosystems for species inventory and conservation. *Endangered Species Update* 10 (3–4):20, 23–25.

American Association for the Advancement of Science, American Institute of Biological Sciences, and Ecological Society of America. 1995. Letter to Representative Don Young, 10 October.

Americans speak out. 1995. (National Wildlife Federation poll results.) *National Wildlife* (April–May): 34–37.

Anacostia History. 1997. Available at http://www.chesapeakebay.net/anacostia/histeco.htm (current as of December 1997).

Babbitt, Bruce. 1995. Interview by Diane Rehm. *Diane Rehm Show*. National Public Radio, WAMU (Washington, D.C.), 3 May.

Barnes, Burton V. 1993. The landscape ecosystem approach and conservation of endangered species. *Endangered Species Update* 10 (3–4):13–19.

Bean, Michael J. 1994. Ecosystem approaches to fish and wildlife conservation: Rediscovering the land ethic. Speech, U.S. Fish and Wildlife Service, Office of Training and Education Seminar Series, 3 November, Arlington, Va.

———. 1995. (Chair, Wildlife Program, Environmental Defense Fund.) Interview by author. 21 June.

Beck, Ben. 1998. Comments at Friends of the National Zoo (FONZ) volunteer meeting.

Benenson, Bob. 1995. GOP sets the 104th Congress on new regulatory course. *Congressional Quarterly* 53 (25): 1693–97.

Bowen, Catherine Drinker. 1986. *Miracle at Philadelphia: The Story of the Constitutional Convention, May to September, 1787*. New York: Book-of-the-Month Club. Original edition, New York: Little, Brown, 1966.

Campbell, Faith. 1991. The appropriations history. In *Balancing on the Brink of Extinction: The Endangered Species Act and Lessons for the Future*, ed. Kathryn A. Kohm. Washington, D.C.: Island Press. 134–46.

Center for Excellence for Sustainable Development. 1999. *The Natural Step*. Available at http://www.sustainable.doe.gov/database/859.html (current as of 11 October 2000).

Chadwick, Douglas H. 1995. Dead or alive: The Endangered Species Act. *National Geographic* (March): 2–41.

Cheater, Mark. 1994. Who cares about conservation? (Nature Conservancy poll results). *Nature Conservancy* (September–October).

Clark, Jaime Rappaport. 1995. (Assistant director, Ecological Services, U.S. Fish and Wildlife Service.) Interview by author. 12 May.

Clark, Tim, and Ann Harvey. 1991. Implementing recovery policy: Learning as we go? In *Balancing on the Brink of Extinction: The Endangered Species Act and Lessons for the Future*, ed. Kathryn A. Kohm. Washington, D.C.: Island Press. 147–63.

Coggins, George Cameron. 1991. Snail darters and pork barrels revisited: Reflections on endangered species and land use in America. In *Balancing on the Brink of Extinction: The Endangered Species Act and Lessons for the Future*, ed. Kathryn A. Kohm. Washington, D.C.: Island Press. 62–74.

Competitive Enterprise Institute (CEI). N.d. Brochure about the organization. Washington, D.C.: CEI.

Corn, M. Lynne. 1995. *Endangered Species: Continuing Controversy*. CRS Issue Brief. Washington, D.C.: Congressional Research Service, Library of Congress (6 April).

Corn, M. Lynne, and Pamela Baldwin. 1990. *Endangered Species Act: The Listing and Exemption Processes*. CRS Issue Brief. Washington, D.C.: Congressional Research Service, Library of Congress (8 May).

Daily War on the Environment. 1997a. E-mail daily, Sierra Club. 14 May.

———. 1997b. E-mail daily, Sierra Club. 3 June.

Defenders of Property Rights. 1995a. *S. 605—The Omnibus Property Rights Act of 1995*. Flyer. Washington, D.C.: Defenders of Property Rights.

———. 1995b. *State by State Legislative Update*. Fact sheet for June. Washington, D.C.: Defenders of Property Rights.

Defenders of Wildlife. 1993. *Saving Endangered Species: A Report and Plan for Action (1992–1993)*. Ed. Ruth Norris. Washington, D.C.: Defenders of Wildlife.

Dingell, John D. 1991. The Endangered Species Act: Legislative perspectives. In *Balancing on the Brink of Extinction: The Endangered Species Act and Lessons for the Future*, ed. Kathryn A. Kohm. Washington, D.C.: Island Press. 25–30.

Dobson, A. P. 1996. *Conservation and Biodiversity*. New York: Scientific American Library.

Dobson, A. P., J. P. Rodriguez,, W. M. Roberts, and D. S. Wilcove. 1997. Geographic distribution of endangered species in the United States. *Science* (24 January).

Dowhan, Joe. 1995. (Biologist and supervisor, U.S. Fish and Wildlife Service.) Telephone interview by author. 22 May.

Egan, Timothy. 1994. Oregon, foiling forecasters, thrives as it protects owls. *New York Times*, 11 October, p. 1.

Endangered Species Act. 1973. 16 U.S.C.A. secs. 1531–44.

Endangered Species Coalition. 1995. *Endangered Species Act Protects US: Going on the Offensive—A Toolkit for Communicating a Winning Message for Reauthorization of a Strengthened Endangered Species Act*. Washington, D.C.: ESC.

Endangered Species Recovery Act of 1997. See U.S. House. 1997; U.S. Senate. 1997.

Environment and Energy Publishing, LLC. 1997a. *Environment and Energy Weekly* (Washington, D.C.), 10 February.

———. 1997b. *Environment and Energy Weekly* (Washington, D.C.), 28 July.

———. 1997c. *Environment and Energy Weekly* (Washington, D.C.), August.

———. 2000a. *Environment and Energy Daily* (E-mail service). (Washington, D.C.) 1 March 2000.

———. 2000b. *Environment and Energy Daily* (E-mail service). (Washington, D.C.) 3 March.

Ernst, John P. 1991. Federalism and the Act. In *Balancing on the Brink of Extinction: The Endangered Species Act and Lessons for the Future*, ed. Kathryn A. Kohm. Washington, D.C.: Island Press. 98–113.

ESA Today. 1995a. A daily Internet/Fax newsletter. Washington, D.C.: Endangered Species Coalition. No. 147 (19 October).

———. 1995b. A daily Internet/Fax newsletter. Washington, D.C.: Endangered Species Coalition. No. 157 (2 November).

ESA Action. 1996a. A daily Internet/Fax newsletter. Washington, D.C.: Endangered Species Coalition. No. 174 (8 December).

———. 1996b. A daily Internet/Fax newsletter. Washington, D.C.: Endangered Species Coalition. No. 177.

Fay, John, and William Kramer. 1995. (Affiliated with the U.S. Fish and Wildlife Service.) Interview by author. 16 August.

Feller, Erica. 1995. (Legislative assistant to Congressman Wayne Gilchrist.) Interview by author. 5 May.

Ferris, Kathy. 1983. *Pro: Groundwater Law Responsible Step Forward*. Phoenix: Arizona Department of Water Resources.

Glick, Daniel. 1995. Having owls and jobs too. *National Wildlife* (August–September): 9–13.

Gordon, Rob. 1995. Listing of endangered species: Testimony to Environment and Public Works Committee, U.S. Senate. 7 March. Washington, D.C..

Gorman, Paul. 1995. Editorial memorandum from director of National Religious Partnership for the Environment to newspaper editorial boards. February.

Grader, Zeke, and Liz Hamilton. 1995. Joint letter from Pacific Coast Federation of Fishermen's Associations and Northwest Sportfishing Industry Association to the Honorable Don Young, 25 January.

Gray, Gary G. 1993. *Wildlife and People: The Human Dimensions of Wildlife Ecology*. Urbana: University of Illinois Press: 1993.

Greenlines. 1995. Daily electronic newsletter. Washington, D.C.: Defenders of Wildlife, Grassroots Environmental Effectiveness Network (GREEN). 20 November. Available at http://www.defenders.org/green/glines/gline-1.html (current as of 11 October 2000).

———. 1996a. Daily electronic newsletter. Washington, D.C.: Defenders of Wildlife, Grassroots Environmental Effectiveness Network (GREEN). 5 January. Available at http://www.defenders.org/green/glines/gline-30.html (current as of 11 October 2000).

———. 1996b. Daily electronic newsletter. Washington, D.C.: Defenders of Wildlife, Grassroots Environmental Effectiveness Network (GREEN). 24 July. Available at http://www.defenders.org/green/glines/gline-173.html (current as of 11 October 2000).

Greenpeace Campaign Report. 1997. *Dishonorable Discharge: The Navy's PCB Poisoning of the Anacostia River*. Available at http://www.greenpeace.org/~usa/reports/toxics/discharg.html (current as of 11 October 2000).

Greenwalt, Lynn A. 1991. The power and potential of the act. In *Balancing on the Brink of Extinction: The Endangered Species Act and Lessons for the Future*, ed. Kathryn A. Kohm. Washington, D.C.: Island Press. 31–36.

———. 1995. (Vice president for international affairs and special assistant to the president, National Wildlife Federation; former director, U.S. Fish and Wildlife Service.) Interview by author. 22 June.

Habitat Conservation Plans: Are They Protecting Species? 1996. Oakland: California Endangered Species Defense Campaign, Environmental Law Foundation.

Hamilton, Joan. 1994. Babbitt's retreat. *Sierra* (July–August): 52–57.

Harbrecht, Doug. 1994. A question of property rights and wrongs. *National Wildlife* (October–November): 5–11.

Hartmann, Thom. 1998–99. *The Last Hours of Ancient Sunlight*. New York: Harmony Books.

Hawkin, Paul. 1997. Natural capitalism: How biological systems will determine business success. Speech, National Academy of Sciences Conference on Nature and Human Society, 27–30 October, Washington, D.C.

Helvarg, David. 1995. The institute for innovative plunder. *Sierra* (March–April): 34–38.

Holmes, Bob. 1995. There is an endangered species on my land! *National Wildlife* (June–July): 8–15.

Hughes, Jennifer B., Gretchen Daily, and Paul R. Erhlich. 1997. The loss of population diversity and why it matters. Speech, National Academy of Sciences Conference on Nature and Human Society, 27–30 October, Washington, D.C.

Interagency Ecosystem Management Task Force. 1995. *The Ecosystem Approach: Healthy Ecosystems and Sustainable Economies*. Vol. 1, *Overview*. (Report of June 1995.) Available at http://128.174.5.51/denix/Public/ES-Programs/Conservation/Ecosystem/ecosystem1.html (current as of 11 October 2000).

Jacobson, Susan K. 1997. Nature conservation through education. In *Principles of Conservation Biology*, ed. Gary K. Meffe, C. Ronald Carroll, and contributors. 2d ed. Sunderland, Mass.: Sinauer Associates.

Joseph, James. 1995. Lucas leaves everybody hanging: *Lucas v. South Carolina Coastal Council*. In *Property Rights Reader*. Washington, D.C.: Competitive Enterprise Institute. 29–30.

Kempthorne, Dirk. 1995. Congress must recapture the original spirit of the Endangered Species Act. *Roll Call* (3 April): 8.

Kohm, Kathryn A. 1991. The act's history and framework. In *Balancing on the Brink of Extinction: The Endangered Species Act and Lessons for the Future*, ed. Kathryn A. Kohm. Washington, D.C.: Island Press. 10–22.

Lapin, Marc, and Burton V. Barnes. 1995. Using the landscape ecosystem approach to assess species and ecosystem diversity. *Conservation Biology* 9 (5): 1148–58.

LaRoe, Edward T. 1993. Implementation of an ecosystem approach to endangered species conservation. *Endangered Species Update* 10 (3–4):3–6.

League of Conservation Voters. 1995, 1996. *National Environmental Scorecard*. Available at http://www.lcv.org/scorecards/index.htm (current as of 11 October 2000).

Lewis, Thomas A. 1992. Cloaked in a wise disguise. *National Wildlife* (October–November): 4–9.

Lovejoy, Thomas E. 1997. Purpose. Speech, National Academy of Sciences Conference on Nature and Human Society, 27–30 October, Washington, D.C.

Lucas v. South Carolina Coastal Commission, 505 U.S. (1992).

Mann, Charles C., and Mark L. Plummer. 1995a. California vs. gnatcatcher. *Audubon* (January–February): 38–48, 100–4.

———. 1995b. *Noah's Choice: The Future of Endangered Species*. New York: Knopf, 1995.

Matthews, Jessica. 1997. Column, *Washington Post*, 13 January.

May, Sir Robert M. 1997. The dimensions of life on Earth. Speech, National Academy of Sciences Conference on Nature and Human Society, 27–30 October, Washington, D.C.

McAllister, Bill. 1995. Clinton announces executive order challenging curbs on EPA. *Washington Post*, 8 August.

McNally, Nancy Macan. 1995. (Executive director, National Endangered Species Act Reform Coalition.) Interview by author. 23 May.

Meffe, Gary K., C. Ronald Carroll, and contributors. 1997. *Principles of Conservation Biology*. 2d ed. Sunderland, Mass.: Sinauer Associates.

Meltz, Robert. 1995. *The Property Rights Issue*. CRS Issue Brief. Washington, D.C.: Congressional Research Service, Library of Congress (20 January).

Meslow, E. Charles. 1993. Spotted owl protection: Unintentional evolution toward ecosystem management. *Endangered Species Update* 10 (3–4):334–38.

Meyer, Stephen M. 1994. The final act. *New Republic*, 15 August.

———. 1995. Endangered species listings and state economic performance. Working paper, Massachusetts Institute of Technology, Department of Political Science, 30 March.

Mossman, Barbara. 199?. Written text of speech, in collected papers from office of Senator Slade Gorton.

National Research Council, Committee on Scientific Issues in the Endangered Species Act. 1995. Report. Washington, D.C.: Department of Interior.

National Wildlife Refuge System. 1997a. *Delineation of Ecosystem Units*. Available at http://refuges.fws.gov/NWRSFiles/HabitatMgmt/EcosystemManagement/Delineation.html (current as of 11 October 2000).

Nature Conservancy, Office of Government Affairs. 1995. *The Workings of the Endangered Species Act: A Summary of Our Findings*. Arlington, Va.: Nature Conservancy (8 February).

Norse, Elliott A. (ed.). 1993. *Global Marine Biological Diversity: A Strategy for Building Conservation into Decision Making*. Washington, D.C.: Island Press.

Northern Spotted Owl v. Hodel, 716 F. Supp. 479 (D. Wash. 1988).

Noss Reports to the NBS. 1995. *eco.logic* (Newsletter of the Environmental Conservation Organization, Hollow Rock, Tenn.), no. 26 (May): 22–23.

Odum, Eugene P. 1993. *Ecology and Our Endangered Life-Support Systems.* 2d ed. Sunderland, Mass.: Sinauer Associates.

Pearce, David W., and R. Kerry Turner. 1990. *Economics of Natural Resources and the Environment.* Baltimore: Johns Hopkins University Press.

Perry, Rick. 1995. Testimony of Texas Agriculture Commissioner Rick Perry to the U.S. Senate Committee on Environment and Public Works. 7 March. Washington, D.C.

Pimm, Stuart L. 1997. The sixth extinction: How large, how soon, and where? Speech, National Academy of Sciences Conference on Nature and Human Society, 27–30 October, Washington, D.C.

Point-Counterpoint on Gorton/Johnston ESA Reform Bill. 1995. Washington, D.C.: Senator Slade Gorton's Office (typewritten).

Preserving environmental justice for all of God's creation: The Endangered Species Act. 1994. *Networker/Interfaith Impact* 4, no. 3 (summer): 1–4.

Press, Frank, and Raymond Siever. 1993. *Understanding Earth.* New York: W. H. Freeman.

Pyle, Thomas J. 1995. (Legislative assistant to Congressman Richard Pombo.) Interview by author. 2 June.

Quigley, Thomas M., and Stephen E. McDonald. 1993. Ecosystem management in the forest service: Linkage to endangered species management. *Endangered Species Update* 10 (3–4):30–33.

Reffalt, William. 1991. The endangered species lists: Chronicles of extinction? In *Balancing on the Brink of Extinction: The Endangered Species Act and Lessons for the Future*, ed. Kathryn A. Kohm. Washington, D.C.: Island Press. 77–85.

Rolston, Holmes, III. 1991. Life in jeopardy on private property. In *Balancing on the Brink of Extinction: The Endangered Species Act and Lessons for the Future*, ed. Kathryn A. Kohm. Washington, D.C.: Island Press. 43–61.

Rosenbaum, Walter A. 1995. *Environmental Politics and Policy.* 3d ed. Washington, D.C.: CQ Press.

Salwasser, Hal. 1991. In search of an ecosystem approach to endangered species conservation. In *Balancing on the Brink of Extinction: The Endangered Species Act and Lessons for the Future*, ed. Kathryn A. Kohm. Washington, D.C.: Island Press. 247–65.

Saperstein, David. 1995. *Testimony before the Endangered Species Act Task Force.* 18 May. Distributed by Endangered Species Coalition.

Saving the Endangered Species Act. 1995. *HSUS News* 40, no. 2 (spring): 5–7.

Sawhill, John. 1995. Wildlife and ways of life: Seeking greener pastures. *Nature Conservancy* (January–February).

Schei, Peter. 1997. Comments at the Workshop on Biodiversity at the Fifth Annual

World Bank Conference on Environmentally and Socially Sustainable Development, October, Washington, D.C..

Scott, J. Michael, Timothy H. Tear, and L. Scott Mills. 1995. Socioeconomics and the recovery of endangered species: Biological assessment in a political world. *Conservation Biology* 9 (1): 214–16.

Seattle Times. 1995. ESA: Is common sense an endangered species? (editorial). 23 April.

Shetler, Stanwyn. 1991. Biological diversity: Are we asking the right questions? In *The Unity of Evolutionary Biology: Proceedings of the Fourth International Congress of Systematic and Evolutionary Biology, July 1990, University of Maryland*, ed. Elizabeth C. Dudley. Portland, Ore.: Dioscorides Press.

Siwolop, Sana. 1994. Are we as rich as we think? *International Wildlife* (May–June): 12–15.

Smith, Zachary A. 1995. *The Environmental Policy Paradox*. 2nd ed. Englewood Cliffs, N.J.: Prentice Hall.

Spain, Glen. 1995. Letter to the Senate from the director of the Pacific Coast Federation of Fishing Associations, 1 May.

Stapleton, Richard M. 1993. Who owns the land? *National Parks* (September–October): 26–27.

Sugg, Ike C. 1995. (Fellow in wildlife and land use policy, Competitive Enterprise Institute.) Interview by author. 11 May.

Suzuki, David, and Peter Knudtson. 1992. *Wisdom of the Elders: Honoring Sacred Native Visions of Nature*. New York: Bantam.

Tear, Timothy H., J. Michael Scott, Patricia H. Hayward, and Brad Griffith. 1995. Recovery plans and the endangered species act: Are criticisms supported by data? *Conservation Biology* 9 (1): 182–95.

U.S. Fish and Wildlife Service. Ca. 1993. Facts: Questions and Answers on the Endangered Species Act. Fact sheet. Washington, D.C.: FWS.

———. 1995. *Endangered Species: Endangered Means There's Still Time*. Information packet. Washington, D.C.: U.S. Department of Interior, FWS.

———. 1997b. Home page. Available at http://www.fws.gov/index.html (current as of 11 October 2000).

———. 2000. Wildlife Restoration, Sport Fish Restoration (revenue and apportionment history for Pittman-Robertson and Dingell-Johnson funds). Available at http://fa.r9.fws.gov/ (current as of 11 October 2000).

U.S. House. 1997. *Endangered Species Recovery Act of 1997*. 106th Cong., 1st sess., H.R. 2351. Introduced by Rep. George Miller (D-Calif.), 31 July.

U.S. Senate. 1997. *Endangered Species Recovery Act of 1997*. 106th Cong., 1st sess., S. 1180. Introduced by Sen. Dirk Kempthorne, 16 September.

Vento, Bruce. 1995. "Dear Colleague" letter to the House of Representatives, July.

Vivoli, Mike. 1995. Putting people last. In *Property Rights Reader*. Washington, D.C.: Competitive Enterprise Institute. 10–12.

Watson, R. T., and V. H. Heywood (eds). 1995. *Global Biodiversity Assessment*. Cambridge, U.K.: Cambridge University Press.

Welch, William M., and Jessica Lee. 1995. GOP rules ride spending bills. *USA Today*, 17 July.

Wicker, Tom. 1994. Waiting for an environmental president. *Audubon* (September–October): 49–54, 102–3.

Williams, Florence. 1993. The compensation game. *Wilderness* (fall): 29–33.

Williams, Nat. 1995. (Affiliated with the Nature Conservancy.) Interview by author. 20 June.

Wilson, Edward O. 1988. *Biodiversity*. 14th ed. Washington, D.C.: National Academy Press.

———. 1992. *The Diversity of Life*. New York: W. W. Norton.

———. 1997. The creation of biodiversity. Speech, National Academy of Sciences Conference on Nature and Human Society, 27–30 October, Washington, D.C.

Wirth, Tim. 1997. Biodiversity and organizing for sustainability in the U.S. government. Speech, National Academy of Sciences Conference on Nature and Human Society, 27–30 October, Washington, D.C.

World Bank Conference on Environmentally and Socially Sustainable Development. 1997a. *Biological Diversity*. Fact sheet published for the fifth annual conference, October, Washington, D.C.

———. 1997b. *Endangered Species*. Fact sheet published for the fifth annual conference, October, Washington, D.C.

Yaffee, Steven L. 1991. Avoiding endangered species/development conflicts through interagency consultation. In *Balancing on the Brink of Extinction: The Endangered Species Act and Lessons for the Future*, ed. Kathryn A. Kohm. Washington, D.C.: Island Press. 86–97.

———. 1997. Why environmental policy nightmares recur. *Conservation Biology* 11 (3):328–37.

The year of unfortunate. 1992. *National Wildlife* (February–March): 33–38.

Index